D1520995

YASUKUNI

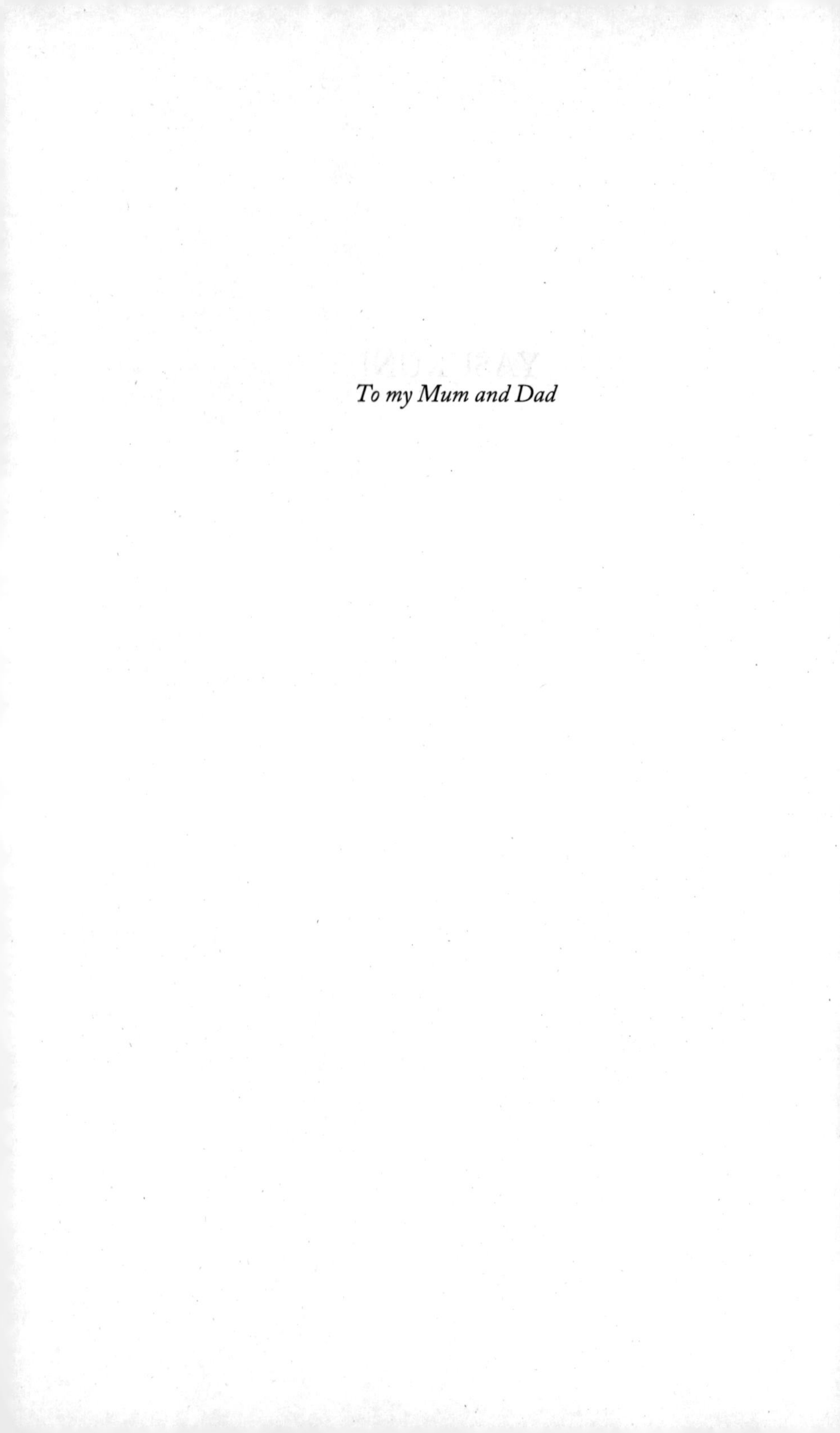

To my Mum and Dad

JOHN BREEN

editor

Yasukuni, the War Dead and the Struggle for Japan's Past

Columbia University Press
New York

Columbia University Press
Publishers Since 1893
New York

Library of Congress Cataloging-in-Publication Data

Yasukuni, the war dead and the struggle for Japan's past / John Breen, editor.
p. cm.
Includes bibliographical references and index.
ISBN 978-0-231-70042-9 (cloth : alk. paper)
1. Yasukuni Jinja (Tokyo, Japan) 2. Shinto and politics. I. Breen, John, 1956–
BL2225.T62Y3727 2008
299.5'6135—dc22

2007044188

∞
Columbia University Press books are printed on permanent and durable acid-free paper.
This book is printed on paper with recycled content.
Printed in India

c 10 9 8 7 6 5 4 3 2 1

CONTENTS

ILLUSTRATIONS

Between pp. 21–3

THE CONTRIBUTORS

John **Breen** is senior lecturer in Japanese at the School of Oriental and African studies, University of London. He specialises in 19th-century Japanese history, and is presently completing a study of the imperial court in 19th-century Japan. He is co-author of a forthcoming history of Shinto (from Blackwells). Among his major publications are 'Meiji tennō o yomu' [Reading the Meiji emperor], *Ratio* 3 (2007), 'Juyondai shōgun Iemochi no jōraku to Kōmei seiken ron' [14th shogun Iemochi's pilgrimage to Kyoto and the creation of the Komei administration] in Meiji ishinshi gakkai ed., *Meiji ishin to bunka*, Yoshikawa kōbunkan, (2005); *Death in Japan* (*Mortality* special issue, guest editor), 9.1.2004; *Shinto in history: ways of the kami* (co-edited), Hawaii University press (2000), and 'The Imperial oath of April, 1868: ritual, power and politics in Restoration Japan', *Monumenta Nipponica*, 51.4.1996.

Kevin M. **Doak** occupies the Nippon Foundation Endowed Chair in Japanese Studies, and is chair of the Department of East Asian Languages and Cultures at Georgetown University. His research interests are modern Japan focused. He specialises in modern Japanese intellectual history, nationalism, fiction and essays, and religion with an emphasis on Catholicism. Research in progress includes an edited collection, *Xavier's Legacies: Catholicism in modern Japan*, an article 'Akutagawa's 'Saiho no hito': a translation and critical commentary' and an article on Tanaka Kotaro's theory of natural law. Among his major publications are *A history of nationalism in modern Japan: placing the people,* Brill (2006), 'Romancing the East, rejecting the West: Japanese intellectuals' responses to modernity in the early

20th century', *Comparative Studies of South Asia, Africa and the Middle East* 26.3 (2006), 'Time, culture and faith: Yoshimitsu Yoshihiko's Critique of Modernity', *University of Tokyo Center of Philosophy Bulletin* I (2003), and *Dreams of difference: the Japan romantic school and the crisis of modernity*, University of California Press (1994).

Nitta Hitoshi earned his PhD from Kokugakuin Univesity in Tokyo and is presently professor in the Department of Literature at Kogakkan University. He specialises in the relationship between state and religion in modern Japan. In addition to many academic and popular articles, he has written several books on subjects such as modern religion and politics, state Shinto and the emperor and the patronage of the Yasukuni shrine by successive Prime Ministers. Recent book titles include the following: *Kindai seikyō kankei no kisoteki kenkyū*, Taimeido (1997), *"Arahito gami", "Kokka Shinto" to iu gensō*, PHP Kenkyūjo (2003), *Shushō ga Yasukuni sanpai shite, dokoga warui*, PHP Kenkyūjo (2005).

Caroline **Rose** is senior lecturer in Japanese Studies and currently Head of the Department of East Asian Studies at the University of Leeds. She received her BA and PhD at Leeds, and has studied at Fudan University in Shanghai and Tsukuba University in Japan. Her specialist field is contemporary Sino-Japanese relations, with particular reference to the history problem and reconciliation. She has published two monographs on Sino-Japanese relations, *Interpreting History in Sino-Japanese Relations*, Routledge (1998) and *Sino-Japanese Relations: Facing the Past, Looking to the Future?* RoutledgeCurzon (2005); and has written widely on Japanese history education, Chinese and Japanese nationalism, and Sino-Japanese relations in the East Asian context. Her current research focus is on reconciliation in North East Asia, citizenship education in Japan, and Japanese diplomatic history of World War I and the inter-war period.

Philip **Seaton** (homepage: www.philipseaton.net) is associate professor in the Research Faculty of Media and Communication, Hokkaido University, Japan. He specialises in representations of World War II in the Japanese media and is currently researching regional war memories in Hokkaido. His first book is *Japan's contested war memories*, Routledge (2007). Major articles include 'Reporting the 2001 textbook and Yasukuni shrine controversies', *Japan Forum*, 17.3, 2005 (winner of the 2006 Daiwa Japan Forum Prize); 'Reporting the "comfort women" issue, 1991-1992', *Japanese Studies* 26.1, 2006; and 'Do you really want to know what your uncle did?', *Oral History* 43.1 (2006).

Seki Hei graduated from Beijing University, came to Japan in 1988 and completed his PhD at Kobe University in the Graduate School of Humanities and Social Sciences. In 2002 he published a groundbreaking book on the growing anti-Japanese sentiment in China and, thereafter, has worked as a critic specialising in Sino-Japanese relations. His books have all been concerned to explore variations on the Sino-Japanese theme: the pathological loathing of the Chinese for Japan, the dangers to Japan of a closer relationship to China and the future of Japan's diplomacy with its Chinese neighbour. Seki Hei is a regular contributor to such journals as *Seiron*, *Voice*, *WiLL* and *Gekkan Nippon*. Among his most recent books are the following: *Watashi wa "Moshuseki no shō hakuse" datta*, Asuka shinsho (2006), *Nicchū no shukumei*, Fusōsha (2006), *"Nicchū yūkō" wa Nihon o horobosu: rekshi ga oshieru "datsu Chūgoku" no hōsoku*, Kōdansha (2005) and *Naze Chūgokujin wa nihonjin o nikumu no ka*, PHP (2002).

Takahashi Tetsuya is professor in the Graduate School of Arts and Sciences at Tokyo University. He specialises in philosophy and the study of culture and its representations. In his recent research he is concerned with a critical exposition of the logic of sacrifice in the field of politics and religion. His publications include books on Yasukuni, education, revisionist history, Derrida, and memory. In the past decade he has published *Yasukuni mondai*, Chikuma shobō (2005), *Kokka to gisei*, NHK Books (2005), *Shōgen no poriteikusu*, Miraisha (2004), *Kyōiku to kokka*, Kōdansha (2004), *Rekishi/shūseishugi*, Iwanami shoten (2001), *Sengo sekininron*, Kōdansha (1999), *Derida: datsu kōchiku*, Kōdansha (1998) and *Kioku no echika*, Iwanami shoten (1995).

Wang Zhixin is Professor of education at Miyazaki University. He taught at Shanghai University before coming to work in Japan in 1985 to study comparative education at Chiba and Tokyo universities. He received his doctorate from Tokyo University in 1993. He has written widely in Japanese on Sino-Japanese relations. Among his many publications are the following books: *"Hannichi kanjō" ka sore tomo "tainichi ken'okan" ka: Nihongawa to no ronsō hatashite dare no mondai na no ka?* Nihon kyōhōsha (2005), (co-authored); *Gendai Chūgoku no kyōiku*, Akashi shoten (2004); *"Tsukuru kai" no rekishi kyōkasho o kiru zainichi Chūgokujin gakusha no shiten kara*, Kyōhōsha (2001) and *Hihan shokuminchi kyōikushi ninshiki*, Shakai hyōronsha (2000).

FOREWORD

My fascination with Yasukuni shrine dates back twenty years, to 21 March 1987 to be precise. This was when, for the first time, I attended the Annual Reunion of the Veterans of the Ōka unit, a suicide squadron in the Imperial Japanese Navy. The squadron survivors, spared by war's end, gathered at Yasukuni to mourn and honour their comrades in the form of a Shinto rite of propitiation (*ireisai*). This was a memorable day because it complicated such limited understanding as I had of Yasukuni till then. For the first time I sat in the worship hall (*haiden*) of Yasukuni and underwent an *oharae* purification; it was the first time I walked through the main sanctuary (*honden*) to pay my own respects to the Japanese war dead, and it was the first opportunity I had to talk to members of the Ōka unit about their experiences of war.

As we waited in the Assembly hall (*sanshūsho*) prior to the start of the rite of propitiation, I was asked to stand and introduce myself. I explained that I came as the guest of Naitō Hatsuho, author of *Kyokugen no tokkōki: Ōka*, and that I taught Japanese history at SOAS.[1] No sooner had I sat down than I felt a tap on my shoulder. Turning round I saw a frail, kindly man who introduced himself as S-san, the father-in-law, it transpired, of a SOAS colleague of mine. She is a fine woman, he said with pride. I concurred willingly with this sentiment, but was amazed to come across a relative of a colleague, at Yasukuni of all places. That her husband, an academic at a famous

1 Naito's book is a moving and sympathetic exploration of the psychology of Ōka pilots like Nonaka Goro, and a trenchant critique of commanders like Okumura Motoharu who sent them to their death. The book has been translated into English as *Thundergods: the kamikaze pilots tell their story*.

private Japanese university whom I knew pretty well, had a father who was in the Ōka squadron I had no idea. This was something the son kept very quiet; his father's past was perhaps for him more a matter of shame and less of pride.

This was also the first time I toured the Yūshūkan war museum, opened to the public just two years earlier in 1985. The exhibits, and especially the models of the Ōka aircraft, which dominated the central hall, made a lasting impression on me. The Ōka, whose noses were packed with explosives, had no engines of their own; they were clamped to the underbelly of the 'mother plane' which got them airborne. The Ōka pilot would squeeze through a trapdoor in the fuselage of the mother plane, and lower himself into the Ōka. On sighting an enemy warship, the pilot would pull a release lever and, with the most primitive of steering mechanisms, hurtle his craft towards his target. The Yūshūkan model of the killing machine helped me imagine not just the murderous capability of the suicide squadrons, but the extraordinary courage of the men I had sat alongside minutes before in the worship hall.

The party of veterans, Naitō Hatsuho and I left the Yūshūkan for Kamakura. Our destination was the Kenchōji, one of the most famous of Kamakura's Zen temples. The priest in charge of the Seitōan 'chapel' of this medieval temple had been an Ōka squadron member himself; he, too, had survived the war. Some years earlier he had died, but the veterans still made a pilgrimage to the Kenchōji every year. A memorial plaque dedicated to all the dead from the Oka squadron stood inside the Seitōan. The veterans on this occasion, too, paid their respects to their comrades once more. The party then headed for a seaside restaurant in Kamakura. Among the veterans whom I spoke with were unrepentant nationalists, several of whom had spent the post-war in the self-defence forces; but there were pacifists and paid-up members of the Japanese Communist party too. There were Christian veterans of the Ōka squadron and Buddhist veterans, as well as atheists. The arguments in which they engaged in that Kamakura restaurant in March 1987 were ones, so Naito Hatsuho told me, which they rehearsed year in year out:

> 'It is so good to be alive'; 'No, I wish I had died; I think so every year in March'; 'No, that is an absurd thing to say.'
>
> 'The Pacific war was a stupid war from start to finish'; 'No, it was a just war; it was just war because it freed Asia from the shackles of British and American imperialism'; 'That is an absurd statement. We were conned into fighting by the militarists; our comrades were victims of the militaristic Japanese state.'
>
> 'One word would have sufficed, but there was nothing; the emperor should have apologised to us for what we all had to endure; he should have said sorry.' 'No, that is absurd; leave the emperor out of it.'

I have been back to Yasukuni on many occasions, and participated in the Great Rites of Spring and Autumn as well as the Mitama matsuri, Yasukuni's own Shinto version of the Buddhist summer festival of All Souls. My first visit in 1987 quickly persuaded me that Yasukuni is a far more complicated place than is frequently allowed in discussions and writings on the shrine in Japanese, English, Chinese and Korean. I subsequently had the opportunity to interview other groups of war veterans, and they confirmed my understanding that Yasukuni is, indeed, a sacred, ritual site, albeit a deeply flawed one.[2] One particular event remains clear in my memory. A shrine priest who was particularly kind and helpful to me in my research at Yasukuni asked if, in return, I would agree to speak in a seminar series organised by the Yasukuni *sūkei hōsan kai*, the shrine worshippers association. I gave this a little thought, and quickly decided it was an opportunity not to be lost, and agreed to speak. At one stage during the question and answer session after my talk, I said that, while mourning and honouring the war dead is a noble undertaking, Yasukuni in its present guise runs the risk of appropriating the war dead for other purposes. A small section of the audience, war veterans whom I had interviewed months before, responded with a ripple

2 For a selection of interviews, see Breen, 'The dead and the living', pp. 88-90.

of applause. The point is that at least some of those men and women who venerate at Yasukuni and regard it as the most sacred of sites, are still aware that it is not without its problems. This is, perhaps, nothing more or less than we should expect.

This book is an attempt to convey, through the voices of various observers and commentators who hold very divergent views, a sense of the real complexity of Yasukuni, and indeed the complexity of the Pacific War as it lives on in contemporary memories.

ACKNOWLEDGEMENTS

I would like to thank Naitō Hatusho for introducing me to Yasukuni all those years ago, and for offering wise counsel on what I have written on Yasukuni and other aspects of Japanese history since then. I would also like to thank Revd. Yamaguchi Tatebumi, now the assistant chief priest at Yasukuni, for the kindness he showed me, and the help he offered in conducting my research. I hope he appreciates the idea behind this book, even if he may be critical of my contribution to it. I would also like to thank the organizers of, and contributors to, several events that forced me to think more carefully about Yasukuni: Professor Marie Conte-Helm for organizing the Daiwa seminar on 'Yasukuni: religion, politics and the legacy of war', at Daiwa House in London, 2005 and Trent Maxey, John Nelson and members of the Yasukuni panel at the AAS conference in San Francisco, 2006. Thanks are due to Professor Mark Selden for his insightful but always constructive criticisms of an earlier version of this manuscript. Yasukuni shrine and Meiji jingū were kind enough to allow me to use illustrations from their archives. The translations from the original Japanese texts were ably done by Jennifer Davies; the exception is Takahashi Tetsuya's chapter which was translated by Dr Nicola Liscutin.

NOTE

1) The war dead are venerated, honoured and propitiated at Yasukuni as *kami*, a word which is often inadequately translated as 'gods'. Here I have used the word *kami* throughout.
1) Japanese names are presented here in Japanese order, with the family name first, followed by the given name.

INTRODUCTION
A YASUKUNI GENEALOGY

John Breen

The Kyōdō news agency reported on 8 May 2007 that the Japanese Prime Minister, Abe Shinzō, had dispatched an offering to the Yasukuni shrine on the occasion of its Great Autumn Rite a fortnight earlier. Abe, who stayed away from the shrine, paid 50,000 yen (c. £250) for a bunch of flowers which Yasukuni priests then offered on his behalf to the *kami* venerated in Yasukuni's Main sanctuary.[1] The *kami* are, of course, the apotheosised war dead; and at Yasukuni they are also referred to as *eirei* or 'glorious sprits'. Why was this newsworthy not only in Japan, but throughout the Asia Pacific and beyond? Because it was the latest episode in the ongoing saga of the post-war Japanese state's patronage of the Yasukuni shrine. It is a 'saga' in that controversy attaches to state patronage: on the one hand, there are grounds for regarding Prime Ministers' visits, like those of Abe's predecessor, Koizumi Jun'ichirō, as breaching the Constitutional provisions for the separation of state and religion; on the other, there is the fraught issue of the Class A war criminals. The Class A war criminals were enshrined in 1978, a generation after the war ended, and are now venerated at Yasukuni shrine along with the war dead. This fact is controversial, above all, in the context of Japan's twenty-first century relationship with China, Korea and even to some extent the USA. The Chinese insist that when Prime Ministers visit

1 Kyōdō tsūshin 8.5.07.

Yasukuni they are tacitly approving the actions of such Class A war criminals as General Matsui, executed for his responsibility for the Nanking Massacre, not to mention those of Prime Minister Tōjō who led Japan to war in the first place.

This latest episode saw Abe innovating: he honoured the war dead, and let it be known he did, but in such a way as to sidestep the opprobrium he would have attracted, domestically but especially internationally, had he followed Koizumi, and gone to the shrine in person, especially if he had done so officially, in his capacity as Prime Minister. Abe's act of 'remote veneration' also risked censure from other quarters, namely from those of a more conservative disposition, who insist he should head boldly to Yasukuni regardless of Chinese views. What appears to explain Abe Shinzō's cautious patronage of Yasukuni in spring of 2007? First, from the start of his premiership Abe went out of his way to cultivate the Chinese, whom Koizumi had alienated and offended.[2] Second, in April 2004, the Fukuoka district court deemed that Koizumi's visit to the shrine in 2001 did, indeed, breach the state-religion separation provision and was, therefore, unconstitutional; the Osaka High Court issued a similar ruling in September 2005. Neither ruling stopped Koizumi returning to Yasukuni in 2005 and again in 2006, of course, and it is unclear whether they had any greater influence over Abe Shinzō. There is one other possible reason for Abe's caution; it concerns recent revelations about the last Emperor, Hirohito and his relationship to Yasukuni shrine and Class A war criminals.

Fragments: Emperor, Yasukuni and Class A War Criminals

On 27 April 2007, the *Asahi* newspaper published two fragments of the diary of Urabe Ryōgo. Urabe was Chamberlain to Emperor Hirohito from 1969 till the latter's death twenty years later. Urabe himself died in 2002, and in his will he entrusted his diary to his heirs, who sold it to the *Asahi* newspaper. The *Asahi* plans to publish all thirty-three volumes, but in April it released two tantalising fragments,

2 As I read the proofs to this manuscript, the Japanese press reports that Abe has decided to stay away from Yasukuni on 15 August, 2007.

both of which relate to Emperor Hirohito and his relationship with Yasukuni. Hirohito was known to be devoted to Yasukuni, which he visited for the Great Rites of Spring and Autumn during the war, and on eight occasions after the war. His last visit was in 1975, and why he never returned to the shrine became thereafter a matter of great public interest. The Urabe diary fragments reveal why. The first fragment, dated 28 April 1988, appears somewhat cryptic. It reads: '[His Majesty] finished eating so we went to [the] Fukiage [quarter of the palace grounds]. After Chief Steward [Tomita Tomohiko]'s audience [with Him there was over], I entered [His presence]: the Yasukuni enshrinement of the war criminals; Chinese criticisms and Okuno's statement'.[3] That Urabe underlined the entire section of his diary in red suggests this was for him an especially memorable day. It seems clear enough that Hirohito discussed with Tomita, and then with Urabe himself, both the enshrinement of the Class A war criminals and the diplomatic row that erupted with China following an inflammatory statement made by Okuno Seisuke a week or so earlier. Okuno, a member of the Takeshita cabinet, bemoaned the fact that Japan was 'still haunted by the ghost of the Occupation forces', and demanded to know 'in precisely what sense' it might be said that Japan was 'the aggressor' in the last war. It took Okuno's resignation before Chinese criticisms of his effective denial of Japanese aggression abated. Of still greater interest are the emperor's views on the Class A war criminals, and their enshrinement in 1978. Urabe failed to elaborate in this fragment, but Chief Steward Tomita himself wrote a highly revealing memorandum after his audience with the Emperor on that very day. The Tomita memo, as it is known, was published in 2006 by the *Nihon keizai* newspaper, but was dismissed as insufficient proof by some commentators. The Urabe diary fragment seems to corroborate the Tomita memo, the burden of which was this: Emperor Hirohito told Tomita he had stopped visiting Yasukuni after 1975 because he disagreed with Yasukuni's enshrinement of the Class

3 *Asahi shinbun*, 27.4.07.

A war criminals.[4] It now seems highly probable that Hirohito told Urabe the same thing on the same day: Hirohito could not approve the Class A war criminals' entering the Yasukuni pantheon alongside the war dead.

The second published fragment of Chamberlain Urabe's diary is dated July 2001, twelve years after Hirohito's death, and it leaves no doubt this was indeed the Emperor's position. 2001 was the first year of Koizumi Jun'ichirō's premiership, and speculation was rife that the new Prime Minister would go boldly to Yasukuni on 15 August, the day of the war's end.[5] In his July entry, Urabe wrote: 'The immediate background to the Emperor terminating his Yasukuni visits was that he did not agree with the enshrinement of the Class A war criminals'.[6] Precisely why Urabe reflected on this matter in an entry for July 2001 must remain unclear till the *Asahi* publishes the diary in full, but this second fragment confirms that Hirohito did indeed object to Class A war criminals' enshrinement, and his failure to visit after 1975 was entirely on this account.[7] The grounds for his objections are a matter for conjecture, however. Did Hirohito believe these Class A war criminals were responsible, and had to be held responsible, for the war; that they should not therefore be venerated alongside the men and women who died fighting on their orders; that their enshrinement was a denial of the responsibility which Japan should accept? Was he merely anxious to avoid conflict with China? Or perhaps his greater concern was to deflect attention from his own involvement in the war? Whatever the reason, the presence of the spirits of the Class A war criminals in Yasukuni was clearly offensive to the Emperor. Of course, whether this fact influenced

4 On the Tomita memo, see the chapters by Takahashi and Seaton in this volume.

5 In fact Koizumi compromised at the last minute, and went on 13 August.

6 *Asahi shinbun*, 27.4.07

7 As I check the proofs for this manuscript, the *Mainichi shinbun* reports that the emperor also told chamberlain, Tokugawa Gikan, that he was opposed to the Class A war criminals' enshrinement. (*Mainichi shinbun* 4.8.07).

Abe's decision to stay away in spring 2007 remains like much else a matter of conjecture.

Removal: the Japan Society for the War Bereaved

What impact this revelation of Chamberlain Urabe, and Chief Steward Tomita before him, will have on Yasukuni in the longer term, is difficult to judge at the time of writing, but some intriguing suggestions of a shift in the position of the Japan Society for the War Bereaved (*Nihon izokukai*) quickly surfaced. The Society has been, in financial and numerical terms, the single greatest sponsor of the Yasukuni shrine in the post-war period. It has a membership of 80,000 (as of 2006); many members are wealthy and influential, and the society's President is invariably a distinguished public figure. The President at the time of writing is former Liberal Democratic Party (LDP) Secretary General, Koga Makoto. Koga responded instantly to the Urabe diary fragments by setting up a Study Group to consider the possibility of removing the Class A war criminals from Yasukuni to some other site. Koga was motivated by a desire, shared by a majority of the Society's members, to see the reigning emperor, Akihito, visit Yasukuni. After all, Japanese soldiers went to war believing that, if they died, the Emperor would go in person to Yasukuni to propitiate them as a reward, as indeed he did during the fifteen years of war with China, Asia and the US. If, however, the Class A war criminals' enshrinement was an impediment to Hirohito's patronage of the shrine in the last decades of his reign, then Akihito too would be beyond persuasion; the Class A war criminals would have to be removed elsewhere.

'Removal' is not a question of transferring human remains, for there are none at Yasukuni. It is a question, rather, of the ritual removal of the war criminals' spirits from the Yasukuni pantheon to another site. In physical terms, it involves transferring the slips of paper inscribed with the names of these men from the Yasukuni Repository to a repository elsewhere. A second point to note is that the Yasukuni priesthood has remained bitterly opposed to removal ever since it was first mooted by Prime Minister Nakasone Yasuhiro around the time of his controversial visit in 1985. Yasukuni priests insist that, in theological terms, spirits once enshrined can never be dislodged. Their favoured analogy is that of the candle and its flame: 'You can transfer the flame of one candle to another, but the original candle continues to burn'. They are also adamant that the state must never be allowed to interfere in its affairs: Yasukuni is after all an independent religious juridical person in law.

Koga's Study Group met for the first time on 8 May 2007, and the *Mainichi* newspaper estimated that eight of its twelve members were in favour of actively exploring how removal might be effected. As one member told the *Mainichi*, 'Our ultimate aim is to clear the way for the present emperor to return to Yasukuni. It is now apparent that the impediment to the previous emperor's visits to Yasukuni was none other than the enshrinement of the Class A war criminals. The [Tomita memo and the Urabe diary] have added impetus to earlier proposals for removing the [war criminals' spirits] elsewhere.'[8] Should the Study Group conclude that removal is, indeed, the way forward, and should they then persuade a majority in the Japan Society for the War Bereaved, Yasukuni priests will be in an impossible position. The Society will argue that removal conforms to the emperor's wishes, and even though the priests of Yasukuni insist now that there can be no removal, they are as devoted to the emperor and the imperial institution as they are to the enshrined war dead. The shrine itself can, moreover, hardly survive without Society's support.

State and religion: the immediate post-war

By a strange coincidence, April 2007 saw the publication of another set of historically important documents on Yasukuni. Compiled by the Diet library with the (somewhat limited) cooperation of Yasukuni archivists, *New edition: a collection of Yasukuni shrine problem documents* (*Shinpen Yasukuni jinja mondai shiryō shū*) is important in

8 *Mainichi* 6.05.07.

the context of the aforementioned saga. The reason is that it attests to the vital role of the state in the post-war apotheosis of not only the war dead, but also of the war criminals. Government ministers always insisted that Yasukuni shrine priests had been the driving force behind the criminals' enshrinement; it now seems the role of the state, specifically Health Ministry bureaucrats, was pivotal. Indeed, Koga Makoto cited this *New edition* as a further reason for launching his Study Group: '[The new Diet library collection has demonstrated the government played a positive role in the apotheosis of the war criminals] and so there is an increasingly strong feeling that now is the time to begin debates about all sorts of things, including the removal [of the Class A war criminals]'.[9] Koga's point here seems to be that, if the state was after all a key player in enshrinement, then it is incumbent on the state to assume a role in removal. The *New edition* disappoints, however, in its failure to reveal details of state-shrine negotiations in the critical decade of the 1970s. Information for the 50s and 60s is there in abundance, but there is a gaping hole for the years 1970-8. When the Diet library asked Yasukuni for documents on this period, a shrine spokesman responded that they had 'looked but were unable to find anything'. The *Yomiuri* newspaper pressed the shrine only to be told it had 'no plans to comment further on the existence or otherwise of any documents not included in the present collection.' The Health Ministry similarly claimed to have undertaken a thorough investigation in its archives, but to have come up with nothing either.[10] The Health Ministry, it should be explained, was (indeed, it remains) responsible for the care of war veterans and the bereaved. It oversees the payments of war pensions, for example; it is also charged with recovering the remains of the war dead from foreign battlefields, and organises tours for veterans and the bereaved to overseas war memorials. This explains why its officials were so intimately involved.

9 *Mainichi shinbun* 6.5.07.

10 *Yomiuri shinbun* 20.4.07.

The *New edition* does, however, reveal that, notwithstanding the Constitutional separation of state and religion, Health Ministry officials and shrine priests met frequently after the end of the Occupation. The enshrinement of those men convicted and then hanged as Class A war criminals was discussed for the first time in 1958. Tajima Norikuni of the Health Ministry broached the subject, but Yasukuni shrine priests responded with caution: 'It all depends on how the media deal with this. The popular reaction could make of this a major issue.'[11] The Ministry's position, it transpires, was that the war only ended with the departure of the American Occupation in 1951. The war criminals were executed during 'war time' and were technically 'war-dead'. Tajima and other Ministry officials returned to the shrine to urge a decision on the Class A war criminals: 'The bereaved are anxious that this should go ahead, and we in the Ministry need you to make up your minds as a matter of urgency.' Nothing happened. When the matter was tabled again in 1961, the shrine insisted that, while the enshrinement of Class B and C criminals might proceed, Class A criminals should be 'kept on hold'. The reasoning is far from clear. Four years later the shrine was still adopting a position far more cautious than the government's, insisting once more that the matter of Class A criminals be put on hold. In 1966, the Health Ministry sought to apply further pressure by sending the shrine the personal details of the Class A war criminals, but still the shrine resisted and it was not till a decade later, 1978, that the war criminals were finally apotheosised. How is the position of Yasukuni to be explained? The answer may well lie in the different dispositions of Yasukuni Chief Priests during the post Occupation period.

Post-war Shinto Orthodoxy: Tsukuba, Matsudaira and Ashizu

Tsukuba Fujimaro was the Chief priest between 1946 and 1977, and he was a very interesting man. The longest serving incumbent in Yasukuni's history, Tsukuba was the third son of Prince Yamashina Ki-

11 *Yomiuri shinbun* 20.4.07.

kumaro, but removed himself from the Yamashina line in the 1920s, became a commoner and assumed the name of Tsukuba. After the war he acquired renown for his involvement in the anti-nuclear peace movement, which took him to Europe in the 1960s.[12] His enduring legacy was in the construction of a new shrine within the main Yasukuni shrine precinct, a simple wooden structure known as the Chinreisha. The Chinreisha is dedicated to the war dead of imperial Japan's erstwhile enemies, none of whom are the object of veneration in those Yasukuni rites that take place in the Main sanctuary. Tsukuba's Chinreisha accommodates two sites for two categories of apotheosised enemy: one is for those who fought against the imperial army in the civil wars of the 1860s; the other is dedicated to the British, American, Chinese, Korean and South East Asian war dead of the Pacific war. In the *Yasukuni* newsletter of New Year 1964, Tsukuba sought to explain the rationale behind the new shrine: 'It is my belief that the *kami* of Yasukuni are active even now as harbingers of peace, standing hand in hand with the spirits of the war dead from all countries of the world. The [construction of the new Chinreisha] renders possible for the first time in Japan the veneration of the glorious spirits of the war dead of all the nations of the earth.'[13] Tsukuba ensured that priests made offerings to the foreign war dead every morning and evening, just as they made offerings to the Japanese war dead in the Main sanctuary; he also established 17 July as the Chinreisha annual festival.[14]

It seems likely that the presence of Tsukuba, who believed the Chinreisha was 'in accord with the wishes of the emperor', explains why Yasukuni resisted Health Ministry pressure to enshrine the war criminals.[15] The least that can be said is that, no sooner did he die in 1977 and the office of Chief Priest pass to former Imperial Navy officer Matsudaira Nagayoshi, than the Class A war criminals' en-

12 *Mainichi* 9.8.06.

13 *Yasukuni*, p. 2.

14 On the Chinreisha, see the chapter by Breen in this volume.

15 *Mainichi shinbun* 9.8.06.

shrinement went ahead. This same Matsudaira threw a steel fence around the Chinreisha, concealing it from view and rendering it impossible for anyone, except shrine priests, to pay their respects there. Matsudaira was also responsible for re-opening the controversial Yūshūkan war museum in 1985, for the first time since 1945.[16] The Yasukuni problem as it is today is then to a considerable degree a legacy of the Matsudaira era from 1977 to 1992. Nonetheless, it is interesting to note that Matsudaira was an outspoken critic of the post-war Japanese state; its interference in shrine affairs he was determined to resist at all costs. He was especially indignant at Prime Minister Nakasone Yasuhiro's interest in removing the Class A war criminals elsewhere. In 1985, when Nakasone made his historic, official visit to the shrine, Matsudaira refused to greet him, though for a different reason. Nakasone's attitude was an insult, Matsudaira insisted, to the spirits of the war dead. In an effort to sidestep the state-religion dilemma, Nakasone declined to undergo Shinto purification by shrine priests, and he refused to bow and clap twice as Shinto etiquette demanded. Instead, he bowed his head and meditated quietly in front of the main sanctuary before turning round and heading back to his official residence. Nakasone's naïve hope was that his actions would somehow 'put an end to the war'. Nothing could have been further from the truth. Instead, he not only antagonised the Yasukuni priesthood, he also stirred the wrath of the Chinese government for venerating Class A war criminals. Such was the Chinese outcry that Nakasone decided that, in the interests of good relations with China, he should never return to Yasukuni. 1985 was, indeed, his last visit.

It might be noted that the position adopted by Matsudaira, at least on the war criminals' enshrinement, was out of tune with post-war Shinto orthodoxy; after all Matsudaira was not a Shinto man. No figure is more representative of that orthodoxy than Ashizu Uzuhiko. He was the leading Shinto intellectual till his death in 1992, and the Shinto establishment today still regards him, and his writings, with

16 On the war museum, see the chapters by Nitta and Breen in this volume.

something approaching awe. He was, for example, the inspiration behind the National Association for Shinto Shrines (*Jinja honchō*), which has defined post war Shinto in its institutional guise ever since its foundation in 1946.[17] Ashizu was determined that Yasukuni should become associated with Japan's peaceful post-war recovery, and not the prosecution of aggressive war against Asia or the West. He wrote a position paper in *Jinja shinpō* in autumn 1946, in which he demanded that any features of Yasukuni that might be associated with 'Fascists, militarism or aggression' should be removed: 'Anything that might lead to misunderstanding in this regard must be eliminated.'[18] Ashizu adhered to this position until his death in 1992. He objected to Class A war criminal enshrinement before it happened, and then penned a protest in its aftermath. In his article, Ashizu insisted Yasukuni's mission was to enshrine those who had fallen 'on the formal orders of the state'; convicted war criminals were altogether different. He dismissed as 'vulgar theory' those who insisted that anybody and everybody who served their country should be venerated in the Yasukuni pantheon.[19] For Ashizu the line was to be drawn at the Class A war criminals. This was precisely the position Tsukuba appears to have adopted up until his death in 1977.

It is easy enough to be distracted by the multi-dimensional controversy in which Yasukuni has found itself embroiled, especially since the late 1970s, and forget that it is a sacred site. It is *the* place, even if it is not the only place, where veterans honour and mourn their comrades, fulfilling war time promises to 'meet again at Yasukuni'; it is the place where the bereaved mourn their loved ones. Indeed, whatever one's views on the Yasukuni shrine, only a cynic would suggest that Prime Ministers when they visit are not motivated, at some level, by a desire to honour the men and women who sacrificed their lives for Japan. It is important, in other words, to allow the possibility

17 Interestingly, Yasukuni is one major shrine that remained structurally outside the umbrella of the National Association of Shinto Shrines.

18 'Yasukuni jinja to heiwa no risō', *Jinja shinpō* 2.9.1946.

19 *Mainichi shinbun* 8.8.2006.

that there are multiple Yasukunis. Adopting an historical perspective on the shrine is essential for underscoring this point. Yasukuni was, at the time of its creation in 1869, a site very different from what it is today.

Revolution: Yasukuni and the Beginnings of Modern Japan

The Meiji Restoration of 1868 effected a complete re-imagining of Japan's religious landscape. The leaders of the new imperial government disestablished Buddhism and its institutions, a process accompanied by much violence; they banned many popular religious practices, too, all in an effort to make space for the new religious construct which we now refer to as Shinto. The early Meiji state declared that all shrines in the land, from the great shrines in Ise dedicated to the Sun goddess Amaterasu, to the myriad local shrines in villages across Japan, were 'sites for the performance of state rites'; they and their priests were placed under the supervision of the modern state. The Meiji government then published a new annual cycle of rites; these were to be performed by the modern Emperor as 'priest king' at the shrine complex in the imperial palace in Tokyo, and emulated by priests at shrines across Japan. All these rites were designed to dramatise the ethnic myth of the emperor's descent from the Sun goddess. Modern Japan's national holidays were duly constructed around these ritual events, as pre-modern feast days were abolished.

The Meiji state in this way effectively legislated a new understanding of shrines as 'Shinto', as entirely distinct, that is, from the Buddhism with which they had been intertwined in both spatial and theological terms in pre-modern Japan. The Meiji state also now created several entirely new shrines, of which the best known are the Minatogawa shrine in Kobe, and Yasukuni in Tokyo. Minatogawa venerates the spirit of Kusunoki Masashige (1294-1336), a medieval warrior whose loyalty and self-sacrifice in the imperial cause were regarded by the new Meiji leadership as exemplary. Yasukuni shrine was similarly dedicated to the spirits of men whose loyalist credentials were beyond reproach: men who had sacrificed their lives on the emperor's behalf in the civil conflicts that accompanied the Imperial Restoration of 1868.[20]

Yasukuni was, from the moment of its creation, distinctive among these shrines either created anew or newly appropriated and transformed by the modern state. It was so in its relationships to the military, to the emperor himself and to society at large. Yasukuni, alone among modern Japan's shrines, was overseen jointly by the Army and Navy ministries, and they ensured that it never wanted for funding. They determined the rituals in the Yasukuni annual cycle, locating them in the first, fifth and ninth months, each marking famous victories of the imperial army over rebel forces in 1868-9. The early celebrants of Yasukuni ritual all bore arms; the first were selected from shrine priest volunteers who fought for the Hōkokutai band of loyalist warriors, and the first *dedicated* Yasukuni chief priest was a samurai from Chōshū by the name of Aoyama Kiyoshi who had no specialist knowledge of Shinto. Aoyama's appointment established a Yasukuni tradition of chief priests frequently hailing from a military background with no Shinto training.[21] In 1879, the shrine assumed the name Yasukuni or 'country at peace', and was granted the status of 'Special state-funded shrine' (*bekkaku kanpeisha*). By this time, the Yasukuni pantheon comprised not only the loyalists from the civil conflicts either side of the Restoration, but also the men who fell in Japan's first overseas adventure in Taiwan in 1874. There were others too who died in the crushing of rebellions against the imperial government: the Saga rebellion of 1874 and the much more threatening Satsuma rebellion of 1877. By 1879, the military victories recorded by the imperial government were too numerous to commemorate, so the shrine's feast days were revised, and re-established as the Great Rites of Autumn and Spring.

---

20 On the modern state's religious policies at the time of the Restoration see Breen, 'Ideologues, bureaucrats and priests'.

21 The aforementioned Matsudaira Nagayoshi was the most recent example of this tradition in practice.

The imperial connection was from the outset more intimate and evident at Yasukuni than at any other shrine in Japan apart from the great shrines in Ise.[22] This was a natural consequence of the fact that Yasukuni was constructed for the apotheosis, propitiation and honouring of men and women who sacrificed their lives in the emperor's name. The Meiji emperor first progressed to the shrine to venerate the Restoration war dead in 1874; he returned in the aftermath of the Satsuma rebellion in 1877, when he presented to the shrine the large mirror that still dominates the main sanctuary today. Hereafter, the practice was established of the Emperor dispatching gift-bearing emissaries to Yasukuni every year on the occasion of the Great Spring and Autumn Rites. The Emperor himself venerated Japan's war dead from the Sino-Japanese war of 1895 and he returned in 1907 to venerate his subjects who fell in the Russo-Japanese war (Fig. 1). Imperial princes were regular participants at the Great Rites of Spring and Autumn, and visitors to Yasukuni were left in no doubt of the shrine's imperial connection: the main sanctuary was draped with banners, and the steps up to it decorated with lanterns, all bearing the sixteen-petal imperial chrysanthemum.

New Tokyo Flourishing

Yasukuni's intimate connections to the military, to the imperial institution and so to death in battle on the emperor's behalf meant that the shrine was identified with the virtues of loyalty, self-sacrifice and patriotism, which the Meiji leaders and their pre-war successors deemed essential to the construction of the modern nation state. In order to ensure the dissemination of these virtues to as wide a sector of society as possible, early Meiji leaders gave to Yasukuni a quality shared by no other state sponsored shrine in the capital or, indeed, the land: the combination of solemn apotheosis and popular entertainment. The very first rites of apotheosis, in 1869, were announced by booming cannon, accompanied by firework displays and

22 For the imperial connection at Yasukuni today, see the chapter by Breen in this volume.

concluded with sumo wrestling matches. In 1871, the space outside the main *torii* gate was converted into a race horse track. At the end of the same year, a lighthouse was erected adjacent to the main *torii.* It was intended as a guide for fishing vessels in Tokyo harbour, but it did much to transform Yasukuni into one of modern Tokyo's most vibrant tourist attractions. In 1873, Hattori Bushō (1841-1908), lecturer at the government's Kaisei institute, visited Yasukuni for the Great Autumn Rite and wrote about that event in his best-selling *Tōkyō shin hanjō ki* (A record of Tokyo flourishing anew), published the following year. Bushō conveys brilliantly the bustle and excitement of Yasukuni as a site of entertainment, as well as the ritual solemnity, without any sense that the two may be incongruous.

The [Great Rites of Autumn] take place over three days. Pilgrims mass at Kudan like clouds in the sky, rubbing shoulders and elbows. It is all so typical of the new flourishing Tokyo. Merchants vie with one another to set up shops, spreading out mats and lining up their goods; others set out stalls with food for sale; people push into one another and there is scarcely room to stand. On the first day, there is a firework display... They let the fireworks off one after another, from noon through till night. Imagine lightning streaking across the sky, or a golden phoenix spitting out fire, flying through clouds of smoke, or a bright red dragon with a pearl in its mouth charging through purple clouds...... Every firework is different; it is an extraordinary sight to behold. The second day they hold horse races.... They mark out a track using wooden fences, and set two horses to race against each other. What decides the winner are the skill of the riders and the innate talent of the horses, some fleet of foot, others sluggish.... Sometimes horse and rider stumble having just left the starting grid; some get half way round and fall off; some are overtaken just a few paces from the finishing line... They are like crazed lions as their hooves kick up the dirt with scuffing sound; they are like goblins in flight, as they race with banners flying... The third day is sumo. This is the event that really pulls the crowds during the [Great Autumn Rite]. What is special is that the greatest wrestlers [*yokozuna*] compete with complete novices [*fundoshi katsugi*]. Sometimes the most powerful wrestlers of all compete with others from their own stable... On this day alone, a *sekiwaki* wrestler from the east might be pitted against a [much stronger] *ōzeki* wrestler also from the east. Often, the managers deliberately pit a weak wrestler against a much stronger wrestler. If an *ōzeki* loses against a *sekiwaki*, he will be shamed for life; if a novice defeats an accomplished wrestler, it is glory for life!

Bushō was exhilarated by his experience of Yasukuni entertainment, but he was keen to dwell on Yasukuni's role as a site of mourning, and of national pride. He understood that the site of Kudan, with its remarkable vista of all Tokyo, was selected in order that the *kami* in the Yasukuni pantheon might more easily watch over the city. The main sanctuary and the chrysanthemum-embossed banners that bedecked the shrine persuaded him that the spirits of national heroes of the new Japan truly dwelt in the shrine's building. Bushō was convinced that they would no longer be wandering ghost-like, lost on the field of battle. 'Their spirits can not now be in the realm of hungry ghosts, suffering the pangs of starvation.' Rather, 'the spirits of the fallen are even now joining their pale hands together in the nether realm, thanking the emperor for his beneficence....' 'Only the man who is envious of the manner in which these heroes died [insists Bushō] merits being called a citizen of the imperial realm'.[23]

Yasukuni's Spaces

When Busho wrote of Yasukuni in the 1870s, it comprised the Main sanctuary, where the enshrined *kami* were propitiated and venerated and a 'spirit garden' (*shōkon saitei*), an open area to which the spirits of the war dead were first summoned by a priest before being transferred to the Main sanctuary, there to be venerated as *kami*. The entrance to the shrine precinct, which comprised these two structures, was marked by a *torii* gate (Fig. 2). Steadily thereafter the shrine underwent a spatial transformation. The Yūshūkan war museum was constructed in 1881 on a site just east of the main sanctuary. In 1893, a towering statue of Ōmura Masujirō (1824-69), the founder of the modern Japanese army, was erected on the central pathway leading to the main sanctuary. Both these new structures helped enhance Yasukuni's reputation as a major tourist attraction of mid-Meiji Ja-

23 Hattori, *Tōkyō shin hanjōki*, pp. 57-9.

pan. (Fig. 3). The Yūshūkan began by displaying weaponry, uniforms and other relics from the Satsuma rebellion, as well as swords of great pedigree; Ōmura's 12m high statue, for its part, acquired renown as Japan's first ever Western-style statue in bronze. But the shrine was to undergo further dramatic spatial transformation. Japan's first modern war, the Sino-Japanese war of 1894-5, marked an initial stage. In 1905, the Meiji Emperor progressed to the shrine to make offerings as the spirits of 1,500 Japanese officers and men were enshrined; many more were to follow. Fireworks, horse racing, sumo and the bustle reported by Bushō thirty years before were fully a part of these events, and indeed all others till the start of the Pacific war in 1941, but on this occasion the shrine precinct bristled with the spoils of victory. The Yūshūkan, too, displayed Chinese weapons, maps and uniforms.[24] It was now that the Army and Navy ministries planned the construction of a new building, able to accommodate large numbers of bereaved pilgrims. The Worship hall, which stands today between the main sanctuary and the *torii*, was duly completed in 1901; eight hundred worshippers could kneel there, undergo ritual purification and then look across to observe the ritual proceedings in the main sanctuary (Figs 4 and 5). A stage for *nō* drama, performances of which henceforth accompanied major shrine rites, was erected in the precinct at the same time. So abundant were the spoils after Japan's victory against Russia in the war of 1904-5 that an annex had to be built to the Yūshūkan to house them all. 88,000 new *kami* were added to the Yasukuni pantheon at the end of that war, which despite ending in Japanese victory exhausted and demoralised Japanese society. Widespread social unrest followed the end to hostilities, but Japan's frequent wars and the continuous production of war dead meant that Yasukuni could only prosper: Japan participated in the First World War on the side of the Allies, and a decade later it began its costly war against China.

It was to celebrate the fiftieth anniversary of the shrine's foundation in 1929 that a new imposing *torii*, wrought of iron and bronze, was

24 On displays of Chinese weaponry see the chapter in this volume by Wang.

built at the foot of Kudan hill (Fig. 6). The *torii*, funded with a donation from the All Japan Sumō Association, stood 20 metres high and weighed some 90 tons, which made it the largest, and heaviest, *torii* in Japan. It served to mark the outer extremity of an expanded precinct of the shrine. In 1923 Tokyo was hit by a massive earthquake, but it left the shrine's sacred spaces and its several structures, new and old, relatively unscathed. The two *torii* gates withstood the tremors; the main sanctuary and Worship hall survived with only superficial damage. However, the Yūshūkan, the only building in the precinct made of brick in Western style, suffered a major hit, and many of its treasures were lost. The museum was subsequently redesigned by the Japanese architect, Itō Chūta (1867-1954), but building work was not completed till 1931. Today one of the most distinctive features of the Yasukuni shrine precinct is the sacred gate or *shinmon*. This extraordinary wooden structure, with its distinctive thatched roof reminiscent of the imperial shrines in Ise, and heavy door embossed with an eye-catching gold chrysanthemum, was erected in 1934 as an offering to the Yasukuni spirits (Fig. 7). Japan was then mired in the early stages of a disastrous war with China, and the protective powers of the Yasukuni *kami* were needed more than ever before. At around this time, too, the spirit garden was moved just outside the sacred gate (Fig. 8). With the completion of this gate, the re-siting of the old *torii* (which had to be moved back to accommodate it), and the relocation of the garden, the Yasukuni shrine assumed pretty much the appearance and the dimensions which it maintains to this day (Figs 9 and 10).[25]

In 1943, the massive iron and bronze *torii* was removed on the instructions of Prime Minister Tōjō Hideki, its raw materials put to military use; other statuary was also surrendered to the war effort.[26]

25 In 1985, the spirit garden and the *torii* and lanterns which had marked the site off as distinctive during the 1930s were paved over and turned into a parking lot. On this transformation, see Tsubouchi, 'Yasukuni', Chapter 1.

26 Kobori, *Yasukuni jinja*, p. 119. The great bronze *torii* that stands at the foot of Kudan hill today was erected in 1978; at 25 metres tall, it is still the largest in Japan.

Devastation again struck Tokyo in the firebombing; but, miraculously, Yasukuni once more escaped barely scathed. Ten days of bombing by American B29s in March of 1945 razed Tokyo to the ground; the firestorms claimed the lives of at least 100,000, but Yasukuni survived. The main sanctuary, the worship hall and the sacred gate, the most vulnerable structures, all avoided a direct hit.

Yasukuni: Post-War

During the war, Emperor Hirohito participated in the Yasukuni Great Rites of Spring and Autumn. By war's end, he had personally witnessed the enshrinement of thousands upon thousands of men and women, but this was a tiny proportion of Japan's total war dead. Yasukuni could only apotheosise those military personnel whose details—name, age, regiment, rank, place and date of death—it possessed, but the fate of hundreds of thousands of soldiers, sailors and non-military personnel, that is the vast majority of those who died in the last year of the war, was still unknown in August 1945. Yasukuni faced a very uncertain fate at the hands of the Occupation forces; indeed, the Occupation contemplated razing the shrine to the ground. It nonetheless granted permission for a performance in November 1945 of a solemn, and possibly final, rite for all the Japanese war dead who were as yet unidentified. Prime Minister Shidehara attended, perpetuating a practice of Prime Ministerial visits to the shrine that traced its origins to the onset of the Pacific war in 1941; Shidehara's cabinet were all in attendance, with senior representatives of the Army and Navy. Emperor Hirohito, too, visited Yasukuni on this occasion, to pay his respects to the war dead. In the following month, the Occupation issued the so-called Shinto directive which abolished 'state Shinto', effectively ending state support for all shrines. Yasukuni lost the special status it had acquired in 1879, and with it the funding it had been guaranteed since early Meiji. It was now reconstituted in law as an entirely independent religious juridical person. This status it holds today, its integrity guaranteed by the Constitution of 1946.

Yasukuni shrine was spared destruction by the Occupation, but its future depended on quickly generating very substantial funds. Immediately the priests set up a Yasukuni Worshippers' Society (*Yasukuni jinja hōsankai*) to this end. With an imperial princess as president, a former Foreign minister as vice-president and a former Prime Minister and company presidents as consultants, it is not surprising that fundraising proved highly successful; so much so that the shrine soon invested in a spacious new reception hall and a new shrine office. In 1953, the Japan Society for the War Bereaved was formed to raise awareness of the economic plight of many of the bereaved, and ensure the state did its duty by them; it also set out to pressure the post-Occupation government to 'renationalise' the shrine and revive state funding for Yasukuni rites. This proposal steadily gathered momentum, and led to the repeated submission of Yasukuni bills (*Yasukuni hōan*) to the Diet by members of the Liberal Democratic Party between 1969 and 1974. On each occasion, however, these bills were defeated. The post-Occupation practice of Prime Ministerial patronage of Yasukuni shrine rites began with Yoshida Shigeru's visit to the Great Rite of Autumn in 1951, and Emperor Hirohito returned to Yasukuni for the first time after the departure of the Americans in autumn of 1952. It was to be the best part of another generation before Yasukuni found itself at the centre of the domestic and international controversy that obtains to the present day.

The Yasukuni Controversy

It is this controversy with which the contributors to this book seek to engage. It should be said at the outset that this is a polemical book, but one with a difference. *Yasukuni, the War Dead and the Struggle for Japan's Past* sets out neither to attack Yasukuni nor, indeed, to commend it. Rather, it seeks to bring together authoritative voices from different points on the Yasukuni spectrum, and asks the reader to judge the merits of the arguments presented. In Japan and overseas there has been very little *debate* about Yasukuni. Scholars and critics each adopt their own more or less persuasive positions, but rarely engage with one another; certainly there exists no single volume in Japanese or English in which a diversity of views is offered. In other words, the interested reader has had, till now, very little opportunity to assess the merits of both sides of the Yasukuni divide. Here Kevin Doak argues the case *for* Yasukuni from the perspective of a practising Catholic. He takes issue particularly with the objections that the Chinese have consistently voiced. Wang Zhixin articulates precisely that Chinese position, drawing on historical sources as well as contemporary perspectives to make his case. Seki Hei is a Taiwan Chinese academic resident in Japan, who is dismissive of mainland Chinese objections, as rooted in an all-too-narrow Marxist perspective. While Seki champions the Prime Ministers' right to visit Yasukuni, Takahashi Tetsuya, the most widely read critic of state patronage in recent years, sees the shrine as the symbol par excellence of post war Japan's denial of responsibility, and its fabrication of history. Nitta Hitoshi by contrast is the most prolific, and persuasive, writer of the pro-Yasukuni lobby in Japan. His chapter insists that hypocrisy infiltrates the arguments of anti-Yasukuni polemicists at every turn, and his contribution includes a sharp rebuke for the editor of this volume, John Breen, whose own chapter explores Yasukuni as a site of memory, and finds it seriously wanting. These polemical chapters are 'book-ended' by contributions from Caroline Rose on the international ramifications of the Yasukuni problem, and from Philip Seaton, who approaches Yasukuni in its domestic dimension through an exploration of Japanese media coverage.

Fig. 1 The Meiji emperor visits the Yasukuni shrine, 17 December 1895 on the occasion of the enshrinement rite for Japanese who died in the Sino-Japanese war (1894-5). Reproduced with permission from the Meiji jingu, Tokyo.

Fig. 2 The Yasukuni shrine, circa 1875. The honden or Main sanctuary was built in 1874 and has survived to this day. Reproduced with permission; from the Yasukuni shrine archive.

Fig. 3 The precinct of Yasukuni, atop Kudanzaka. This is a *nishiki'e* painting by the artist Ikuhide and dates from 1889. The Yūshūkan war museum is the building just visible on the right of the picture. From the Yasukuni shrine archive; reproduced with permission.

Fig. 4 The honden or Main sanctuary, 1897. Prior to the building of the Haiden or Worship hall, the bereaved and other visitors to Yasukuni accessed the Main sanctuary directly. From the Yasukuni shrine archive; reproduced with permission.

Fig. 5 The bereaved enter the Main sanctuary, in this painting by Seta Sanshirō. The painting shows the bereaved accessing the Main sanctuary from the Worship hall, just visible on the left. From the Yasukuni shrine archive; reproduced with permission.

Fig. 6 The great Yasukuni torii. From the Yasukuni shrine archive; reproduced with permission.

Fig. 7 The Sacred gate or *shinmon*, circa 1934. This picture postcard from the second decade of the Showa period (1926-89) clearly shows the sacred gate and, through it, the chrysanthemum drapes of the Worship hall are just visible. From the Yasukuni shrine archive; reproduced with permission.

Fig. 8 The sacred garden or Saitei, 1936. On the evening of 26 April 1936, shrine priests offer up prayers to summon the spirits of the Japanese military who fell in China. The following day shrine priests transport the sprits to the central shrine within the Main sanctuary, and worship them as kami. From the Yasukuni shrine archive; reproduced with permission.

Fig. 9 Yasukuni shrine precinct, 1937. This illustration of the lay out the shrine in 1937 is by Uehara Furutoshi. It was designed as a wall chart for use in primary schools. The illustration shows (from the bottom up) the First torii, the statue of Omura Masujiro, the Second torii, the Sacred gate, the Worship hall and the Main sanctuary. Just visible to the left of the Worship hall is the Sacred garden. From the Yasukuni shrine archive; reproduced with permission.

Fig. 10 The Yasukuni precinct as it is today. The Main sanctuary, the worship hall, the Sacred gate, the statue of Omura Masajiro and the great *torii* are all visible.

1

STALEMATE: THE YASUKUNI SHRINE PROBLEM IN SINO-JAPANESE RELATIONS

Caroline Rose

Former Prime Minister Koizumi Jun'ichirō's annual visits to the Yasukuni shrine from 2001 to 2006 prompted much criticism from the Chinese leadership and the Chinese public, and led to a stalemate in high-level relations between the two countries even as China emerged as Japan's largest trading partner. Hu Jintao said in 2005 that the Yasukuni shrine issue was the single problem preventing China and Japan from moving ahead, and Li Changchun, member of the Politburo Standing Committee of the Chinese Communist Party (CCP), told Nakagawa Hidenao, Chairman of the LDP's Policy Affairs Research Council in February 2006 that Prime Minister Koizumi's Yasukuni visits represented 'the most serious difficulty since the normalization of diplomatic ties.'[1] By late 2005 Chinese leaders were refusing to meet Koizumi even on the sidelines of East Asian regional meetings. Koizumi's final visit to the shrine, before he stepped down as prime minister, took place on the anniversary of Japan's surrender on 15 August 2006 and elicited one of the most strongly worded protests by the Chinese

1 Przystup, 'Looking beyond Koizumi'.

Foreign Ministry. Koizumi's visit was described as an 'act that gravely offends the people in countries victimized by the war of aggression launched by Japanese militarists and undermines the political foundation of China-Japan relations.'[2]

The political foundations of the relationship, though shaken, were not totally destroyed by Koizumi's actions. Since becoming prime minister in September 2006, Abe Shinzō has adopted a determined strategic ambiguity regarding his plans to visit the shrine. As of early summer 2007, he has stayed away from the shrine, choosing instead to dispatch offerings and have shrine priests present them to the war dead on his behalf.[3] In so doing he has appeased, at least temporarily, his Chinese critics. One of Abe's first tasks as new prime minister was to mend relations with China and South Korea. Within one month of taking office, Abe found himself among friends in Beijing where he met with Wen Jiabao and Hu Jintao and talked of the need to 'look at past history squarely'.[4] However, the revival of top-level exchanges between Japan and China, though to be welcomed, does not mark the end of the stalemate on the Yasukuni shrine issue, and it is not yet clear what would transpire should Prime Minister Abe choose to visit the shrine in the future.

The Yasukuni shrine problem has been ongoing domestically in Japan since the end of the Occupation, but emerged as a diplomatic issue between Japan and its neighbours, particularly China and Korea, in 1985 when Prime Minister Nakasone Yasuhiro visited the shrine. With the exception of Prime Minister Hashimoto Ryūtarō's visit to the shrine in 1996, the problem reverted to the domestic agenda in Japan until Koizumi's visits once again drew vocal opposition from abroad. The issue goes to the very heart of debate about Japan's war responsibility and its perceived inability to reconcile with its Asian neighbours. In this chapter, I argue that the issue can also be viewed within the context of domestic politics (and politicking) in both Japan

2 Xinhua, 'FM on Koizumi's shrine visit'.

3 See Breen, 'A Yasukuni genealogy', pp. 1-2

4 Abe, 'Press conference by Prime Minister Abe Shinzō'.

and China. The chapter looks at the way the issue has been instrumentalised in domestic political and foreign policy circles in both countries, thereby perpetuating and exacerbating the problem. It begins with a brief description of the Yasukuni shrine problem first as a Japanese domestic issue, and then as a bilateral issue with China. It then examines the domestic politics of the issue in Japan and China. In particular, it is concerned with two areas in which the Yasukuni issue appears to serve the interests of domestic political agencies in both countries: first, as a means of legitimisation by appealing to popular sentiment, and second, as a means of reinforcing domestic and foreign policy goals of Chinese and Japanese leaders.

The Yasukuni Shrine as Domestic Problem

The Yasukuni shrine was founded in the Meiji period 'for the worship of the divine spirits of those who sacrificed themselves for the country.'[5] Specifically, the religious role of the shrine was to pacify the spirits of the war dead to prevent them from seeking retribution on the living. As Shinto became the official religion of the state under the Meiji government, the shrine became the central site for commemoration and worship of the 'divine spirits', that is, Japanese military and military-related individuals who had died for Emperor and nation since 1853. Enshrined there today are the spirits of approximately 2.5 million war dead, including, since 1978 the spirits of fourteen Class A war criminals. The shrine receives approximately 8 million visitors per year, and is considered a central site for national memory in Japan.[6] It is a powerful symbol of pre-war State Shinto and Japanese militarism, and for this reason it divides the nation, going to the core of contested interpretations of Japan's role in the Second World War, and the recreation of a national identity in the post-war period. Crudely put, the struggle is between those on the left, the progressives who view Japan's actions during the Second World War as aggressive and are in

5 http://www.yasukuni.or.jp.

6 Harootunian, 'Memory, mourning and national morality', p.150.

favour of a strict separation between state and religion, and those on the right who view Japan's role in the Second World War as part of the struggle against colonial domination of Asia and who favour state support for the Yasukuni shrine. This is, of course, far too simplistic a view, and obscures the many shades of opinion on Yasukuni and its various meanings. Certainly, neither camp is monolithic and there is much less consensus on these issues than is assumed. For the purpose of this chapter it is worth highlighting two of the more contentious aspects of the issue: the legal and constitutional status of the shrine itself; and problems relating to the politics of history, remembrance and commemoration.

The post-Second World War Constitution ensured a strict separation of state and religion, and guaranteed freedom of religion to all. The Yasukuni shrine became a religious juridical person (*shūkyō hōjin*), independent from the government. The formation of the Japan Society for the War Bereaved (*Nihon Izokukai*) and the emergence of a conservative coalition in the mid-1950s, however, led to various attempts over the next generation to pass a bill in the Diet to renationalize the shrine, and to institutionalize prime ministerial and ministerial visits. The bills failed, stymied by opposition from, among others, the Japan Socialist Party (JSP), and Christian and Buddhist groups. Nonetheless, the Japan Society for the War Bereaved and other groups continued to push for the regularization of official visits to the shrine.[7]

It was, in fact, common practice for Japanese prime ministers, cabinet ministers, and indeed Emperor Hirohito (till 1975) to make regular visits to the Yasukuni shrine in the post-occupation period.[8] Such visits passed off with little controversy till the 1970s when

7 Pye, 'Religion and conflict in Japan', p.11; Tanaka, 'Yasukuni shrine, the Prime Minister, and the Constitution'; and *Yomiuri Shinbun*, 'Yasukuni: behind the *torii*'.

8 Between 1951 and 1985, with the exception of Hatoyama Ichirô and Ishibashi Tanzan, every Japanese prime minister visited Yasukuni during either the Great Spring or the Great Autumn Rites. Since 1985 only Miyazawa Kiichi (in secret), Hashimoto Ryūtarō and Koizumi Jun'ichirō have visited.

several factors combined to heighten public awareness and concern. These included the ambiguity surrounding the status of prime ministerial visits (that is, whether they were undertaken in a private or official capacity), the choice of dates for Yasukuni shrine visits, and the enshrinement of the spirits of fourteen Class A war criminals in 1978. Prime Minister Miki chose to visit the shrine on the anniversary of Japan's defeat on 15 August 1975, the first prime minister to do so. Miki maintained the visit was undertaken in a private capacity in that he used a private car, made a financial offering with his own money, and signed the visitor's book without adding his official title, but his visit nonetheless sparked debate in Japan which endured. Visits to the shrine by subsequent prime ministers attracted media attention, particularly if they failed to clarify whether they were private or official. This ambiguity served only to blur the supposed constitutional separation of state and religion. There was nothing ambiguous, however, about Prime Minister Nakasone's official visit to the shrine on 15 August 1985. Quite apart from provoking strong protests from China, his actions resulted in a number of domestic lawsuits. In several cases, notably the ruling on the Ehime suit by the Supreme Court in 1997, and later rulings by courts in Fukuoka in 2001 and Osaka in 2005, official visits were judged unconstitutional.[9] Prime Minister Koizumi's visits in the 2000s prompted similar lawsuits, and on two occasions (Fukuoka 2001 and Osaka 2005) similar verdicts. But Prime Minister Koizumi paid them no heed.

The Yasukuni shrine also provokes controversy because of its association with a particular interpretation of the past. The way a state, or sub-sections of the state, remembers its past is central to the (re-)formulation of its national identity. In Japan, the struggle between left and right for mastery over a national narrative is still ongoing. The symbolism of the Yasukuni shrine, in addition to the version of history presented in the Yushukan museum sited in the shrine precinct, embodies the 'affirmative view' of Japan's role in the Second World War, that is the view that Japan's role in Asia was

9 Tanaka, 'What is the "Yasukuni problem?"'

one of liberation rather than aggression. Though not necessarily the mainstream, this is a persistent opinion which hinders attempts to produce a more balanced approach acknowledging Asian suffering at the hands of the Imperial Japanese Army. As Saaler states, in the post-war period the Yasukuni shrine and the Yūshūkan have come 'to play a central role in the political, religious and cultural re-affirmation of the nation.'[10]

The shrine's role in the state's approach to remembrance and commemoration is additionally problematic since the way a state remembers and commemorates its past impacts on the way in which others perceive its intentions. According to Lind, the more apologetic or contrite a state is, the more benignly its intentions are perceived. By contrast, the more a country teaches nationalistic history and glorifies its past behaviour, the more threatening it appears. Where approaches to remembrance and reconciliation are contested domestically, for example, if the government appears contrite, but society does not, this creates ambiguity and leads to confusion.[11] In Japan's case, it is the representatives of the state who appear, by visiting the Yasukuni shrine, to lack contrition and repentance for the past. Although Yasukuni is seen as the main, indeed the quasi-national, site of commemoration for Japan's war victims, overshadowing other memorial sites, such as Chidorigafuchi, the cemetery for 'unknown soldiers',[12] Yasukuni's status does not imply a consensus on the national story. Particularly problematic for some is the fact that enshrinement of

10 Saaler, *Politics, memory and public opinion*, p. 122.

11 Lind takes policies of remembrance to include the following 'policy instruments': apologies, trials, education, and commemoration. Lind, 'Sorry states: apologies in international politics'.

12 The Chidorigafuchi cemetery for the war dead receives far fewer visitors than Yasukuni, numbering approximately 180,000 compared to Yasukuni's several million per year. A memorial ceremony is held at the cemetery in early August and is attended by government representatives and religious groups, but the official memorial ceremony held by the Japanese government takes place on 15 August at the Budōkan next to Chidorigafuchi cemetery, and is attended by, amongst others, the Emperor and prime minister. Saaler, *Politics, memory and public opinion*, p. 103.

the spirits of the military and military-related personnel who died for the Emperor in Japan's wars took place regardless of their actions during war or their religious leanings and beliefs. A quite different issue concerns Taiwanese and Koreans who object to Yasukuni's unilateral enshrinement of their loved ones alongside Japanese war criminals. This has produced much anguish within Japan and overseas, not least for families of Taiwanese and Korean servicemen or for those of Japanese Christian or Buddhist soldiers who actively oppose enshrinement.[13] In addition, there is much opposition to the enshrinement of Japanese Class A war criminals at Yasukuni, and this lends an even greater ambiguity to prime ministerial visits: who and what is the prime minister worshipping and honouring when he visits the shrine?

Yasukuni Shrine Visits as a Bilateral issue with China

Prime Minister Nakasone's visits to Yasukuni in 1982 and 1983 provoked domestic controversy in Japan, particularly since he did not clarify whether they were undertaken in an official or private capacity. Nakasone was viewed as generally supportive of the attempts by the Japan Society for the War Bereaved and right-wing groups to restore state support for the shrine. He authorised a study committee to investigate the question of official visits, and the report's conclusion, published in November 1984, exacerbated the situation with its finding that official visits might be constitutional. A further report, this time produced by a private advisory committee set up by the cabinet secretary, published its findings on 9 August 1985. Though inconclusive, it nonetheless provided Nakasone with sufficient grounds to make an official visit along with most of his Cabinet on 15 August 1985, which for the first time prompted the Chinese government to raise the issue directly with Japan. Although the Chinese made no official protest—this, according to Whiting, was because of concerns over the possible reaction of the Chinese public—there

13 See the chapter by Takahashi in this volume and, for example, O'Brien and Ohkoshi, *To dream of dreams.*

had been some attempt on the part of the Chinese Ministry of Foreign Affairs in the run up to Nakasone's visit to persuade the Japanese government to 'handle the matter with prudence'. Chinese concerns about Nakasone's actions, seen within the general context of a more assertive Japanese foreign policy aimed at 'settling post-war accounts', were enunciated by the Chinese leadership at various commemorative events held on or around 15 August, to mark the fortieth anniversary of the end of the war, and were couched in terms of the attempts of 'a handful of Japanese' to revive militarism. Specific reference was made to Japanese government officials who paid homage at the Yasukuni shrine 'where, among others, the chief Japanese war criminals [are] venerated', an action which 'hurt the feelings of the Chinese people'.[14] The Chinese media also reported widely on Nakasone's Yasukuni visit, and maintained a steady flow of articles relating China's victory in the War of Resistance against Japan.

The fortieth anniversary activities in China continued into September, as did the criticisms of the Japanese government as expressed by Chinese leaders in meetings with a Japan Socialist Party (JSP) delegation and the Dietmen's League for Japan-China Friendship. The summer's events culminated in a series of anti-Japanese demonstrations in Beijing, where students rallied against Nakasone and Japanese militarism. As is widely recognised, demonstrations in China are often used as a means to register criticism of the domestic government. The anti-Japanese demonstrations were no different in this regard, and students were also venting their anger over the high cost of living, corruption, and slow reforms. However, the demonstrations, and the manifestation of genuine anti-Japanese sentiment, nonetheless sent a strong signal to the Japanese government, and to Nakasone in particular, that Japan's Asian neighbours were not prepared to accept official Yasukuni visits.[15] In explaining his decision not to visit the Yasukuni shrine for the autumn rites in October 1985, Nakasone referred to the need to

14 Whiting, *China Eyes Japan*, p. 54. See also Shibuichi, 'The Yasukuni shrine dispute', pp. 206-8.

15 Whiting, *China Eyes Japan*, pp.76-7.

avoid provoking further anti-Japanese demonstrations in China since they could be detrimental to the pro-Japanese General Secretary Hu Yaobang; this would not be in Japan's interests.[16] Nakasone had underestimated the strength of domestic and foreign opposition. Following sustained protests from within and beyond Japan, he chose not to return to Yasukuni. Subsequent prime ministers followed his lead, with the exception of Hashimoto in July 1996, and, of course, Koizumi between 2001 and 2006.[17]

Koizumi's annual visits to the shrine caused considerable damage to Japan-China relations, and the lack of in-country summits after 2001 was certainly symbolic of a rupture between the two protagonists. However, Koizumi did have occasion to meet Chinese leaders at regional and international forums where discussions took place. Some meetings were cooler than others, but in the latter stages of his term of office, the Chinese leadership refused to meet Koizumi even on the sidelines. The impact of the Yasukuni problem could be felt beyond the official level, too, and appeared to have a negative influence on popular perceptions, reinforcing unfriendly feelings amongst the Chinese and Japanese people as revealed in various opinion polls, but more obviously in the anti-Japanese demonstrations in China in April 2005. These were the culmination of several incidents provoked in no small part by the actions of Japanese businessmen, students, and politicians (including Koizumi's Yasukuni visits), and showed how popular sentiment against Japan is easily inflamed in China.[18] By the same token, the demonstrations produced an angry backlash in Japan, prompting the Japanese government to seek an apology and compensation from China for the damage caused to Japanese businesses.[19]

16 Itagaki, *Yasukuni kōshiki sanpai*, pp. 161-70 and Shibuichi 'The Yasukuni shrine Dispute', p.207.

17 See Nelson, 'Social memory as ritual practice', pp. 457-8 for a discussion of Hashimoto's visit.

18 Gries, 'China's "New thinking on Japan"', pp.843-7.

19 Przystup, 'No end to history'.

Chinese governments since 1985 have been consistent in their criticism of Japanese leadership visits to Yasukuni, and their protests have frequently referred to the enshrinement of the spirits of Class A war criminals. For the Chinese leadership, the enshrinement of war criminals, the ambiguity accompanying prime ministerial and cabinet ministers' visits as to their official or private status, and the level of right-wing support for the visits, all signal the inability or unwillingness of certain Japanese to move away from past militarism and accept responsibility for the war. The Yasukuni issue is, therefore, inextricably intertwined with the 'history problem'. In the view of Beijing, Japan's failure to 'adopt a correct view of history', or to 'take history as a mirror and look forward to the future', continues to 'hurt the Chinese people'. Thus for China, the 'Yasukuni shrine is a symbol of (Japan's) war of invasion' and 'the key point about Yasukuni visits is that they affirm Class A war criminals.'[20]

Thus, the Yasukuni shrine, and in particular Prime Minister Koizumi's patronage of it since 2001, have posed problems at both domestic and bilateral levels. Shrine visits are used to advance domestic political and foreign policy-related agendas in both countries, which helps to explain why the problem cannot simply be resolved by cessation of prime ministerial visits or the creation of a non-religious national memorial.

The Domestic Politics of the Yasukuni Issue in China and Japan

The Chinese government has often been accused of attempting to play the history card in its dealings with Japan. Yet in regard to Yasukuni, both sides exploit historical grievances for such divergent domestic political goals as enhancing party or individual legitimacy, seeking popular or intra-party support, introducing or developing a particular foreign policy stance, or reinforcing a particular interpre-

20 Jin, 'Canbai', p. 24. For detailed accounts of the Chinese response to Nakasone's 1985 visit see Itagaki, *Yasukuni kōshiki sanpai*, pp. 161-70 and Whiting, *China Eyes Japan*. For contrasting views, the chapters by Seki and Wang in this volume.

tation of history and shoring up national identity. Such behaviour makes a political solution more difficult, and furthermore, pits Chinese public opinion against Japanese public opinion, exacerbating the poor state of relations.

Several recurring themes emerge from a reading of Chinese-, Japanese-, and English-language media, journals, articles and books on the Koizumi visits to Yasukuni since 2001. The most common explanations focus on the use of the Yasukuni issue by both governments as a means of legitimising the ruling party or individual leaders, and appealing to popular sentiment, on the one hand, and of reinforcing domestic and foreign policy goals, on the other.

Legitimisation and Populism

Prime Minister Koizumi's stance towards Yasukuni was seen as a means to help him gain power in the LDP presidential elections, and maintain his high levels of popular support as prime minister of Japan. During the LDP leadership contest in April 2001, all four candidates were asked if they would consider visiting Yasukuni if elected. Koizumi pledged that he would do so, and, it is argued, he continued to win support from at least one section of the electorate on the basis of his annual visits to the shrine. A number of Chinese analysts interpret Koizumi's visits as opportunities to buoy up his popularity and earn him votes in the short term.[21] The Japan Society for the War Bereaved is seen as an important source of support, and Bu Ping considers the Yasukuni visits as a 'political necessity' to keep such voters on the government's side.[22] Others argue that the LDP had to show its conservative credentials in the face of the growing popularity of the Democratic Party of Japan (DPJ) in 2003; it was also able to use Yasukuni patronage as a means of displaying a strong foreign policy stance when threat perceptions were high among the

21 Zhou, 'Xiaoquan neige de waijiao zhengce xianxi', p.31.

22 Bu, 'Riben jingguo shenshe wenti', p. 180.

Japanese, for example in relation to North Korea and China.[23] Similar arguments are extended to those in Koizumi's circle, and in particular to Minister Aso Tarō's proclamations on Yasukuni-related matters. Not well-received by the Chinese press and academics, Aso's rebuttal of Chinese and Korean criticisms of Koizumi's visits are explained by Liu Jiangyong, for example, as appeasing the Japanese right wing in the hope of raising Aso's own political popularity. Aso, according to Liu, 'must use some tactics to show his hard-line foreign policy catering to emerging nationalism and fishing for political capital in the next prime ministerial election.'[24]

It is true to say that Koizumi's shrine visits gained support, not surprisingly, from the right wing, and specifically the pro-Yasukuni interest groups such as the Japan Society for the War Bereaved and the Glorious War Dead Society (*Eirei ni kotaeru kai*). [25] It would also appear that the visits garnered increasing support from the Japanese public over time, as some opinion polls suggest. Thus, a poll taken by the *Asahi shinbun* in August 2001 revealed that 65% of those polled opposed Koizumi's visit while only 26% were in favour. By 2005 the support rate had increased to 36% of those polled, those opposed to the visits having dropped to 48%.[26] Headlines in the *Daily Yomiuri* and *Mainichi Daily News* after Koizumi's 15 August 2006 visit announced a 50% support rate.[27] While polls should be approached with

23 Zhai, 'Riben zimindang reyi canbai qingguo shenshe', p. 36.

24 Cited in Ni, 'Who is doing the threatening?'

25 The right wing in Japan is not a monolith. For an analysis of the different right wing groups and their activities see Shibuichi, 'The Yasukuni shrine dispute'.

26 Shibuichi ('The Yasukuni shrine dispute', p. 212) notes that public opinion has tended favour official visits, citing for example an *Asahi shinbun* poll of October 1985 in which 50.5% of those polled thought it was good that Nakasone officially visited the Yasukuni shrine, while just 23% thought it was problematic.

27 The *Daily Yomiuri* found that 53 % of the respondents either 'supported' or 'somewhat supported' Koizumi's visit to the shrine, while 39 % were opposed ('Over 50% approve of Yasukuni Shrine visit', 17 August 2006). The *Mainichi Daily News* results showed 50% in favour, and 46% against Koizumi's visit

caution, the gradual shift in favour of support for prime ministerial visits to the shrine suggests that the attempts of the Japan Society for the War Bereaved, and Koizumi himself, to 'regularize' visits, and in doing so acclimatise, or desensitise, Japanese public opinion have been successful. Some Chinese observers are concerned that if official visits become customary, the Chinese and Korean governments may abandon their protests, thereby allowing Japan to throw off its historical burden without fully settling the history problem.[28]

Although Koizumi appeared to win some popular support by keeping to his pre-election pledge, he did not gain universal support at home. In fact, he was subject to increasing criticism from senior LDP members, business leaders, academics, policy advisers and journalists. Senior members of the LDP objected to his visits, and advised him against them, while several former prime ministers, including Nakasone, former Foreign Minister Tanaka Makiko, party elder Nonaka Hiromu, former Chief Cabinet Secretary Fukuda Yasuo and many others objected to his plans to visit the shrine.[29] New Kōmeitō Party leader Kanzaki Takenori advocated a measured approach to Japan's dealings with China, and popular news magazines published the dialogues between the editors of Japan's leading newspapers *Yomiuri shinbun* and *Asahi shinbun* (Watanabe Tsuneo and Wakamiya Yoshibumi respectively), both of whom were extremely critical of Koizumi's stance.[30] Former Prime Minister Nakasone criticised Koizumi for attempting to use Yasukuni visits for populist ends.[31] Political commentator Iwami Takao also considered populism one of the reasons for Koizumi's insistence on visiting the shrine, in addition to his desire to be 'exceptional'. In Iwami's view, Koizumi 'stands out'

('50% of Japanese support Koizumi's visit to Yasukuni shrine', 17 August 2006).

28 Zhou, 'Xiaoquan neige de waijiao zhengce xianxi', p. 31.

29 Shibuichi 'The Yasukuni shrine dispute', p. 210-11.

30 See also Kuriyama, 'Reconciliation'. For other aspects of Yasukuni reporting in the Japanese media, see Seaton's chapter in this volume.

31 Nakasone, 'Koizumi kun', p. 45.

precisely because he resists the external and internal pressure not to visit, and thereby aims to gain public sympathy or support.[32] Such domestic opposition was insufficient, however, to deter Koizumi. External pressure also failed to persuade him of the need to refrain from official patronage, and Koizumi viewed Chinese, and Korean, protests merely as attempts to interfere in domestic politics.

While the Yasukuni issue may appear to be a diplomatic dispute largely of Japan's own making (after all, by visiting the shrine, Koizumi cannot but provoke a response from China and other Asian neighbours), the issue nonetheless affords Chinese leaders opportunities they are able to instrumentalise for their own domestic purposes. This is not to say China has no desire to see an end to this problem, but since a resolution did not seem possible under Koizumi's leadership, the shrine visits enabled the CCP to reinforce messages about its own credentials and legitimacy as well as that of particular leaders.

The legitimacy of the CCP is grounded very firmly in anti-Japanese nationalism; it originated in the May Fourth Movement in 1919 and reached its apogee in the War of Resistance against Japan. Given a perceived weakening of ideology (Marxist, Leninist and Mao Zedong thought), the party has, since the 1980s, regularly invoked the spirit of anti-Japanese resistance as a means of unifying the people and ensuring loyalty to the party. This has taken various forms: socialist spiritual civilisation campaigns under Deng Xiaoping; patriotic education campaigns under Jiang Zemin; anti-Japanese media campaigns during the textbook issue of 1982; and leadership speeches made on key anniversaries. An example of the last is President Hu Jintao's commemorative speech of 3 September 2005, in which he criticised Japanese leaders' Yasukuni visits, and referred twelve times to China's War of Resistance against Japan.[33] Koizumi's visits to Yasukuni provide the Chinese leadership with numerous opportunities to recount China's Second World War history, not least the role of the CCP in bringing about

32 Iwami, 'Koizumi Yasukuni seisaku', p. 53.

33 *Yomiuri shinbun*, 'Yasukuni shrine' and Hu, 'Hu Jintao zai jinian'.

victory in the War of Resistance against Japan, and remind the Chinese public of the need to remain vigilant against a possible resurgence of Japanese militarism.

A recurring theme in the literature on Sino-Japanese relations is the tough position Chinese leaders adopt towards Japan as a means of legitimising their personal power, or gaining the upper hand in a domestic power struggle. There are several examples of this sort of phenomenon. Deng Xiaoping's tactics during summer 1982 when he adopted a hard-line position on the Japanese history textbook issue can be seen as a means of deflecting domestic criticism from, say, the People's Liberation Army (PLA) and consolidating the new leadership triumvirate in the form of Deng Xiaoping, Hu Yaobang and Zhao Ziyang.[34] Similarly, Jiang Zemin's insistence on tackling the history problem, in particular the issue of an apology, during his summit meeting with Obuchi Keizō in Japan in 1998 can be viewed in the context of succession politics and Jiang's need to demonstrate his anti-Japan credentials to gain support from the military.[35] By contrast, Chinese leaders who have become too close to Japan or have taken too soft an approach have sometimes jeopardised their careers. This was exemplified by General Secretary Hu Yaobang whose fall from grace in 1987 was precipitated by his pro-Japanese stance and fears among other leading figures in the CCP that a Sino-Japanese friendship event planned by Hu in late 1986 would lead to anti-Japanese demonstrations and perhaps escalate, as they had done in 1985, into anti-CCP demonstrations.[36]

Hu Jintao's response to the Yasukuni problem has also been assessed in terms of his need to build a power base. Hu Jintao emerged, along with Wen Jiabao, as one of China's new, fourth generation leaders in 2003. Hu was keen to create friendly relations with Japan, if only to realize the economic potential that cooperation could bring, but he was also described as having the weakest power base of

34 Rose, *Interpreting history*, pp. 146-50.

35 Rose, 'Japan's foreign policy, 1998-9'.

36 Whiting, *China Eyes Japan*, pp. 150-2; Hughes, 'Rivalry and realpolitik'.

any Chinese leader since Hua Guofeng in the 1970s. In addition, Hu Jintao had relatively limited experience in foreign policy matters and would have needed to rely heavily on his foreign policy experts in the first instance.[37] Hu's tough stance on Yasukuni, as manifested during his talks with Koizumi in November 2004 at the APEC meeting in Chile, has been explained by Japanese observers in the context of his need to satisfy domestic constituents, such as anti-Hu forces in the PLA, and build support at home.[38] Similarly, analysis in the *Mainichi shinbun* also suggested that since Hu had recently taken over the top three posts in China he needed to show a strong stance in order to consolidate his domestic base.[39]

A number of conspicuous cancellations of high-level meetings or visits in 2005 further highlighted the Chinese government's position *vis-à-vis* Koizumi's China policy. A visit by State Council Vice Premier Wu Yi was cut short the day before she was due to meet Prime Minister Koizumi on 24 May. The explanation provided by the Chinese Embassy at the time was 'urgent public business', but the Chinese Foreign Ministry later explained that Japanese leaders had made statements that rendered the atmosphere no longer conducive to a meeting with Koizumi.[40] On 3 September 2005, Hu Jintao delivered a particularly hard-hitting speech to mark the sixtieth anniversary of China's victory in the War of Resistance against

37 Nathan and Gilley, *China's new rulers,* pp. 84, 242 and Bachman, 'New leaders', pp. 128-9.

38 Hu specifically asked Koizumi to act 'in an appropriate manner', particularly in light of the upcoming sixtieth anniversary of the end of the war. This was the first time that Hu mentioned the Yasukuni shrine directly. See Matsumoto, 'Yasukuni to iu nanmon', p. 39. Tanaka and Okamato suggest that the anti-Japanese demonstrations of April 2005 (which, in their view, had been government-orchestrated) were also related to Hu Jintao's need to consolidate his power in the face of internal opposition ('Hannichi Chūgoku ga ochiitta kiki', pp. 34-5).

39 The three posts are president of the PRC, general secretary of the CCP, and chair of the Central Military Commission. Foreign Press Centre, Japan, 'Leaders of Japan and China meet'.

40 Przystup, 'No end to history'.

Japan, and in October, after Koizumi's visit to Yasukuni on the 17th, Beijing abruptly cancelled Japanese Foreign Minister Machimura Nobutaka's forthcoming visit to China.

These symbolic gestures serve to underscore China's tough policy on Japan, and signal to the Chinese and Japanese people that the Chinese government will not back down. This links to another explanatory factor in China's official response to Yasukuni problem, that is, the growing importance of public opinion in China since the 1990s. The CCP is increasingly mindful of public opinion, and can not afford to take too moderate a stance on Japan in the face of the sort of popular anti-Japanese sentiment and public protests witnessed in April 2005. By maintaining a firm position on Japan, the CCP is appealing to, or attempting to appease, popular sentiment in order to secure the party's longevity. But this has also made more difficult any governmental attempts to bring about some sort of resolution or reconciliation. An attempt to float a new way of thinking about Japan had appeared in the form of a series of articles in the Chinese journal *Strategy and management* in 2002 and 2003, in which *People's Daily* journalist Ma Licheng and two leading professors in the fields of international relations and Japanese studies articulated the need for friendly relations with Japan. In so doing, as Hughes points out, these 'establishment intellectuals' were elaborating upon an official CCP line of maintaining peace and stability in the international arena. In effect, the 'new thinking' on Japan was a 'trial balloon'; but this was soon shot down by an angry public response and an internet campaign in which Ma was branded a traitor. This signalled to the CCP that the time was not right for any radical change in China's Japan policy, particularly in light of Koizumi's Yasukuni visits.[41]

Some Japanese commentators see China's concern for internal stability as explaining its response to Yasukuni visits. Matsumoto frames China's response in 2005 in terms of the need to deal with 'internal contradictions.' He describes, for example, the difficulties

41 For a detailed discussion of the 'new thinking' debate see Gries, 'China's "New thinking on Japan"'.

the CCP was experiencing in the form of numerous outbreaks of rural violence, high levels of corruption, and the widening gap between the urban rich and the rural poor; and he argues Japan was used as an 'external enemy' to deflect attention away from domestic problems, and thereby maintain some social cohesion.[42] On the other hand, there are limits to which the Chinese government can fan anti-Japanese sentiment given the potential for such activities to develop into anti-government protests, as happened in the 1980s. Thus the *Sankei shinbun*, referring to the high levels of social unrest in China in 2004, suggested that Hu Jintao had wanted at the APEC meeting to secure an agreement from Koizumi that he would 'act in an appropriate manner' *vis-à-vis* Yasukuni, precisely to prevent the outbreak of anti-Japanese protests which could escalate into anti-CCP protests.[43]

Reinforcing Domestic and Foreign Policy Goals

Koizumi's persistent visits to Yasukuni symbolised an assertive stance towards China and Korea and an unwillingness to engage in the sort of 'grovelling' foreign policy some of his predecessors had been accused of from within the LDP ranks.[44] This stance also helped him at a time when China was perceived as a threat in some circles in Japan. In fact, Koizumi regularly stressed that China's rise represented an opportunity rather than a threat to Japan. An LDP position paper produced in January 2006 also stated that China did not represent a threat, but it did note seventeen years of double-digit defence spending in China, and called for greater transparency in China's military expansion, thereby hinting at a potential threat.[45] Koizumi's approach to the Yasukuni

42 Matsumoto, 'Yasukuni to iu nanmon', p. 38.

43 Foreign Press Center, Japan, 'Leaders of Japan and China meet'.

44 For a discussion of Japan's assertive policy towards China see Lam 'Japan's deteriorating ties'.

45 Other Japanese government papers have identified China, obliquely, as a threat. The Ministry of Foreign Affairs Diplomatic Bluebook 2006 called attention 'to an arms build-up "that will directly affect Japan's national

issue *vis-à-vis* relations with China was that it represented just one aspect of an otherwise strong and healthy relationship. He maintained that Chinese protests represented interference in Japan's domestic affairs, and expressed an inability to understand why the visits should pose such a problem to the Chinese government. Moreover, Koizumi had no aversion to offering apologies to the Chinese for Japan's actions during the Second World War, but it was the mismatch of his words and deeds to which the Chinese objected. For example, during his one day visit to Beijing in October 2001 Koizumi went to Marco Polo bridge, the site of the outbreak of fighting between the Chinene and Japanese troops in 1937, and the Memorial Hall of the War of Resistance against Japanese Aggression. He offered a 'heartfelt apology and mourning' for the Chinese people.[46] The following spring, however, he visited Yasukuni, thereby casting doubts on his sincerity. Similarly, at the Asia-Africa summit held in Jakarta in April 2005, Koizumi issued a heartfelt apology to the audience for the 'tremendous damage and suffering' caused by Japan's colonial rule and aggression. His meeting with Hu Jintao the following day was judged to be fairly positive. It was overshadowed, however, by the fact that while the meeting was taking place, several Japanese Diet members were visiting the Yasukuni shrine for the Great Rites of Spring.[47]

Seen in broader terms, Yasukuni visits can be linked not just to the attempt to adopt a more assertive China policy, but to Japan's overall domestic and foreign policy agenda under Koizumi. He represents the post-war generation that has no personal, living memories of the Second World War. Koizumi always insisted his visits to the shrine were to pay his 'respects to those who died in the war, with the conviction

security"'; and the Japan Defence Agency's Defense White Paper cited China's lack of transparency. In February 2006, the DPJ adopted as Party position the view that China represented an actual threat to Japan. Przystup, 'Looking beyond Koizumi'.

46 'President Jiang Zemin met with Japanese PM Koizumi', 8 October 2001, available at http://www.chinaembassy.org.zw/eng/xwdt/t148656.htm.

47 Przystup, 'No end to history'. See also the chapter by Wang in this volume.

that we must never wage such a war again.'[48] Saaler suggests that the highly symbolic nature of his visits meant he was 'translating communicative memory into a permanent cultural memory.'[49] This process occurs when living memory gives way to memory based on media such as monuments, memorials, museums etc., but, as we have seen, it is problematic when the past is contested both domestically and internationally. It is even more problematic if, as some argue, there is a deeper political purpose to his visits. Takahashi suggests that Koizumi's visits to the Yasukuni shrine can be linked to 'national politics', specifically the movement in favour of constitutional revision which will in turn pave the way for Japan to become a 'nation that can go to war'. Takahashi further argues that Koizumi's political act of worship at Yasukuni is aimed at promoting acceptance of sacrifice for one's country in the national interest.[50] Tanaka similarly contends that prime ministerial visits represent the 'readying of a contrivance to reconcile the Japanese people to 'new deaths' in the wake of anti-terrorism legislation and Japan's despatch of Self-Defence Forces (SDF) to Iraq.[51]

A number of Chinese academics also make the link between Japan's domestic and foreign policy goals and Koizumi's decision to visit Yasukuni. They argue that his visits symbolise the shift to the right in Japanese politics since the mid-1990s and the pursuit of 'normal nation' status.[52] In particular, by patronising Yasukuni, Koizumi is seen as attempting to raise the spirits and confidence of the Japanese people and deflect their attention away from the social and economic 'crises' of the 1990s and 2000s.[53] The need to raise the patriotic spirit of the

48 Fackler, 'Japanese court rules'.

49 Saaler, *Politics, memory and public opinion*, p. 91.

50 Takahashi, 'National politics', and Takahashi's chapter in this volume.

51 Takahashi, 'National politics', p. 157; Tanaka 'Yasukuni shrine'.

52 This is a recurring theme in the Chinese academic literature on Koizumi's visits to the Yasukuni Shrine. For a representative sample see Kou and Wei, 'Qingguo shenshe'; Ren, 'Canbai qingguo shenshe'; Wu and Zhang 'Canbai qingguo shenshe'; and Shi, 'Neighbours at Odds'.

53 Ren, 'Canbai qingguo shenshe', p. 287.

Japanese is also linked to the attempts of neo-nationalist groups, supported by some in the LDP, to re-write history textbooks in such a way that Japanese children can take pride in their country's history. The legalisation on the national flag and anthem, and the revision of the Fundamental Law of Education are given as further examples of this trend.[54]

For China also, domestic and foreign policy aims can be furthered by the Yasukuni shrine problem. As noted above, the visits provide the CCP with an opportunity to reiterate, via the media or key leadership speeches, a view of Japan or, rather, of Japanese leaders as untrustworthy, unrepentant and unable to adopt a correct view of history.[55] Chinese leaders, like Japanese leaders, are also translating communicative memory into permanent cultural memory. The way in which the Sino-Japanese war has been depicted officially in China has changed significantly over the last fifty years or so. The initial focus was on the role of the victorious CCP as opposed to the weakness and treachery of the Guomindang (GMD). This has shifted since the 1980s and the GMD's role in the war is now acknowledged and even highlighted; this is an essential development if Taiwan is to be incorporated into Greater China. Instead there is much greater focus on the 'real' common enemy, that is Japan, and what the Imperial Japanese Army did in China. The Yasukuni problem, and the way it is reported in the Chinese media and dealt with by the CCP, feeds therefore into patriotic education campaigns and reinforces what the younger generation of Chinese has been taught in schools. Frequent references

---

54 Bu Ping, 'Riben jingguo shenshe wenti', pp. 181-2. The reference here is to groups such as the Atarashii rekishi kyōkasho o tsukurukai (Society to Write New History Textbooks) whose controversial *Atarashii rekishi kyōkasho* (*New history textbook)* was authorised by the Japanese Ministry of Education in 2001 amid much domestic and international criticism over the watered-down descriptions of Japan's aggression in the Second World War.

55 For example, at a press conference held on 14 March 2006 after the National People's Congress, Premier Wen Jiabao stated that the problem regarding the Yasukuni Shrine does not lie with China, nor with the Japanese people, but with the *leaders* of Japan (author's italics) *Xinhua*, 'Sino-Japanese relations'.

to Japan's aggression, and reminders that Japanese leaders have yet to fully recognise war responsibility, serve to bring the nation together as it remembers collectively the horrors of the war and the extent of the damage inflicted by Japan. Far from receding into memory, commemoration of the war, as with many other countries, is a growing business in China; many new memorials, museums, and patriotic education sites, virtual and real, have been established or refurbished in the last ten to twenty years, and the sixtieth anniversary saw a proliferation of commemorative acts and saturation coverage on television of war-related documentaries and dramas.[56] As in Japan, the new post-war generation of leaders in China sometimes find it politically expedient to recall the country's past glories and heroic deeds in order to re-create cultural memory.

Not only does the Yasukuni issue highlight China's problems with a certain Japanese interpretation of the past, but the prime ministerial visits also raise concerns among the Chinese leadership, and indeed the Chinese public, about Japan's future intentions in the region.[57] In this view, a country that does not or cannot fully and properly reflect on the past cannot act responsibly in international affairs. This raises questions for the Chinese about Japan's suitability to have a permanent seat on the United Nations Security Council (UNSC), which became a focus of some of the student demonstrations in April 2005. Indeed the Chinese government is firmly opposed to Japan's bid to gain permanent membership of the UNSC precisely because of its approach to the history problem. Other moves by the Japanese government, such as the plans for constitutional revision, the strengthening of Japan's security arrangements with the US, and the quest to become a 'normal nation' with greater military power raise no little alarm among Chinese bureaucrats, who consider these plans to be part of a comprehensive foreign policy aimed at containing China.[58] This, in turn, enables Beijing to articulate its own foreign policy position, in stark contrast to

56 Curtin, 'Koizumi'.

57 Kou and Wei, 'Qingguo shenshe', p. 19.

58 See Ni, 'Who is doing the threatening'.

Japan's, in terms of a peaceful rise, or peaceful development, and as a counter to those in Japan who portray China as a threat.[59]

Conclusion

The Yasukuni shrine issue shares a common characteristic with some of the other contentious issues in Sino-Japanese relations, such as the history textbooks and territorial disputes, in that they tend to be cyclical in nature. As of early 2007, the Yasukuni problem appears to have receded once again into the background. It remains unclear as to whether Prime Minister Abe will visit the shrine in future. In spring and summer 2007, at least, he declined to do so. However, it is not unreasonable to assume, as do some Chinese observers, that the issue will recur, not least because Japan's domestic opposition to the visits is perceived to be too weak to put a stop to them.[60]

In the meantime, a number of practical solutions have been discussed in both countries. The Chinese, for example, have asked that the Class A war criminals be dis-enshrined. This has also been the focus of discussion in Japan for many years. Chairman of the Japan Society for the War Bereaved, Koga Makoto, advocated such an approach at a meeting of senior Society members in October 2006. This proposal remains highly contentious in Japan and the group did not appear to take the suggestion further.[61] By late October Koga proposed alternative solutions such as the construction of a new secular war memorial or the use of Chidorigafuchi cemetery as an alternative site 'to which all Japanese can visit without discomfort.'[62]

The Chinese have indicated that they would welcome a national non-religious memorial as suggested by Koizumi's 2004 commission (Discussion Group to Consider Memorials and Other Sites for the Commemoration of the War Dead and Praying for Peace, Chair:

59 For example, see Hu, 'Hu Jintao zai jinian'.

60 Zhou 'Ribenren', p. 23.

61 See the discussion of this issue in Breen , 'A Yasukuni genealogy'.

62 Przystup, 'Ice breaks at the summit'.

Imai Takashi). This would not prevent Japanese prime ministers from making visits to Yasukuni, and nor would a new memorial remove Yasukuni's status as the central site for mourning the war dead. However, it would provide a *neutral* site for shared commemoration to take place. As Lind points out, 'non-accusatory' and non-symbolic sites of remembrance are needed in order to remove the focus from sites of barbaric acts, or sites that venerate those who committed the acts.[63]

The prospects for a political solution are less obvious. Although there were signs that some Chinese leaders would have preferred to adopt a more moderate stance towards Japan in the early 2000s, the CCP has in a sense become hamstrung by its own emphasis on patriotic education and war memorialisation. Contradictions thus emerged between what some in the Chinese government may have wanted to do pragmatically (that is, pursue a more friendly relationship with Japan) and what they were bound to do for ideological reasons and political expediency. Similarly, the complexity and divisive nature of Yasukuni as a domestic problem in Japan have hindered progress on the issue. Nakasone suggested that Koizumi could have demonstrated greater courage by choosing *not* to visit the shrine. Although this may well have scored points in China, it would have undermined Koizumi's own arguments for visiting the shrine and left him vulnerable to domestic attack. Furthermore, he would have been seen as giving into foreign pressure thereby leaving himself open to the very criticism he wished to avoid.

The instrumentalisation of the Yasukuni shrine by both governments as a means of shoring up national identity at times of social and economic uncertainty, and of reinforcing broad domestic and foreign policy agendas, has hindered any genuine attempts to resolve the issue. With neither a political nor a practical solution immediately forthcoming, it is difficult to foresee anything but a stalemate in this particular aspect of Sino-Japanese relations.

63 Lind, 'Sorry states', pp. 36-7.

2

A RELIGIOUS PERSPECTIVE ON THE YASUKUNI SHRINE CONTROVERSY

Kevin Doak

Introduction

Most people today discuss the Yasukuni shrine controversy from a political perspective. I can add nothing to that debate. I am neither a politician nor a diplomat, so I am not the right person to contribute to that kind of argument. Nor am I a Japanese citizen, so politically, it is none of my business. I am an American professor of Japanese studies. That perspective suggests to me the need to take a more dispassionate look at the issues at hand. The Yasukuni problem stirs up all sorts of passions, though I am not entirely sure why it does so, and some distance from the problem is essential if we are to reflect on Yasukuni in a more constructive way. Since Yasukuni is a shrine, and prime ministerial visits are about mourning the war dead, a perspective that is not merely historical but also religious or spiritual is called for.

The Catholic Church and Yasukuni

The Yasukuni shrine in the post-war period is a rather different site from what it was before the Second World War. Then it was maintained and managed by the state; since the war it has been run as a religious juridical person.[1] There are nonetheless important continuities, not least in the realm of controversy. Whether or not Prime Ministerial visits to Yasukuni amount to the imposition of a specific religion, or whether they violate an individual's freedom of religion are not only a matter for debate today; they were so before the war, too.

Freedom of religion in Japan did not begin with the post-war era. Article 28 of the Meiji Constitution of 1889 guaranteed freedom of religion to the Japanese people. Many Westerners and even Japanese forget that there was, as a result, freedom of religion throughout the wartime period. It was not a mere gesture. In fact, Christians such as Imanaka Tsugimaro served on Tōjō Hideki's wartime Cabinet Planning Board, and the Catholic law professor Tanaka Kōtarō remained in his government post at Imperial Tokyo University throughout the war. There were others as well, such as the Catholic Admiral Yamamoto Shinjirō of the Imperial Navy. There is no evidence that these patriotic Christians suffered any official discrimination because of their religious beliefs. Evidently, then, there was freedom of religion even at the height of the war.

So what relationship, if any, should Japanese who do not adhere to Shinto have with Shinto shrines and particularly with Yasukuni shrine? Must they completely reject them as evil, or at least consider shrine visits incompatible with their monotheistic faith? It is widely assumed that Christians in particular can only have an antagonistic relationship with polytheistic Shinto. They believe that Christianity is a narrow, exclusive religion; but this is not true. Catholics, in particular, were permitted under certain circumstances to visit shrines in wartime Japan, as they are today. One of the most illustrative examples of the Catholic position on Shinto shrines involves the Catholic Sophia University in the early 1930s.

On 5 May, 1932, about sixty Sophia University students in the Army Reserve Student Corps were being prepared by Colonel Kita-

1 See Breen, 'A Yasukuni genealogy' for a discussion of the involvement of the Health Ministry in shrine affairs in the post-war period (ed.).

hara Hitomi, the military attaché to the university, to visit Yasukuni shrine to pay their respects to those who had died in military service. Some Catholic members of the Reserve Corps hesitated, and asked Fr. Herman Hoffman, President of Sophia University for his advice. Fr. Hoffman initially took a cautious approach, suggesting they should not visit Yasukuni if they felt their consciences would not permit it. But he also sent an inquiry to his religious superiors to find out whether or not permission might be forthcoming for Catholic students to participate in Yasukuni rites. In September 1932, Jean-Baptiste-Alexis Chambon, the Archbishop of Tokyo, made a formal approach to the Japanese Ministry of Education seeking clarification as to whether or not such visits were essentially religious in nature. He received a written reply from the Ministry of Education on 30 September: 'Our requirement for students to visit shrines is for educational reasons... Their salutes (*keirei*) involve nothing more than a demonstration of patriotism and loyalty.' The Japanese government report contained the words 'there is nothing more involved' (*mono ni hoka narazu*); so visits to the Yasukuni shrine were not religious acts.

On receiving this response the Vatican, which was well informed about religious affairs in Japan, acted through the Sacred Congregation for the Propagation of the Faith (SCPF). As luck would have it, the prefect of the SCPF at the time was none other than Cardinal Pietro Fumasoni-Biondi who was quite familiar with religious issues in Japan, having served as the Apostolic Delegate in Tokyo during 1920-2. On 26 May 1936, the SCPF released an official document called *Pluries Instanterque* that noted that 'since ceremonies of this kind are endowed with a purely civic value, it is permissible for Catholics to join in them, and act in accord with the other citizens.' In other words, the SCPF found no religious impediment to Japanese Catholics visiting Yasukuni shrine. The Vatican has a long history of experience in diplomatic relations and, as a City-State itself, fully appreciated the importance of a declaration from the relevant national authorities on the meaning of an act like visiting Yasukuni shrine. Such an act was always open to various interpretations by all sorts of people, but the Vatican knew that the interpretation that ultimately mattered was that given it by those in positions of responsibility, the legitimate representatives of their nation.

The implications of this directive were far reaching, and extended beyond the immediate issue of Japanese military reserve students, and even beyond the wartime. *Pluries Instanterque* was disseminated as an instruction on the duties of Catholics toward their fatherland. The document also allowed bishops in Japan to sanction their priests to assist at patriotic ceremonies in Shinto shrines, as well as at marriages and funerals. The underlying logic of this cross-religious approach provides the justification for the exceptional permission given today to Catholic priests in Japan to officiate at weddings of non-Catholic Japanese in Catholic churches. So, the policy of the Catholic Church has been consistent, whether considering the weddings of non-Christians in Catholic churches or visits to Shinto shrines where dead Christian soldiers are among those honoured.

Much of the recent controversy among Christian Japanese over Yasukuni results from two misapprehensions: first, that the Vatican was under pressure by the Japanese state to issue this 1936 directive. There is little evidence to support this assumption, and much to refute it, including the post-war testimony of Tanba Kōzō, advisor to the president of Sophia University in 1936. Second, there is the idea that there was no justification for the war, and thus no good Christian could support it. I return to this issue below, but it should be noted that the Vatican understood Japan as taking a leading role in the struggle against atheism and Communism on the Asian continent, which explains why, for example, the Vatican officially recognized the state of Manchukuo. In brief, there was no official Church proclamation against Japan's role in the Second World War, and thus participation in that war was, as always, left up to the moral judgment of individual citizens and the lay faithful.

Hence the 1936 directive was not merely a political calculation by the Vatican concerned about the persecution of Christians by the Japanese state. Rather, Cardinal Fumasoni-Biondi's determination stemmed from a deep familiarity with Japanese political and religious culture on the one hand, and from the Catholic Church's long-standing approach to inter-religious dialogue on the other. One striking example of this broad-minded attitude toward Shinto concerns the role of Father Gustav Bruno Maria Bitter. The Jesuit Father Bitter was the Vatican's representative in Japan in the immediate post war period, and he was personally responsible for persuading General Douglas MacArthur to stay his hand and not raze Yasukuni to the ground. Bitter insisted that burning Yasukuni would constitute a blemish on the history of the American military; his advice was that each and every person who had died for the nation was entitled to have their spirits propitiated at Yasukuni, regardless of their religion.

Thus, it is not surprising that in 1951, even after the Religious Corporation Law was implemented and state Shinto dismantled, Cardinal Fumasoni-Biondi, still speaking as the Prefect of the SCPF, reaffirmed the 1936 directive permitting Japanese Catholics to visit Shinto shrines. The Vatican consistently maintained a broad-minded approach to the shrine question, recognizing that patriotism and respect for the sacrifices of those who died for their country were good things and worthy of praise. This approach to inter-religious relations was stated definitively by Pope Paul VI fourteen years later, and remains the authoritative Catholic teaching on the issue: 'The Catholic Church rejects nothing that is true and holy in these [non-Christian] religions. She regards with sincere reverence those ways of conduct and of life, those precepts and teachings which, though differing in many aspects from the ones she holds and sets forth, nonetheless often reflect a ray of that Truth which enlightens all men.'[2]

While studying in Japan I too visited shrines and felt no particular sense of awkwardness about doing so. Prime Minister Ōhira Masayoshi was a devout Christian, yet he visited Yasukuni on many occasions after the war, while Sono Ayako, the famous Catholic author, does so too. Many Japanese find this difficult to come to terms

2 Pope Paul VI, *Nosta Aetate: Declaration on the Relation of the Church to non-Christian Religions*, 1965.

with, but it is not actually contradictory at all given the historical background referred to above, and the typically tolerant nature of Catholic theological thought.

From my perspective as a Catholic the visits to Yasukuni shrine by successive prime ministers do not constitute a challenge to the constitutional separation of religion and state.[3] Visits to Yasukuni do not violate the individual's freedom of religion, whether that individual is Buddhist, Christian or an adherent of any other religion; and just because the Emperor or Prime Minister, Foreign Minister or Diet members visit Yasukuni, it cannot mean that their actions violate, or pose a threat to, the religious rights of others.

'Secularisation Theory' and the Sacred

Christians are numbered among those who have taken legal action against former Prime Ministers, alleging their visits were in breach of the Constitution. There is a tendency among Protestants, in particular, to worry that these Yasukuni visits pose a threat to the position of minority religious groups, though this fear seems overblown. The overwhelming majority of Japanese citizens are not Christian; many do not profess a particular creed; and yet they see Japan becoming more and more secularised. Some think it is dangerous for religion to be granted access to any kind of public place but, in so believing, they run the risk of idealising an excessively rigorous separation of religion and state. In this author's opinion, a more subtle and flexible approach is called for. People should be much more mindful of the fact that humans never simply lead the superficial secular existence of economic animals.

Yoshimitsu Yoshihiko, a Catholic philosopher who is said to have had a major influence on the popular Catholic novelist Endō Shusaku, commented before the war how people yearned for a complete or 'integral' humanism. He took up the theme in the famous 1942 symposium on *Kindai no chōkoku* (Overcoming modernity), where he

3 For a contrasting view, see Seaton's chapter in this volume (ed.).

argued that modernity was to be identified in the universal problem of atheism, which only offered humans an 'incomplete humanism.' Atheist Communists were already prominent at the start of the 20th century across the world, of course, and nowhere more so than in the Soviet Union. The Communist Party rules China to this day, and atheism predominates there too—along with a very incomplete humanism. If it is fortunate that atheism never dominated in this way in Japan, it is unfortunate that post-war Japan has been deluged with secularism, since it is incapable of offering fundamental answers to questions about human life and death. Such questions demand a more satisfactory, human and religious approach.

I am an American and a practising Catholic, but I do not feel threatened in the slightest by Japanese people treating Yasukuni as the sacred place it is, nor by their visiting Yasukuni to mourn the war dead using traditional Shinto methods; in fact, I welcome it. After all, offering up one's life for another human being, to die for the protection of one's family friends or fellow countrymen is the most sacred of acts. Former Prime Minister Koizumi Jun'ichirō made a point of stating he visited Yasukuni precisely to pay his respects to those men and women who gave up their lives in the last war. He may not have intended to identify these acts as 'sacred'. But we miss much of the picture if we only look at his visits through the lens of secularism.

In any democratic society, individual rights, civil rights and religious freedom are premised on showing respect for the dignity of others. In particular, if those others are the deceased, then it is common decency not only in Japan, but in the USA and in all countries of the world, to act with humility and refrain from passing moral judgements on them. It is anyway pointless to criticise the dead. If the dead in question are the men and women who sacrificed their lives for their country in war, then their mourning demands a response that is both universal, transcending particular denominations, and is yet accompanied by some recognition of the sacredness of life and death. This much is—or ought to be—human instinct.[4]

4 For a similar perspective, see Nitta's chapter in this volume (ed.).

It seems to me that in this regard Koizumi's Yasukuni visits were always a halfway measure: he avoided the 'secular trap', but he stopped at least one step short in his approach to the sacred. Some claim that the Prime Minister's visits were unconstitutional, and there have been lawsuits challenging the constitutionality of his visits. His 2006 visit was certainly a response to these. On this occasion, he felt unable to enter the shrine's Main sanctuary; he wore a suit rather than the more formal *haori* and *hakama* and took out change for the offertory box from his trouser pocket. But it was always the Prime Minister's right to decide of his own volition what form of prayers he offered at the shrine. Indeed, I wish that he had abandoned his reserve and visited Yasukuni monthly or even weekly, instead of the annual visits of his premiership, to gain a greater familiarity with the sacred nature of the sacrifices that are commemorated there. Newspaper columns reporting the Prime Minister's movements through the week revealed he often spent Sundays in his official residence reading the newspaper or listening to music. Could he not have visited Yasukuni or other shrines once in a while? Had he done so on the holy day of Sunday and with much greater frequency, he could have made it clear to the world that his actions were not intended to glorify war or militarism, as is claimed by the Chinese, for example; rather that they were a spiritual response to issues of life and death. That in turn would have required him to be far more positive and confident about his beliefs. In order to pay one's respects to the war dead, prayers that transcend this world are necessary. And the sacred site of Yasukuni shrine has a vital function in this regard for the Japanese people. If this point were to be made with due care, most people, I think, would have understood.

Arlington and the endorsement of past wrongs

What are we to make, though, of the arguments in favour of an alternative national site to Yasukuni, and of suggestions that the prime minister should visit only the grave of the unknown soldier at Chidorigafuchi cemetery? These arguments seem designed to parry criticism from China, but they fall into the trap of secularism. To mourn the war dead at that kind of secular, artificially and mechanically produced site would be an insult to the families of the deceased and to the souls of those who made the ultimate sacrifice for their nation.[5]

The funeral rites and acts of mourning that take place at the Arlington National Cemetery in the USA are, to some degree, displays of religious faith. On the whole, Christian clergymen conduct the prayer services, but no problems at all arise when non-Christian politicians visiting the USA participate in Arlington ceremonies and, say, lay wreaths. In Japan, too, funeral services may be carried out in Buddhist temples or Shinto shrines, but Christians and Muslims may also visit to pay their last respects. All that is happening here is a universal practice that transcends the everyday in order to make a spiritual link to the dead. The point of such events is certainly not to prioritise one specific religion over and against the others. Similarly, Yasukuni shrine priests have never refused visits from people of religions other than Shinto; they allow anyone to visit and pay their respects freely. This single fact serves to prove that Yasukuni does not exclude those who are not adherents of Shinto; it exists, rather, as a place for the profound expression of mourning that historically has transcended religious denominations in a way appropriate to the particular history of the Japanese people.

The Class A war criminals and the Tokyo war crimes tribunal

Those of us alive today should adopt a more humble attitude towards issues of life and death. We may criticise the actions of those who passed away a long time ago, but they have no way of defending themselves. Yasukuni venerates the spirits of all those who lost their lives fighting for their country, and not just Class A war criminals like Tōjō Hideki. Is it really possible for future generations to stand God-like in judgement over our predecessors, according to some absolute criteria in order to determine their good or evil? Does visiting Yasukuni to

5 For an alternative argument in favour of a new national site, see the chapter by Breen in this volume (ed.).

express one's gratitude to the departed souls (including even the Class A war criminals) really constitute one's full-hearted approval of all the things they did during their lives? Of course, it does not by any means. The paying of respect is an act of mourning their death and of praying for their souls. Can the Chinese leaders and those who argue that the Class A war criminals should be removed from Yasukuni really be so arrogant as to believe that they themselves are perfect human beings? Will they themselves not need our prayers some day?

Soldiers of the Confederate army are laid to rest in the Arlington National Cemetery. These men fought to protect the system of slavery, and yet a succession of US presidents have officially paid their respects at the Cemetery. Still, though, I have never heard stories of individual African-Americans or representatives of the various African nations protesting against the visits. This is for the obvious reason that American presidents are not advocating the return of slavery. To suggest this would be absurd. Why then do we accept similar arguments that a Japanese Prime Minister's visit to Yasukuni means endorsement of the war, in spite of explicit denials of such meaning by the Prime Minister himself?

Kikuchi Kan made the point in his short story *Onshū no kanata ni* (Beyond revenge) about a son seeking revenge for his father's death, and we should note with him how strange it is to be obsessed with past events in the matter of mourning the dead, even if the dead in question was once an enemy. One of the arguments deployed against Koizumi's visits to Yasukuni was that the enshrinement of Class A war criminals at Yasukuni was linked to a return of militarism and the endorsement of the war of aggression. But what happens if we apply this argument to the Arlington cemetery and the American and foreign statesmen who visited it? Japanese Prime Ministers too have paid their respects at Arlington on state visits to the United States, so does this amount to their endorsement of slavery and racial discrimination? Of course it does not.[6] Most Japanese are aware that

6 For a very different Arlington comparison, see McGreevy, 'Arlington National Cemetery and Yasukuni Jinja'.

it is completely twisted logic to assume that mourning and paying one's respects to all those who have died in past wars, be they civil wars or foreign conflicts, is to endorse the aspirations of the deceased or the policies that led to the wars in which they died. It is not the deeds of the Class A war criminals that are venerated at Yasukuni shrine, but their departed souls. We all have souls, and they extend beyond this life to the next world. They are all of equal value, regardless of their nationality in this life. It is not for us to judge as good or evil such departed souls.

On the question of the Class A war criminals, it is an indisputable fact, as Massachusetts Institute of Technology Professor, John Dower, has pointed out, that the verdicts of the Tokyo War Crimes Tribunal that defined them as such were a case of victor's justice. The legitimacy of the verdicts is highly questionable from a legal perspective, given that they were judged according to *ex post facto* law; it is only natural that some Japanese oppose the verdicts, even though they do not necessarily justify the war. Human judgement is in the final analysis imperfect, but there are nonetheless very few Japanese who dismiss today's America out of hand just because the Tokyo War Crimes Tribunal was a disgrace. They distinguish between the War Crimes Tribunal on the one hand and America itself on the other. A similar sort of distinction should be made between those declared to be Class A war criminals on the one hand and the Yasukuni shrine on the other. But we should also remember that not everyone who did evil things in this life was labelled a 'war criminal.' Would removing 'war criminals' from Yasukuni 'purify' the shrine of all bad spirits? What kind of hubris leads one to think so?

Chinese atheism and the struggle for the Sacred

The Yasukuni problem is, of course, less easily understood by the Chinese, living under atheistic Communist regimes, which profess faith in Marxist-Leninism.[7] After all, even ordinary Japanese and

7 Wang's chapter in this volume is a clear articulation of the mainland Chinese perspective on Yasukuni (ed.).

Americans find it difficult enough to approach the sacred. But it is not the case that all Chinese are atheist. One should not assume that contact with the sacred will never happen even for those who are today members of the Chinese Communist Party. If Abe Shinzō and his cabinet ministers do not cave in to the twisted logic of the CCP, but persist in their visits to Yasukuni and make manifest their determination to draw near to the sacred, then who knows but that CCP members and the Chinese populace, too, will not one day come to a better appreciation of the sacredness of human life.

The Japanese themselves adopt extremely diverse views of the shrine and its significance, depending on their standpoint. There are nationalist, Catholic and (pro-Communist) leftist perspectives represented by the likes of Watanabe Shōichi, Sono Ayako and Wakamiya Yoshibumi, for example. But the long and the short of it is that prime ministerial visits to Yasukuni are not a problem in terms of the Constitution and its provisions for the separation of religion and state; nor are they problematic from any other sort of legal perspective. This much is clear from the majority of verdicts handed down by various courts in recent years.

Korean and US opposition to Yasukuni

South Koreans and Taiwanese represent a rather different case to the Chinese in this context. 26% of South Koreans are Buddhist, and another 26% are Christian, and the ethos of Confucianism is also deeply rooted, so the majority of South Koreans do have some kind of religious life. And yet some Koreans, at least, express bitter opposition to Japanese prime ministers' visits to Yasukuni shrine. With the Korean peninsula divided between north and south, and with North Korea repeatedly denouncing the fact that the Republic of Korea was established by people like Park Chung Hee in collaboration with Japanese imperialism, the Republic of Korea is anxious to send the message to the North that its people, too, are truly nationalistic Koreans and thus anti-Japanese. This broader question of ethnic unification of the Korean peninsula provides the necessary background for understanding South Korean denunciations of the Yasukuni visits. It is significant that the leaders of Taiwan (which was a Japanese colony fifteen years longer than Korea was) have voiced no criticism in recent years. Perhaps because Lee Teng-chin, the older brother of former Taiwan President Lee Teng-hui (a devout Christian), is amongst those enshrined at Yasukuni, even ordinary Taiwanese visiting Japan today go to Yasukuni. Naturally, some take exception to Yasukuni's enshrinement of fellow Taiwanese who fought and died for the Japanese army. For most Taiwanese, though, freedom of faith is very important. After all, when Taiwan was under Japanese rule, people were at greater liberty to believe in Christianity than they ever were in China under the rule of Mao Tse-tung and the Chinese Communist Party. In a country with such traditions, absurd objections to the Yasukuni visits simply do not arise; and the same can be said for the rest of Asia, outside China and Korea that is.

The fact that former Prime Minister Koizumi visited Yasukuni and that his successor Abe is likely also to do so does not mean that the maelstrom of criticism will spread worldwide. Editor-in-Chief of the *Asahi* newspaper, Wakamiya Yoshibumi, penned an article in 2006 entitled 'Dear Prime Minister Koizumi, will you be able to talk about Yasukuni in the USA?' He wrote how Henry Hyde, Chairman of the House International Relations Committee, sent a letter to the speaker of the House of Representatives, expressing his view that Koizumi should not be allowed to speak at Congress during his visit to the USA unless he promised not to conduct his 15 August visit to Yasukuni.[8] The intention behind Wakamiya's article was to criticise Koizumi: 'Does Koizumi not realise that many Americans frown upon the Yasukuni visits? Are recent critical comments by America's intellectuals not obvious enough for him?' Congressman Hyde spoke with the concerns of one who had fought against the Japanese in the Pacific war, of course, but the fact is that his views were representative of only a small minority in Congress. Indeed, Hyde's comments came just as he was due to retire from Congress (which he did in 2007). One might

8 *Asahi shinbun*, 27.5.2006.

just as easily cite the case of former Deputy Secretary of State Richard Armitage who is a supporter of Yasukuni visits. His appointment as deputy to the Secretary of State might suggest that his are the views that represent more of the mainstream of US national public opinion than those of a Congressmen from a single district in the Midwest. Indeed, Hyde's views may have received so much media attention precisely because they were so unexpected (a 'man bites dog' story).

A just war: who decides?

The actions by the Japanese during the Pacific war can in no way be likened to those of the Nazis in Germany, but there is nonetheless a tendency to claim that visiting Yasukuni defends erstwhile Japanese militarism, and has no place in democratic Japan. However you think about it, though, Japan is now a peaceful nation, and it is impossible to imagine a revival of the militarism of the past. I even think there would be dangers if pacifism were to become too powerful in Japan. In Catholicism, there is the concept of a 'just war', and not to fight in a 'just war' is morally wrong. In modern-day Japan, there are some who believe that Japan should not even fight a 'just war'.

According to the Catholic Catechism, military action may be considered a 'just war' so long as four conditions are satisfied:

1) the damage inflicted by the aggressor on the nation or community of nations must be lasting, grave, and certain;
2) all other means of putting an end to it must have been shown to be impractical or ineffective;
3) there must be serious prospects of success;
4) the use of arms must not produce evils and disorders graver than the evil to be eliminated; the power of modern means of destruction weighs very heavily in evaluating this condition.[9]

It is possible to use these four conditions to judge whether or not Japan's attack on Pearl Harbor constituted a just war of defence. The Japan containment strategy, and the oil embargoes and other

9 *Catechism of the Catholic church*, #2309.

sanctions imposed by President Roosevelt before the attack on Pearl Harbor are precisely the kinds of acts that were considered under traditional international law as constituting acts of war. Some may thus view the surprise attack on Pearl Harbor as a legitimate defence stratagem taken by Tōjō Hideki. To avoid any misunderstanding, I should make it quite clear that I myself am not advocating such an interpretation; I only wish to point out that it is possible to make such a case in good faith.

Similarly, with regard to the war in Iraq and whether or not it is a just war, it is possible to take the position of President Bush, whose view may be summed up as follows: 'In light of the coordinated simultaneous terror attacks of 9/11, and the fear of further terror attacks in the future, it is impossible to defend our nation without removing Saddam Hussein, who has possessed weapons of mass destruction and shows a willingness to use them against us'. In this case, as in all cases, according to long-standing Catholic teaching, the judgement as to whether or not the war meets the criteria for a just war is made by politicians and national leaders entrusted with political power by their citizens, rather than religious leaders such as bishops or the Pope. But how might one assess the war responsibility of these leaders? It may be, as it is said in Japan, that 'the victor in war is always right', but there is no guarantee that moral legitimacy is on the victor's side. Although there must be good prospects of victory, victory itself is not proof that a war was 'just.'

After the war in Bosnia, there was a flurry of activity to hand down verdicts on wicked war criminals through the application of international law in internationally organised courts, but there are very serious problems involved here. Above all, there is the question of just who has the right to pass judgement on political leaders who always have to make difficult political decisions? In Catholic doctrine, that right is not even reserved to the Pope. The fact remains that when any legitimate government determines that a war meets the criteria for a just war, citizens must then make their own decision: face prison as conscientious objectors or fight and so run the risk of being killed in a war they may, or may not, consider to be just.

The USA dropped atomic bombs on Hiroshima and Nagasaki, and burned out Tokyo in the Great Tokyo Air Raid. This deliberate extermination of non-combatants is surely open to criticism as a war crime; it is far more difficult to reconcile with the conditions for 'just war' of Catholic doctrine than a pre-emptive war against Iraq. There are Japanese who approve of Japan's actions in the Pacific War, and believe that, even if mistakes were made, the war was necessary. But it remains that we are all sinners: none of us is completely innocent, regardless of the innocence or guilt a court may determine. I cannot say that Tōjō and the other 'war criminals' alone should be punished as evil people and that the rest of us are all innocent victims. What I will say, rather, is that the war is now over, and it is incumbent on the living to pray for the souls of the dead, and through such prayers to renew our appreciation for the sacredness of all life.

In essence, this is a question of 'the human heart', and it takes precedence over denominational affinities. No person with a 'human heart' would ever violate the grave or the corpse of the most evil man after his execution, no matter how heinous the crimes he committed. I still believe that most Japanese, regardless of whether they are followers of an organised religion or not, understand this and fundamentally respect the sacred; and it is precisely for this reason that they commemorate the war dead at Yasukuni. Their visits to Yasukuni, to other shrines, temples, and churches are evidence of what is most noble in 'the human heart.'

Yūshūkan: facts and history

The government of the PRC distinguishes arbitrarily and in the most self-serving way between good and bad, treating Tojo and the others as evil and insisting that Class A war criminals be removed from Yasukuni. It is vital to be aware that, if Japan were to appease the Chinese on this matter, it would imply not only a loss of dignity for Japan as a nation, but also the loss of the dignity of the person, which is the very heart of a democratic society. Such dignity comes not from politics, or even from historians 'getting their facts right.' It comes from the Sacred who is the author of life and the sole judge of the dead. I therefore welcomed Koizumi's visits to Yasukuni as part of a democratic culture. Recently, Americans have begun to claim that the Yūshūkan war museum located in the grounds of Yasukuni is disgraceful in that it glorifies the war, but we should take the Prime Minister at his word when he insisted his visits to Yasukuni had nothing to do with the Yūshūkan, and he did not intend to glorify war; and that he visited simply in order to perform memorial services for the war dead.[10]

I have yet to visit the newly refurbished Yūshūkan, but have checked the contents of the museum on the museum's website.[11] While I cannot give my approval of the displays in every respect, the fact remains that Yūshūkan is not a government-run museum. If it does glorify and emphasise the actions of the Imperial soldiers and sailors who died in action in kamikaze suicide attacks or as human torpedoes, it does so in recognition of the fact that these actions actually took place and took the lives of those involved; of that there can be no doubt. If the exhibits help clarify the reasoning behind Yasukuni's commemorating the souls of the war dead, then this is a good thing.[12] Far more problematic are the unfounded claims by Marxist historians in Japan, China and Korea, who insist that 'Emperor Hirohito was planning from the outset to invade mainland China', and that the 'Tanaka memorandum' was true. The latter was a document allegedly submitted by Prime Minister Tanaka Giichi to the Shōwa emperor in 1927, arguing the need to occupy Manchuria as the first step to conquering China and then the world. This has been proved

10 For a view which impugns former Prime Minister Koizumi's motives, see the chapter by Wang in this volume (ed.).

11 http://www.yasukuni.or.jp/english/yushukan.html.

12 For a more critical take on the Yūshūkan and its aims, see the chapter by Breen in this volume (ed.).

beyond doubt to be a forgery.[13] The exhibitions in the history and peace museums built during the Communist era in Eastern Europe were all distorted and often entirely without foundation, although this is now being rectified. The anti-Japanese museums throughout the PRC are an even more outrageous example of the distortion of history in the interests of nationalism. Compared with these Communist bloc museums, the Yūshūkan displays are more factual and sombre. Of course, there is no such thing as a 100% accurate view of history. While I was studying at Tokyo University, I specialised in Japanese history and learned about the Hull Note, the ABCD line formed of the Americans, British, Chinese and Dutch, and the economic sanctions imposed on Japan. This was quite a surprise to me. But not entirely. When I was a child, my grandfather often said that President Roosevelt forced Japan into a corner because he wanted to enter the war—against Nazi Germany; this was his strategy for dragging isolationist America in the war. I doubt my grandfather's view was unusual among those of his generation.

Japan became a member of the free world as a result of the terms of the San Francisco Peace Treaty, and has since become rather pro-American. In recent years, the PRC has begun to insist that Japan should obey *its* every whim, and today Japan finds itself trapped between the two. Certain experts propose Japanese prime ministers should take the pragmatic course, and stop Yasukuni visits to avoid antagonising the Chinese. But it is highly inadvisable for Japan to pander to the PRC. There is the question of Japan's dignity, but also that of a democratic culture that fosters the dignity of the person and a relationship to the sacred. There are serious problems inherent in becoming independent of America, only to come under the PRC's sphere of influence. It is not my intention to criticise those Japanese who wish to revise Article 9 of the Constitution, to become a more fully independent state; but neither do I wish to see Japan become snagged under the PRC's umbrella, as some American opponents of revising Article 9 apparently do. At the risk of repeating myself, Ja-

13 See for example, Hata, *Shōwashi no nazo o ou.*

pan should not yield to the PRC opportunistically, out of short-term political and economic considerations. Unlike the textbook issue, the Yasukuni issue is one which concerns our attitude toward life and death; in other words, the dignity of the individual person. None of us, Japanese or not, may compromise on that issue.

Christians, the Yasukuni kami and PRC hypocrisy

The key question for Christians visiting Yasukuni or any other Shinto shrine is 'What is involved?'. Catholics are not permitted to pray to a deceased soldier as a *kami*, or to any other Shinto *kami*. And they are not permitted either to leave the impression that, in their visits to Yasukuni, they are participating in a Shinto prayer to a Shinto *kami*. But if they visit to pay respects to the dead, to show patriotism, that is fine. And if they put their hands together and offer a silent prayer to Jesus Christ, or make the Sign of the Cross, that too is acceptable, so long as there is no cause for misinterpretation of their actions. The Japanese Constitution provides for freedom of religion and, on my own visits to Shinto shrines, I have never been coerced into any Shinto prayer. There is thus no obvious reason why Catholic Japanese cannot visit Yasukuni and offer (Christian) prayers for the deceased.

Christians cannot accept the deification of individuals, but Catholics, at least, have a strong tradition of communion with the dead. Those among the deceased who led good lives of service to others may become saints in heaven. Catholics are encouraged not only to think of saints but to pray to them for their intercession on our behalf. The *Catholic Catechism* has this to say on the Communion of Saints: 'In the communion of saints, "a perennial link of charity exists between the faithful who have already reached their heavenly home, those who are expiating their sins in purgatory and those who are still pilgrims on earth. Between them there is, too, an abundant exchange of all good things." In this wonderful exchange, the holiness of one profits others, well beyond the harm that the sin of one could cause others. Thus recourse to the communion of saints lets the contrite sinner be more promptly and efficaciously purified of the punishments for sin.'[14] Praying for the dead, even notable sinners, is not only encouraged, it is a moral requirement as one of 'the spiritual works of mercy.' This moral requirement is not limited to praying for dead Christians, or those among the non-Christian deceased whom we admire or respect. Indeed, it is incumbent on Japanese, whether Christian or not, to pray for Tōjō Hideki and others who were condemned as 'Class A war criminals.'

After the war, Japan accepted the verdicts of the Tokyo War Crimes Tribunal, but whether these verdicts were just or not is a separate matter. Humans have no choice but to accept injustices on a daily basis, but accepting them does not make them just. I too believe that the Tokyo War Crimes Tribunal was unjust, but I commend Japan for accepting it, for concluding the San Francisco Peace Treaty and for developing as a free and democratic independent nation. Nevertheless, it is important that the souls of even the war criminals are mourned equally. The distinction between the different grades of war criminals, Classes A, B and C, is utterly meaningless. Can the Class A criminals be three times worse than the Class C? Every human is born after all with original sin. I have neither the intention nor the right to condemn the actions of deceased soldiers like Tōjō Hideki, but certain leaders of the PRC seem convinced they have the right to pass judgement on deceased individuals on the grounds that they (or their fathers or mothers) were victims half a century ago. But today the PRC government severely suppresses religious freedom, even imprisoning Catholic priests and bishops. In brief, the PRC does not allow the free *practise* of religion, although their regulations cynically promise the freedom of religious 'belief' so long as one does not act on that belief.[15] Any connection whatsoever to the sacred in China is a difficult and dangerous act. Is the real threat to peace and human dignity in East Asia today from annual visits to a Shinto shrine by a democratically elected Prime Minister?

14 *Catholic Catechism*, #1475.

15 Cf. Regulations on Religious Affairs, adopted at the 57th Executive Meeting of the State Council on 7 July 2004, effective 1 March 2005.

Surely even Chinese people should be allowed to pray for the souls of the war dead once a year? And who knows whether the sight of Prime Minister Koizumi and his successors visiting Yasukuni time and again might not gradually awaken the Chinese people to a deeper relationship with the sacred? The PRC continues to build anti-Japanese museums nationwide and encourages its people to visit them frequently. The purpose of these museums is to incite hatred towards Japan and to propagate the myth that it was the Chinese Communist Party that achieved China's independence. Also, it is a matter of concern that these museums contain no religious aspect but are thoroughly secular. In contrast, the Yasukuni shrine does evoke the sacred in its very structure of being. This difference explains why I expect little good from these anti-Japanese museums, while I do have hopes for the peaceful potential of Yasukuni to enhance a sense of the sacred among the Japanese people.

How can we explain the fact that the embalmed corpse of Mao Tse-tung, who killed twenty million of his own people, is displayed in Tiananmen Square to be worshipped, even though Communists do not believe in a human soul? What is the point of venerating a corpse that has no soul?[16] Prime Minister Koizumi never mowed down his own people with tanks like the Chinese leader did; quite the contrary: his Japanese Self-Defence Forces risked their lives as part of international peace-keeping activities in Iraq and elsewhere. The hypocrisy of the Chinese government is a thing to behold. The Chinese government blatantly interfered in Japanese internal affairs by, for example, indicating their preference for Fukuda Yasuo over Abe Shinzō as Koizumi's successor, on the grounds that Fukuda was less likely to visit Yasukuni. At one and the same time, it has continuously dismissed as 'interference in Chinese internal affairs' criticism from other nations over its suppression of Chinese Christians, Tibetan Buddhists, and the Falun Gong. Prime Minister Koizumi always made it clear that he would respond to reasonable demands

16 For a development of this argument, see Seki's chapter in this volume (ed.).

from the Chinese, but had no intention of responding to unreasonable ones. Abe Shinzō must be no less unequivocal in his response.

Even though Mao Tse-tung was responsible for the invasion of Tibet and the heinous murder of his own people, the Chinese should not be denied the right to mourn him if they so wish; it is no business of foreign governments and peoples to interfere. In the same way, the Japanese people should be allowed to mourn their war dead, including those such as Tōjō Hideki who were executed after the war. There is no inherent danger in young Japanese people visiting the Yūshūkan and developing a certain respect for the actions of the former Japanese army. But it is also important for them to see the A-bomb museums in Hiroshima and Nagasaki, and to learn of the horror of war. Above all they must recognize that Japan already has the kind of democratic society that allows its citizens to learn of multiple perspectives on war. My own personal relationship with Japan goes back two or three decades, and every single one of my Japanese friends has been a pacifist; I have never even met a militarist. It is hard to imagine Japan again engaging in a reckless, aggressive war. That cannot, unfortunately, be said of all its neighbours in Asia.

In this sense, too, I cannot condone China's attempts to intervene in the way that the war dead are commemorated in Japan, and I fail to understand how low-key yearly visits by political leaders of a democratic nation to Yasukuni to pray for peace can be construed as a revival of militarism.

Conclusion

I wish to return finally to the issue with which I began, namely the deeper non-political significance of prime ministerial visits to Yasukuni. This is a matter of much greater importance than the issues raised in the usual debates. The Yasukuni shrine holds up a mirror to the soul of each individual. How each person, whether politician or ordinary citizen, Japanese or foreigner, regards Yasukuni reflects how that individual regards 'those who have gone before', and thus how that person values himself and others who are alive today. This spiritual encounter with the dead, which is implicit in any reflection on Yasukuni, is also an opportunity to experience the sanctity of life, not merely the everyday lives that absorb us so much of the time, or the people we encounter everyday. Rather, Yasukuni provides a genuine opening to experience the sacredness of Life, Life in its eternal dimension. How one comes to terms with Yasukuni is fundamentally a question of how one comes to terms with the sacred. While there are many religious traditions through which we approach the sacred, my own reflections on Yasukuni shrine prompt me in all earnestness to invite everyone, and not just former Prime Minister Koizumi Jun'ichirō and his successor Abe Shinzō, to encounter the sacred much more frequently in our everyday lives.

3

CHINA, JAPAN AND THE SPELL OF YASUKUNI

Wang Zhixin

The Origin of the problem

Koizumi Jun'ichirō stepped down as Prime Minister in September 2006, having visited the Yasukuni shrine every year since taking office in 2001. Japan's post-war stance of war renunciation and campaigning for peace has gone far in establishing trust between Japan and its neighbours, China and Korea, but the former Prime Minister's visits wrecked these links, and brought the Japan-China relationship, in particular, to the brink of collapse.

But how devoutly did Koizumi believe in this act of visiting Yasukuni? It was not as if he had gone there every single year before becoming Prime Minister. In fact, he was criticised for using Yasukuni as a tactic in his own political battles. Holding little sway within the Liberal Democratic Party (LDP), Koizumi had challenged for the position of LDP President twice, and failed both times. Then, aiming for a turnaround, on 18 April 2001, he set out his campaign pledge in the debate session for the next LDP Presidential election: 'Once I take office as Prime Minister, I will definitely visit Yasukuni on 15 August, however much criticism I face.' This was the sort of surprising statement Koizumi was wont to make on becoming Prime Minister. After that, negotiations with Korea and China failed and once the issue escalated, it became impossible for him to stop visiting the shrine.

In total, Koizumi visited Yasukuni six times. In 2006, before stepping down, he went on his sixth and final visit. Out of all the possible days he had chosen in the past—13 August, 4 April, 21 April, 14 January, 17 October, the Great Rites of Spring and Autumn, and New Year's Day—for his parting gesture in 2006 he opted for 15 August. This was the day on which Japan declared its unconditional surrender, and China and the other Asian nations achieved victory against Japan's war of aggression. The politician Koizumi Jun'ichirō had honoured his campaign pledge and kept his promise, and this marked a decisive end to his term as Prime Minister.

Properly speaking, Japanese politicians should have used that very day to promote peace in Asia and reaffirm the lessons learned from the Second World War. Koizumi, however, headed off boldly to Yasukuni, with its Class A war criminals, and venerated the shrine. Asian nations, and particularly China, cannot forgive such an outrage.

Yasukuni glorifies past wars of aggression; and Yasukuni is where war criminals who inflicted untold damage on the peoples of Asia, including Japan, are enshrined. Prime Ministerial patronage of the shrine not only severely damages Japan's political relations with its Asian neighbours, but wounds the feelings of the peoples of those countries. The suspension of summit talks, and the protests and demonstrations against the Yasukuni visits that took place in various Chinese provinces in 2006, were an expression of the feelings of the Chinese people. Koizumi chose to dismiss this message from his neighbour as 'external pressure' and 'interference in the internal affairs of another nation'; he fanned nationalism among Japanese which he used to bolster his approval ratings. The effect was to undermine greatly Japan's domestic politics and international relations.

Koizumi made no attempt to pacify the opposition and anger of his neighbours. For example, in October 2001, he visited the anti-Japanese war memorial at Marco Polo Bridge in Beijing. There he acknowledged Japanese aggression, reflected on the war, and expressed his sorrow and regret. He also visited Korea and expressed his remorse. No sooner had these words left his lips than he repeated his Yasukuni mistake, reprehensible in emotional and rational terms, unforgivable in both Eastern morals and international ethics.

Prime Minister Koizumi was simply unable to understand why the Koreans and Chinese were angry. Prime Minister though he was, he visited Yasukuni, praying for the war criminals even as he prayed for peace. His actions were a blatant display of twisted logic; he belittled and offended the feelings of the people of the war-damaged nations. His actions were a serious challenge to pacifism, to peace and to democracy.[1]

In this chapter, I should like to problematise the history of modern-day relations between Japan and China, in order to decipher the problem of Yasukuni. Furthermore, by analysing the logic of the visits to Yasukuni made by Koizumi and other Japanese politicians before him, such as Nakasone Yasuhiro, I shall attempt to find a way to remove the obstacles impeding Sino-Japanese relations.

A Chinese Perspective on Koizumi Jun'ichirō's Yasukuni visits

On each occasion Prime Minister Koizumi visited Yasukuni, the Chinese government voiced strongly worded protests through all available channels. From its point of view, patronage of Yasukuni and its Class A war criminals severely wounds the feelings of the citizens of those nations that suffered under Japanese militarism and aggression. Given that the visits undermined the foundation of Japan-China relations, the Chinese government was in no mood to forgive. After all, the Class A war criminals enshrined at Yasukuni were the strategists and leaders responsible for Japanese militarism

1 The chapters by Doak and Nitta share a different perspective on the implications for peace of prime ministerial patronage (Ed.).

and the wars of aggression in the 1930s. They were the main culprits who inflicted massive damage on Asia and beyond. Koizumi's defiant disregard for the interests of, and opposition from, international society, Japan's Asian neighbours and the Japanese people themselves, posed a serious challenge to international norms of justice and trampled on human decency.

Yasukuni is offensive to the people of the war-damaged nations, and state patronage eats away at Japan-China relations. For China, this is a matter of principle and of emotion. Japan's militaristic aggression in the Second World War gave rise to 35,000,000 casualties in China. There is no mistaking the fact that inflicting this tragedy was a crime; the Tokyo War Crimes Tribunal determined it so to be, and its rulings found the support of every nation in the world, including Japan itself. I wonder if there exists anywhere in the world a single family not devastated by the loss of a father or a mother. This extreme pain inflicted by the Japanese must be documented. The Chinese people respect forgiveness, and have no wish repeatedly to bring up the events of this tragic past, but when they see senior Japanese politicians venerating those people who once inflicted injury on their own parents, it is no wonder they cannot accept it. Such emotion is natural and universal to all humankind. China was the country worst affected by Japan's militarism and war of aggression; the Chinese people endured immense suffering. Appropriate acknowledgement and treatment of this history are the foundation stones for the post-war revival and rebuilding of Sino-Japanese relations. It is a prerequisite for both countries to look towards the future, but Koizumi injured the feelings of the Chinese people time and again, and this lost him the trust of both the international community and the Japanese people and seriously damaged Japan's image and its national interests.

In actual fact, Koizumi deployed all sorts of sophistry to justify his visits to Yasukuni. For example, he said they were a question of the heart, and it was not for other countries to interfere; for him this was an issue in which foreign governments had no right to speak up. The visits were a question of 'personal freedom' and of internal Japanese affairs, and had nothing to do with China-Japan relations. Only China and Korea were opposed, Koizumi insisted, as he venerated at Yasukuni in the name of peace. However, sophistry will never prevail: fabricated untruths cannot conceal the facts. Koizumi's sophistry served only to deceive himself and others.

Thirteen of the fourteen Class A war criminals enshrined at Yasukuni, men who inflicted the gravest harm on the Chinese people in its modern history, had hands soiled with Chinese blood. So why should the Chinese, who suffered so grievously, not say no to Koizumi? It is not the case that all Japanese politicians share his views. Eight former Prime Ministers have expressed their disapproval of the damage being done to international relations by what Koizumi insists on referring to as his 'personal religious beliefs'. In comments about Koizumi's visits to Yasukuni, Kōno Yōhei, the Chairman of the House of Representatives, said: 'The Prime Minister needs to exercise extreme caution. This is an extremely unfortunate state of affairs. And, it is clear even from surveys in the media that his visits to Yasukuni are not representative of public opinion.'

Were Koizumi's visits to Yasukuni simply a question of his personal freedom to act, when and how he wished? Normal citizens may have that personal freedom, but the Prime Minster is the leader of a nation and a public figure. His very act of visiting Yasukuni was calculated to reflect the feelings of the whole of Japan, and embodied the attitude of the Japanese government towards Japan's war of aggression and the Class A war criminals. It is irresponsible in the extreme to describe this serious issue of political principle as one merely of Koizumi's personal freedom.

But were Koizumi's visits to Yasukuni ever merely a question of Japanese internal affairs? The fourteen Class A war criminals enshrined in the Yasukuni pantheon, including Prime Minister Tōjō Hideki, were found guilty by the International Military Tribunal for the Far East. This is why the issue of Japanese politicians visiting Yasukuni can never simply be a question of internal Japanese affairs;

rather, it is one of universal norms of justice and human decency, which transcend the narrow boundaries of internal politics. The peoples of Asia experienced immeasurable suffering on account of Japan's aggression, and it is only natural that they exercised their right to demand that Koizumi stop visiting Yasukuni in a Prime Ministerial capacity, and that his successor similarly refrains from doing so.

Did Koizumi's visits have nothing at all to do with China-Japan relations? Tōjō Hideki and most of the other thirteen Class A war criminals were involved in the war of aggression in China, and most held key posts in those units that physically invaded China. Four were Staff Officers or Commanding Officers in the Kwantung Army, men who committed acts of immense cruelty against the Chinese people, and it is only natural that the Chinese have opposed visits by the Prime Minister to Yasukuni, where these war criminals are enshrined. It was of course impossible for Koizumi's visits not to have a negative impact on the friendship and mutual cooperation between China and Japan. How can the Chinese people have felt affection for a Japanese Prime Minister who continued to hurt their feelings? It was particularly difficult to understand how as Prime Minister Koizumi could visit China's anti-Japanese war memorial in October 2001, apologise to the Chinese people, acknowledging Japan's acts of aggression, and just six months later on 21 April 2002, make a public visit to Yasukuni. These entirely contradictory actions severely damaged China-Japan relations.

Is it the case, as Koizumi insisted, that only China and Korea were opposed to the visits? In April 2006, Congressman Hyde of the US House of Representatives sent a letter to J. Dennis Hastert, the Speaker of the House, demanding that Prime Minister Koizumi give assurances that he would conduct no more visits to Yasukuni, as a precondition for his addressing Congress during his visit to the USA. There are many others, like Congressman Hyde, who oppose Japanese politicians' visits to Yasukuni, and Koizumi's insistence that only China and Korea opposed them was completely unfounded. Koizumi's visits to Yasukuni attracted criticism from politicians, citizens and mass media in America and many countries in Europe and Africa. No one of sound judgement could forget the multitude of crimes against humanity committed by Japanese militarists in the 1930s.

Were Koizumi's Yasukuni visits in the name of peace? The international community has never raised any kind of objection to Japanese Prime Ministers mourning the war dead at the Chidorigafuchi National Cemetery, or taking part in memorial events in Hiroshima or Nagasaki, but Yasukuni is a different matter. Until the end of the war, Yasukuni was a national, militarist facility. And after the war, too, not only has Yasukuni enshrined the Class A war criminals, but it also houses the Yūshūkan war museum, which declares the 'Great East Asia War' to have been one of self defence. Yasukuni considers the Class A war criminals, stained as they are with the blood of the peoples of Asia, as glorious spirits (*eirei*). Yasukuni and its apologists would have us believe that today's peace is founded upon their sacrifice, which is nothing if not a fraud directed at the world, a sacrilege against human decency.[2] In fact, Prime Minister Koizumi's Yasukuni visits encouraged the extremists who advocate a revival of the ideas of the Great East Asia Co-Prosperity Sphere. His patronage of the shrine acted as a spur to the extreme right-wingers who deny history. And besides this, the purpose of Koizumi's visits to Yasukuni was always to signal an assertive diplomatic stance, in other words, a stubborn refusal to yield to Chinese or Korean pressure. This was all in the name of going down in history as a Prime Minister who stood up for Japan's political interests.

It is unprecedented that China's Premier, President, and other senior leaders have made repeated reference to Yasukuni in recent years, denouncing the outrage committed by Koizumi. Such criticisms were quite without parallel in the relations between the two countries in peace time. After the opening of the China's National People's Congress in March 2004, the Chinese Premier held a press conference in the Great Hall of the People, at which he condemned Prime Minister

2 On this point, see also Breen's chapter in this volume (Ed.).

Koizumi's patronage of Yasukuni in these terms: 'A major issue in China-Japan relations is that Japan's leaders have repeatedly visited the Yasukuni Shrine, where Class A war criminals are enshrined, and this deeply offends the feelings of the Chinese, and people from other Asian countries.' He then acknowledged that this was the reason for the suspension of diplomatic visits between the Chinese and Japanese leaders. The Premier went on to affirm that 'there is no denying that mainstream relations between China and Japan are healthy', citing bilateral trade, travel between the two countries, and the increasing numbers of twinned cities. Then he referred to the suffering inflicted by Japan during the war in which 'over 20,000,000 people died in China'. 'Japanese leaders must not be allowed to influence adversely the normal reciprocal visits between senior politicians and the normal development in the relations between our two countries. I sincerely hope that they will respect the bigger picture when it comes to China-Japan relations', he continued.

At the China-Japan summit held in Chile in November 2004, President Hu Jintao demanded bluntly that Prime Minister Koizumi stop visiting Yasukuni. Koizumi responded by declaring that 'In the future I shall deal with the matter in an appropriate manner', and thus avoided answering the critical question of whether or not he would return to the shrine. At the Asian-African Summit in April 2005, President Hu Jintao once again deplored Koizumi's public visits and presented 'five demands' in connection with China-Japan relations. The Secretary General of the Chinese Communist Party (CCP) and China's President, Jiang Zemin, is on record for having denounced Koizumi's visits to the shrine, saying: 'This is an issue of two nations and two histories'; 'Prime Minister Koizumi must not dismiss this as a simple problem. I can never condone Prime Minister Koizumi's visits to the Yasukuni shrine.'

While he was the Chinese Vice Minister of Foreign Affairs, Dai Bingguo, held a summit meeting with the Chairperson of the Kōmeitō political party, Kanzaki Takenori, to discuss Koizumi's Yasukuni visits, and offered a candid expression of the Chinese position on the matter.

Bingguo expressed his extreme displeasure, denounced the visits, voicing the view that Koizumi must stop visiting the shrine forthwith: 'It is difficult to comprehend why Japanese leaders have visited Yasukuni over and over again. We are opposed to the (Prime Minister's) visits to Yasukuni no matter what the circumstances, the method and the timing. Whether the visits are in the spring or in the autumn, they are essentially the same. We expect the visits not to be repeated, and hope for a fundamental move in the direction of solving this problem.'

The visits even came to exert a negative influence on bilateral economic trade. A situation where political relations were frozen and mutual visits by the Chinese and Japanese leaders suspended even cast a shadow on corporate trade activities: the 9.9% growth in China-Japan trade in 2005 was not only below the growth of trade with Europe and America, but was 15 points lower than the 25.7% growth of 2004. In 1994, trade with Japan accounted for 20% of Chinese overseas trade, but by 2005 this had fallen by 7 points to just 13%.

Koizumi persisted in patronising Yasukuni, and in order to legitimise his actions, he determined to set off on the day of *hatsumōde*, the first day of the year when Japanese traditionally pay their first visit to a shrine. The date, 1 January, enabled him to merge his visit to Yasukuni with the New Year custom, saying: 'Well, it's a Japanese tradition, is it not, for people to pay a visit to their local shrines at New Year?' It is perfectly understandable that normal people mourn their family and friends. Indeed, the bereaved families of the Japanese war dead insist their own visits to Yasukuni are in order to pay tribute to family and friends; for their part, they strongly opposed the enshrinement of Class A war criminals. The Chinese are an honourable people, and distinguish between the Japanese nation and a minority of militarists in their midst, between the general populace and right wing elements. Our position has always been that Yasukuni visits by normal Japanese citizens do not have historical repercussions, but that Yasukuni patronage on the part of the Japanese Prime Minister is of a different order. It is not simply a question of mourning the war dead; this is why Yasukuni is not an issue of Japanese internal affairs alone. Rather, it is a problem of principle and relates to Japanese political leaders' attitude towards Japan's history of aggression and the war crimes committed by the Imperial Japanese army in the Second World War.

When taken to task about the negative influence he exerted on Japan's neighbouring countries, Koizumi was wont to explain that it was not right for China to criticise 'the values attached to the history, traditions and customs of a particular country… I am sure you will understand what I mean. Even if it takes time, I will do what I can to reassure you of my actions.' There are active in Japan numerous scholars and commentators who advocate theories of Japanese cultural uniqueness, and who try to deceive us into thinking the Yasukuni issues are incomprehensible to non-Japanese. However, it is incumbent on the political leader of a country not merely to stress the value of its own history, traditions and customs, but to recognise the values held dear by other countries. Chinese leaders repeatedly urged Prime Minister Koizumi not to hurt the feelings of the Chinese, but Koizumi refused to take heed, and hurt our feelings time and time again.

Within Japanese culture there always existed a native ideology of the *kami*, which holds that the people are the treasures of the realm. There are shamanistic principles at work here in seeking the origins of humankind in heaven, but they lead to the definition of humans as beings who appear in this world with *kami* 'spirit' embodied in the flesh. It followed naturally, then, that when this physical object, the human body, decayed and was beyond use, it returned to the ground whence it came, and the spirit or soul returned to heaven. The human spirits in this theory have their origins in heaven, and they return to heaven; and the power that rules heaven is venerated as a great *kami* or god. In later ages, it was understood that the spirits of the dead themselves became *kami*. The term 'body' exists in Japanese, of course, where it is rendered as *karada*, which is significantly homophonous with 'empty' and 'shell'. The idea is that just like the larva of a cicada discards its skin leaving it hollow, so too when the soul departs this world, the bodily form which acted as its vessel is rendered empty and hollow.

There is another variant mythology in Japan which insists that when people die they become Buddhas; none are ever judged for the good or evil of the acts they committed in this life. It is this variant idea which is deployed to argue that there is no need to pursue the war crimes committed by the Class A war criminals, and no earthly reason therefore not to visit Yasukuni. It is clear that this idea was cultivated by State Shinto, of which Yasukuni was the epitome during the 1930s and 40s, but the idea is a woeful distortion of ancient Shinto, which predates Yasukuni. Ancient Shinto taught that there were two categories of spirits: gentle spirits which brought tranquillity on human kind, and violent-tempered, ferocious spirits which brought calamity.

In Japan's traditional Shinto-influenced religious culture, there were also two types of *kami*: good *kami* and bad *kami*. The former, *kami* of good, have much in common with the aforementioned gentle, peaceful spirits and the ancestral spirits, while the latter, the *kami* of evil, share much with the violent-tempered, ferocious spirits, and those so-called angry spirits of men and women who perished in war, or on account of epidemic diseases or other calamities. These diverse *kami* cults involved divergent practises: spirit propitiation (*irei*) which had its origins in a sense of gratitude towards ancestral spirits and so was common to all Japanese, while spirit pacification (*mitama shizume*) involved pacifying those violent-tempered sprits in order to transform their nature from violent to gentle and good. It is unfortunate that Japanese nowadays fail to understand the way of thinking integral to traditional Japanese religious culture; most cannot even pronounce the names of the various types of spirits and *kami*. It is deeply ironic then that men like Koizumi Jun'ichirō should advocate, as they often do, the revival of traditional Japanese culture. Let it be known that the Yasukuni shrine does not enshrine the spirits of all people, but very specifically only the 'glorious spirits' of fallen war heroes, those killed in action who sacrificed their lives for their country.

A Historical Perspective on Chinese Views of the Yasukuni Shrine

So the Prime Minister's patronage of Yasukuni shrine caused China-Japan relations to worsen to the brink of collapse. The Japanese typically responded by shamelessly ascribing blame to the Chinese government, alleging that the Chinese play Yasukuni like a trump card for their own domestic, anti-Japanese purposes. However, the Chinese people saw through the real nature of Yasukuni from the time of its inception; it is not as if they have only just begun to oppose official patronage.

Ever since its inauguration in 1869 as *Tokyo shōkonsha* or the Tokyo 'spirit summoning shrine', Yasukuni was subject to the critical gaze of the Chinese. During the Japan-learning boom at the end of the Qing Period (1644-1911), many Chinese visited Japan to learn the lessons of Japan's modernisation. Naturally, these men included Yasukuni in their tours of Tokyo. Historical records do not reveal which Chinese was the first to lay eyes on Yasukuni, and there is no way of pursuing the matter. But the first man to record his impressions was Wang Tao (1827-1897), an intellectual active in the Westernisation movement at the end of the Qing Period, and a pioneer of Chinese journalism. Wang Tao was exiled to Hong Kong for the crime of conspiring with the Taiping rebellion. In 1867, he toured various countries including the United Kingdom, France and Germany, and in 1874, he founded the *Xunhuan Daily* in Hong Kong. As Editor in Chief, he worked to introduce modern science and foreign affairs from the West, and championed the Hundred Days Reform Movement of 1898. Wang Tao, who advocated taking from the West its best features, acquired renown as the author of *Pu-fa zhanji* ('Records of the Franco-Prussian War'). He was invited to Japan as the outstanding scholar of his day, well versed in the affairs of the West, and was also held in very high esteem by numerous Japanese intellectuals. Oka Senjin (1832-1913), for example, described him as second only to Wei Yuan (1794-1856), the Chinese intellectual whose book *Haiguó túzhì* ('Illustrated treatise on the maritime kingdoms') made a major contribution to Qing enlightenment. Shigeno Yasutsugu (1827-1910), believed Wang was Wei Yuan's intellectual superior.

Wang Tao spent over four months in Japan, and inspected various shrines including the Minato shrine, where the spirit of the medieval loyalist Kusunoki Masashige (1294-1336) is venerated. He diligently recorded his observations from his travels and, on his return, edited his notes and published them under the title *Fusang yuji* ('Records of my travels in Japan'). He visited Tokyo's 'Spirit summoning' shrine with friends from the *Hōchi* newspaper, and *Fusang yuji* contains the following passage.

> When you get past this point, you arrive at the Spirit summoning shrine. Its purpose is to venerate the state's martyrs, those devoted warriors who sacrificed their lives for their country at the time of Japan's Imperial restoration. They built altars in both Tokyo and Kyoto, and called the sites *shōkon* or 'spirit summoning' shrines. They perform rites there three times a year to mark the days on which the battles of Fushimi and Ueno commenced, and Aizu castle fell.[3] Subsequently they added a day to mark the suppression of the rebellion in Kagoshima.[4] So, now there are four feast days. On these days, there is sumo wrestling and horse racing; clouds of smoke fill the air, and visitors queue up and everything is bustling and alive. It is easy to understand the intention behind the Japanese government's enshrining of the war dead: the enthusiasm of the masses will flourish, and their loyalty will never be found wanting.

At the time of Wang Tao's visit to Yasukuni, Japan was baring its fangs at Asia, in readiness for the Sino-Japanese war of 1894. The Japanese state was now defined by the emperor's twin roles as ritual celebrant and political ruler, and Wang was especially impressed to see how government leaders deployed the imperial rituals of Yasukuni to rally the morale of the general populace. He honestly perceived Yasukuni in the tenth year of its creation to be

3 These were key engagements in the Restoration wars of 1868-9 .

4 This is a reference to the Satsuma rebellion led by Saigō Takamori in 1877.

the unique shrine that it was, a sacred site for the veneration of those loyalists who died in Japan's civil conflicts. Wang Tao also, incidentally, articulated his strong feelings of dissatisfaction and regret over the Satsuma rebellion.

At the start of the twentieth century, many Chinese followed in Wang's footsteps and came to Japan on inspection tours to study the key to Japan's economic and military might. The first Chinese person to discern the true nature of the Yasukuni shrine and to issue a warning was Yang Fu, who toured Japan in 1907. Yang Fu hailed from Yangzhou province, the same as the great eighth century Buddhist monk, Ganjin; he passed the civil service exam to become a government bureaucrat. He then held various posts, such as minister of military affairs, before he used the 1910 Xinhai Revolution as his pretext to resign from government. During the Japan-learning boom of the early twentieth century, Yang Fu was commissioned by Duan Fang, governor of the three provinces Jiangsu, Anhui and Jiangxisheng, to head an inspection party to Japan. He crossed the Japan Sea on the steamship *Hakuai* (Philanthropy), landing at Nagasaki, and subsequently visited Kyushu and both Kansai and Kantō regions. Over 106 days, Yang Fu inspected many Japanese institutions in minute detail, including nursery, primary and secondary schools, schools for the profoundly deaf, Imperial universities, hospitals, museums, libraries, parks, police stations, prisons, the Mint Bureau, and even paper factories. His observations and impressions were recorded every day without fail, and on his return, these records were published under the title *Fusang shixun ji* ('Records of 100 days in Japan'). His memoirs, with their fine detail and beautiful style, were valued highly by all; even the great reformer, Liang Qichao (1873-1929), endorsed them wholeheartedly.

Fusang shixun ji sets out Yang Fu's observations of Japan in the exquisite detail, but especially worthy of note are the impressions he formed, from three different visits, of Yasukuni. On his first visit, Yang Fu expressed surprise that 'weapons from the Russian army and arms from our country seized by Japan's colonial governors over many years of warfare are on display for the general public in and around the precinct of the shrine, accompanied by clear documentation of the weapons' capture.' He wrote that the spoils from the battle of Port Arthur in 1894, such as Chinese torpedoes and firearms, were particularly striking. And, on the subject of the Yūshūkan war museum, he wrote of his dismay on seeing there 'many more captured items on display, such as firearms and military uniforms'. 'Even many maps of military strategy from the wars won are magnified for everyone to see. On the surrounding walls, there are countless pictures praising the benevolent rule of the envoys in the various areas of Fengtian Province'.

Yang Fu returned to Yasukuni once more to observe first-hand the Meiji Emperor's visit to the shrine and then for a third time solely to visit the Yūshūkan war museum. On this third visit, Yang Fu wrote that 'there are countless Chinese guns of all sizes exhibited here. There is even a cannon used in the attack on Jin Long. It has a description attached describing it as one of the Qing dynasty's most important pieces of artillery, seized in 1900.' 'There are countless other cannon, and they have even produced and displayed small-scale models of the battery at Port Arthur and the battery at Heshand Island in Dalian'. At the same time, Yang Fu observed the 'large charts on display setting out the conditions at the time of the invasion of Taiwan. He mentioned that he had seen these or similar diagrams at the museum in Ueno. Indeed, the latter was exhibiting the torpedoes, firearms and other spoils of war for which there was no room at Yasukuni. There were many antiques there, too, and items of cultural value that had been plundered from Beijing by the Imperial army during the Boxer Uprising in 1900. Japan of course had played a major role in the Eight nation alliance that invaded China at that time. Other exhibits included large ropes used by the naval fleet, and Yang Fu noted that 'they were made from hair donated by Japanese women. The intentions of the Meiji government come through loud and clear: they are clearly seeking to rouse a spirit of fervent support for the war amongst the masses'. Yang Fu took great umbrage at the fact that the Yasukuni shrine stimulated the war of aggression, and thus showed contempt for China, Russia and other nations.

At around the same time, another Chinese visitor to Japan, Lou Liran, governor of Sichuan Province, visited Yasukuni and left the following account:

'Yasukuni was built to enshrine those who have died in the imperial cause from the Kaéi Period (1848-1854) till the present day...There the Emperor personally performs rites to honour their memory. Bereaved families from all over the nation are invited, and spirit summoning rites are performed. The whole nation of Japan believes there is glory in this. Chief of staff Yamagata Aritomo wrote a memorial piece in which he said the following: "The Imperial guard, whom the rebels feared most in the Satsuma rebellion, fought the good fight of heroes. Recently, men from the Japanese military got together to erect a monument to mourn the war dead and honour their achievements. The Emperor bestowed on them special Imperial funds, which financed the expenses incurred". Nearby is the Yūshūkan war museum, which houses spoils from the Sino-Japanese War, including the banner displaying Li Wenszhong's rank, and Ye Zhichao's letter of surrender.'[5]

Governor Lou, on observing all this, said:

'Every human being must die. But to die in this way in order to preserve one's honour, even after death! I was genuinely surprised by this view of life and death. I had heard previously that Japanese soldiers are famous for being unafraid of death, but it was only on visiting the Yasukuni shrine that I came to understand the secret behind that fact.'

So, from the start of the twentieth century, the Chinese people were quick to perceive Yasukuni as a stratagem to hasten the Japanese populace to the field of battle for the sake of the Emperor, all under the guise of traditional Shinto. In March 1908, the government official Wang Sanrang (dates unknown) from Lulong City, Yongping in Zhili province (now Qinhuang Dao city, Hebei province) went to Japan for three months under instructions to study and observe the structure and working of local government. Before arriving in Japan, Wang Sanrang read extensively and prepared meticulously; so not only did his general observations yield good results, but he

5 Li (ed.), *Qiang'an Dongyou diary*.

also made a detailed study of Yasukuni. He edited the results of his observations and published them under the title *Youdong ji* (Youdong diary), which included his observations and reflections from his time in Japan, and also his own analysis of the country. The best known chapter was 'The Yasukuni shrine: three considerations'.

> The first consideration exposes the Meiji government's aim in building Yasukuni. Wang points out that the latter, 'after careful consideration', concocted a plan that would locate Yasukuni as the font of the entire population's spirit.

> Nowadays, the precinct of Yasukuni is spacious and lined with trees. There is a constant stream of men and women visiting the shrine. Visitors worship the glorious spirits of the departed war heroes, and recall lovingly their faces. All this helps foster a militaristic spirit among the people. The descendants of the glorious spirits remember the bravery of their ancestors, feel pride, and there arises naturally a sense of fearlessness before death. And, they feel deep shame if these feelings fail. In this way, Yasukuni helps to ensure the population is in a frenzy; there is not a single person not prepared to devote himself to the imperial cause, and none who lack courage. This is surely the key to Japan's successes in the series of modern Japan's conflicts.

Wang's second consideration concerns Yasukuni's militarism:

> There are old and new firearms, sharp and blunt swords, bullet-proof clothing and helmets, all lined up on display. There are model reproductions of the towns and fortresses where battles took place, and also exhibits of small scale models of warships. Good and bad, new and old, sharp and blunt, they have retained every single item. These devoted people have worked hard, and if they compare and make improvements then, it goes without saying that Japanese military weaponry can only get better.

Wang Sanrang's third and final consideration involves his questioning the purpose of the Yūshūkan war museum: 'The question is with what object in mind did the Meiji government ever build such a shrine as Yasukuni [with its adjacent war museum]? If one looks around, there are large scale diagrams of battlefields filled with the dense smoke of canons; they look like plans for a new museum. The flags from the two opposing armies stand apart, and the armies confront each other in a microcosm. Additionally, retreat and victory, offence, defence and pursuit have each been painstakingly illustrated, and the details of the battles are drawn in an extremely lifelike way. These detailed images are burnt into the minds of visitors. As visitors look upon the sights before them, a spirit of admiration for bravery and valuing death wells up from within. Watching Asia for an opportunity is now a thing of the past, perhaps, but the items on display here are certainly not simply for the sake of commemoration.

Wang continued:

> Patriotism and passionate nationalism are important and indispensable but, generally speaking, all the affairs of this world depend on the use to which they are put. Things are affected by the purposes for which they are deployed. In our country, too, after the Sino-Japanese war of 1894-5 and the Boxer Rebellion of 1900, we should have drawn up charts, constructed models and pledged to avenge our defeat and vent our hatred. But we did not do this, while Japan did. Even so, if we use this technique belatedly to bolster our spirits and strengthen our resolve, then in the future, we will enhance the glory of our flag and bring great honour to the history of our nation. We only need to get started now, and the results will soon stun everyone. In any case, the problem really only lies in how we might avail ourselves of this technique.

Wang Sanrang warned that patriotism was a doubled edged sword, and harboured doubts about Japan doing as a victor what was perhaps more appropriate for nations to do in defeat. As I mentioned above, Wang visited Yasukuni three times. The third time, he made a point of visiting in May on the day of the Great Rites of Spring, and carefully observed the veneration and the rites of consolation (*iresai*) that were performed on that occasion. He came to believe that there were several issues at stake, but that they were beyond his own understanding.

Firstly, although 'every country honours their war dead both socially and historically, but in Japan this never had any relation to Shinto whatsoever. So why does the modern state resort to Shinto ceremonies?' Secondly, 'Why are those enshrined at Yasukuni referred to as "Yasukuni *kami*" rather than "Yasukuni people"?' After careful observation and profound consideration, Wang Sanrang came to the following conclusions: 'It is true that since long ago Japan has had a traditional religion called Shinto, and this permeates people's hearts and their faith is extremely devout. If [those enshrined at Yasukuni] are referred to as "Yasukuni people", this would only emphasise the world of the living, but call them "Yasukuni *kami*", and they will be treated with respect for evermore. And, if this practice becomes customary, it is bound to exert an enduring influence on people, and so it is not, after all, strange that the Japanese should be so unafraid of death and honour valour. Accordingly, there is a constant stream of visitors to the shrine, and sumo, drama and other displays of traditional national sports and art are rendered aesthetic. Service men make solemn visits to the shrine, and bereaved families make sincere and pious visits, and this is purely for form's sake. What the real spirit of Yasukuni strives for is not aesthetic expression nor solemnity for form's sake; rather it seeks the inspiration of patriotism, valour and undying loyalty for the emperor. Those that live on the border between human life and the *kami*, they are the ones whose solidarity is strongest, so strong that it is capable of withstanding any assault.'[6]

Conclusion: Towards a Solution to the Yasukuni Issue

The Chinese people clearly recognised at a very early stage the fundamental nature of the unique institution that is the Yasukuni shrine. In short, Yasukuni was a realisation of the policy of unifying ritual performance with politics. Enshrining people who died on the battlefield for the sake of the Emperor as 'Yasukuni *kami*' diminished the value of individual lives. Yasukuni enshrinement planted in the citizens of the modern Japanese nation a spirit of fearlessness before death; it urged the masses towards the field of battle, and encouraged them to sacrifice themselves for the emperor and, in time, to carry out massacres.

Over sixty years have passed since Japan's defeat in the Second World War, and Japan now stands at an important crossroads in its

6 Wang, *Youdong ji*.

diplomatic history, as it seeks to join the United Nations Security Council. As the world's second largest economy, Japan now wants to play a bigger role in the international community. This in itself does not warrant criticism. However, if Japan cannot come to terms with its history, and if it persistently resorts to blatant trickery when it comes to historical issues, if it betrays the promises it has made to the countries of Asia and their peoples regarding these issues, then I have no choice but to express my grave doubts and fears over Japan assuming a weightier role as a major global power. Only when it has reflected seriously on its history of aggression, and shows it can tread the path of peace and development, can Japan hope to gain the trust of the countries of Asia and their peoples and make a bigger contribution to the international community.

I cannot avoid concluding that the shortcomings of post-war peace and democracy in Asia are encapsulated in the fact that there is very little difference between the Yasukuni as observed 120 years ago by Chinese visitors and the Yasukuni of today, more than sixty years since the end of the war. And I cannot help wondering how it transpired that the anti-war, pro-peace movement that took off in Japan after the war passed the Yasukuni shrine by. Unless 'the spell of Yasukuni' is broken, Japan will never see true democracy or peace. It stands to reason that solving the Yasukuni problem will require the cooperation of the Japanese people themselves. They must join hands with the people of neighbouring countries who suffered directly at the hands of the war criminals enshrined at Yasukuni and work alongside them towards a solution. This is the one and only sure route that will lead to a resolution of the Yasukuni problem.

4

PLUMBING THE DEPTHS OF THE YASUKUNI CONTROVERSY IN CHINA

Seki Hei

Introduction

It is no exaggeration to say that for the five years after Koizumi took office as Prime Minister, Sino-Japanese relations revolved entirely around the issue of his visits to the Yasukuni shrine. On each occasion that he did so, he drew strong condemnation from the Chinese government whose stance of opposition grew more resilient year by year. The result was that political relations between the two countries became even chillier. And then, when Koizumi made his fifth visit to the shrine as Prime Minister in October 2005, the Chinese government adopted a hard-line attitude towards Japan that can only be described as unreasonable; it refused all forms of talks with Japan's Prime Minister and Foreign Minister purely on the grounds of these Yasukuni issues. For example, at an Asia Pacific Economic Cooperation (APEC) forum held in Pusan, Korea on 14 November, a Chinese Foreign Ministry spokesman said of the possibility of a Sino-Japanese summit that it was 'quite out of the question'; he also made it clear that a Foreign Minister level meeting was extremely unlikely.

Integral to the thinking behind the Chinese leadership allowing the situation to develop to this degree of gravity was undoubtedly that they intended to deploy the issue of the Yasukuni visits as a political card with which to trump Japan. In short, by returning again and again to 'issues of historical understanding' which, of course, included the Yasukuni problem, to bash Japan, the Chinese were resorting once more to the all too familiar of trying to gain the upper hand in Sino-Japanese relations.

However, China's extremely rigid attitude towards Japan, persisting with its protests over the issue of the Yasukuni visits to the point where it refused all political negotiations with Japan, backfired. It worked in quite the reverse direction since it had the effect of constraining the further development of China's own diplomatic relations with Japan. The key player, Prime Minister Koizumi, remained resolute and refused to buckle under pressure from the Chinese. Indeed, he launched a merciless counter offensive, articulating the most logical of arguments. His position was that it was odd for the Chinese to refuse all talks because of a single discrepancy in views between the two countries. At a press conference on 5 December 2005, for example, Koizumi offered the following critique of the Chinese position:

> 'What is odd is that Sino-Japanese relations should come a cropper on the issue of the Yasukuni shrine alone. Every country is bound to disagree with the views of another, or dispute the views of the other, on one or two issues. Surely, diplomacy is all about continuing the relationship in the midst of such disagreements? It is distinctly odd for the Chinese leadership to insist that the visits I make to Yasukuni shrine are 'odd' for anyone who respects freedom.'

It was, indeed, Chinese President Hu Jintao and his leadership who were responsible for creating the impasse in the first place by declining to lower the fist they raised in defiance, and refusing to negotiate.

Then, in the summer of 2006, there was a flurry of activity on the Chinese side, with the Chinese effecting a complete volte-face and sanctioning talks at the Foreign Minister level with Japan. On 10 June of 2006, President Hu Jintao, who could hardly bear to set eyes on the Japanese Prime Minister, had talks in the Great Hall of the People with Ninomiya Yūji, the Japanese ambassador to Beijing, in which he suddenly, and quite unexpectedly, expressed an interest in making a state visit to Japan. There is no doubt about it; this was proof of Hu Jintao's anxiety to break through the deadlock in China-Japan relations that his own side had created. Until that point, Yasukuni had proved to be a shackle on Chinese diplomatic relations with Japan; far, indeed, from the diplomatic trump card China had envisaged. China's quite abnormal obsession with the issue of prime ministerial Yasukuni visits resulted in its government being forced into a cul-de-sac in terms of its diplomacy with Japan.

One cannot escape the conclusion that the Chinese leadership must have had some other more deep-seated agenda in persisting as it did with the Yasukuni issue, apart from their wish to use it for diplomatic advantage. If it were a trump card and nothing more, then surely they should have been able to deploy it in a more imaginative fashion. This chapter, then, sets out to shed light on these other, more opaque reasons.

The Material and the Spiritual

Closer scrutiny of the statements made by the Chinese government in protest at Koizumi Jun'ichirō's visits to Yasukuni reveals that their principal objection was that 'the visits are destructive of the political foundations of Sino-Japan relations'. So, for example, on 7 December 2005, Vice President Zeng Qinghong held talks with a visiting delegation of Japan Socialist Party members, and took the opportunity to make critical reference to the Yasukuni problem: 'Japanese leaders' worship at Yasukuni shrine wounds the feelings of the Chinese people, and has undermined the political foundations on which relations between the two countries have been built.' The Chinese leaders insistence that 'the issue of the Yasukuni visits is an impediment to political relations between China and Japan' was voiced so frequently as to become clichéd. The Chinese, in other words, believed the Yasukuni visits to be a supremely political issue between the two countries. The Japanese, on the other hand, tended to see them as an essentially religious type of endeavour, only related in the vaguest way to today's worlds of politics and diplomacy. The living pay their respects to, and propitiate the spirits of, the 'glorious war dead', venerated at the religious establishment known as a Shinto shrine: how could this be described as anything other than a religious undertaking? Within Japan, too, of course there were those who criticised the Prime Minister's visits from the perspective that they violated the Constitutional provisions of the separation of religion and state. Such criticisms as these were evidently predicated on an understanding that the nature of the visits was nothing if not religious.

Leaving aside the issue of whether these criticisms were justifiable, why did the Chinese government need to take up the visits, which are religious acts that pivot around the relationship between the living and the spirits of the dead, as a political issue, integral to the foundations of its relations with Japan? How did the leaders of the Chinese Communist Party (CCP) administration, or the Chinese government, really view the visits to Yasukuni that took place in Japan?

An important point lurking concealed behind the issue of the Yasukuni visits is that members of the CCP, and the leaders of the CCP administration, are fundamentally both materialist and atheist, and they thus categorically reject the legitimacy of all religious acts. In this materialistic world view, which serves as the guiding ideology for the CCP leadership, the very existence and legitimacy of religion are denied in every respect, and the existence of gods and spirits is unequivocally refuted. These materialists believe that the existence of a person's mind or spirit is predicated on the existence of a material foundation, namely the human body. Once a human dies, their body ceases to exist and that person's mind or spirit also vanishes into eternity. There is no spirit left behind after death.

In this world view, there is no possibility for any sort of relationship between the living and the deceased; all such linkages are severed. Only those who currently possess human form exist; those whose bodies have died simply do not exist, and there can thus be no possibility of a mutual relationship of any sort. To put it another way, given that the spirits of the dead do not exist, it is utter nonsense to pay one's respects to, or console, the spirits of the deceased; such activities are entirely devoid of meaning. Why on earth would it be necessary to console spirits or souls that have never existed in the first place?

This is the sensibility that sustains these materialists, namely the top-ranking CCP party members. Thus it is hardly to be wondered at that their understanding and interpretation of the meaning of Prime Ministerial patronage of Yasukuni is totally at odds with that of most Japanese people, including former Prime Minister, Koizumi Jun'ichirō. They dismiss as utter poppycock the possibility of religious significance in consoling the spirits of the deceased, which is after all the point of worship at Yasukuni; and they deny any genuine religious sentiment behind Koizumi's insistence on his wish to pay tribute to the memory of those who died in action entirely against their wishes. The result is the Chinese leadership's complete disregard for the religious nature of Yasukuni visits; rather, they understand them to be very real human acts that take place within the confines of this secular world in which we all live.

Since any real human act that takes place in this real world must have real motivation and rationale behind it, it stands to reason that the Yasukuni visits by political leaders, like former Prime Minister Koizumi, must be political acts deriving from some sort of equally real political motivation. *Kami* and the glorious war dead are nothing if not impossible fabrications, hence Koizumi cannot have visited the shrine purely for the purpose of propitiating and consoling those spirits. Koizumi was always wont to explain his motives for worshiping at Yasukuni in terms of his personal desire to pay tribute to the memory of the deceased. For example, at Prime Minister's questions in the Diet on 19 October, he referred to his Yasukuni patronage in the following terms: 'I, Koizumi Jun'ichirō, visit Yasukuni as a citizen of this nation, and I do so to pray for peace, to offer my sincere feelings of respect and gratitude to those who fell in the field of battle'. From the perspective of the leaders of the Chinese state, this level of explanation constitutes little more than expedience and lies.

The world view held in common by each of the leaders of the CCP administration was only able to refute the essentially religious nature of Koizumi's patronage of Yasukuni, and so they treated his successive visits as supremely political acts with supremely political significance in this world. Thus we have stumbled upon the most important dimension of the issue of the Yasukuni visits that has continued to stymie Sino-Japanese relations.

The Chinese Communist party and the Japanese war of Aggression

Here, it is particularly noteworthy that when compared, say, with Deng Xiaoping and his ilk from the older generation, President Hu Jintao and other current leaders are all the more staunchly atheist. Most of Deng Xiaoping's generation of CCP leaders adopted Communism as one type of political ideology after they reached adulthood. As with the rest of their generation, their early years were spent growing up in a traditional society not yet poisoned by this so-called materialism, so they must have been influenced to no small degree by traditional Chinese religious notions of spirits and spirit propitiation. Thus while Deng Xiaoping and his peers may have converted to Communism, it is easy to understand that a fundamental capacity to comprehend religious sentiment continued to reside spiritually somewhere deep inside them. The same certainly cannot be said for Hu Jintao and his comrades in power. Fifty-eight years have already passed since the establishment of the People's Republic of China, and so the current leaders, who are on average in their early sixties, were brought up, ever since they reached the age of reason, in an education system that was Communist through and through. Of course, not every citizen of their generation who received such education became a staunch Communist, but these men were quite special. By this, I mean that they were prize pupils who were truly immersed in Communism heart and soul; it was precisely because of this total immersion that they stepped onto the fast track within the CCP pecking order and ascended the Party's leadership rungs. It is likely that you will find no one anywhere today who possesses such an unwavering conviction in Communism, or such a materialistic make-up as these men do.

There is a further element that has served to strengthen this materialistic make-up. This may be a fact little known in Japan, but if one examines the educational background of the nine members who currently make up the Politburo Standing Committee, that is the top ranking leaders of the CCP, each and every one of them moved into politics from a science background. So, for example, the President of the People's Republic of China, Hu Jintao, graduated with a degree in hydraulic engineering from Beijing's Tsinghua University. Hu worked for Sinohydro Engineering Bureau no. 4 as an engineer. His number two, Wu Bangguo, the Chairman of the Standing Committee of the National People's Congress, majored in electron tube engineering at the Department of Radio Electronics of Tsinghua University. Subsequently, he worked at Shanghai No. 3 Electronic Tube Factory where he was chief of the technical section. Wen Jiabao, the Premier of the State Council, graduated with a master's degree in geological structures from the Beijing Institute of Geology; he began his career in the Gansu geology bureau. Zeng Qinhong, the vice-president of the PRC, graduated from the Automatic Control Department, Beijing Institute of Technology, and is an engineer, specialising in automatic control systems. Apart from these senior figures, consider the academic backgrounds and early careers of these men: Huang Ju, vice premier of the PRC, attended Qinghua University from 1956-63 and graduated in Electrical Engineering; Wu Guanzheng graduated with a degree in thermal engineering from Qinghua University; Li Changchun, the propaganda chief of the Communist Party of China, graduated with a degree in electrical engineering from the Harbin Institute of Technology, and Luo Gan studied engineering at the Beijing Steel and Iron Institute.

These strait-laced scientists and Communist devotees are nothing but a gang of materialistically-driven atheists. Given their make-up, these current leaders have no concern for, or understanding of, religion. Gazing from afar across the seas at the island of Japan, they have always seen the visits to Yasukuni by Japanese prime ministers as nothing more than a charade, a ruse designed to achieve their political ambitions. These Communist leaders, whose responsibility it is to steer China's diplomatic relations with Japan, devote their undivided attention to deciphering these political ambitions.

So, just how does the CCP administration view the political significance of Koizumi's visits? Unquestionably, they regard the issue of the enshrinement of those people designated Class A war criminals to be the most problematic. So, for example, the Chinese government issued an immediate protest against Koizumi's visit to Yasukuni on 17 October 2005, Koizumi's fifth as Prime Minister. The statement stressed the Class A war criminal connection in its opening sentence: 'The Japanese Prime Minister Koizumi Jun'ichirō once again paid his respects at Yasukuni, that shrine where the Class A war criminals are venerated.'

But bearing in mind the world view of the CCP leaders, it is strange indeed that they judge this enshrinement to be in any way problematic, given that they reject out of hand the very existence of the spirits of the dead. Surely it should be a matter of no consequence to them whether the Class A war criminals' spirits are enshrined or not. Herein lies the real problem. The leaders of the CCP do not recognise the existence of spirits of the deceased nor attach any religious significance to them, and so they, along with most Japanese, in fact, have no awareness of the spirits of Tōjō Hideki and others war time leaders as being enshrined in Yasukuni. The fact is that their world view, and the limits it places on linguistic expression, gives them little option but to translate the religious enshrinement into political language. They speak thus in terms of 'remembering' and 'honouring' but never of 'enshrining'. So, 'Tōjō Hideki and the other Class A war criminals, the leaders of the war of aggression, are to this day remembered, and publicly honoured, at the Yasukuni shrine.' In other words, since the leaders of the CCP cannot accommodate the notion that 'after people die, they become spirits of a different nature to living people', they cling to the belief that Tōjō Hideki and the others venerated at Yasukuni are today the same Class A war criminals and the leaders of the war of aggression against China as they were before their deaths. This in turn means that they cannot view the connection created by former Prime Minister Koizumi in his visits to Yasukuni shrine as one of a religious nature between Koizumi Junichirō, as a living person, and the spirit of the late Tōjō Hideki and the others enshrined there. Rather, the relationship can for them only ever be of a political nature between Prime Minister Koizumi as a serving politician, and Hideki Tōjō and the others as one-time war leaders.

In other words, by resolutely visiting the shrine, Koizumi Jun'ichirō, the erstwhile leader of Japan, honours the memory of the leaders of the war of aggression and thereby establishes a political relationship with them. And this is nothing other than Koizumi expressing his tolerance and glorification of the crimes of the war of aggression prosecuted by these men, and his identification with, and approval of, the strategies of aggression which they deployed. The Chinese judge that Prime Minister Koizumi's political relationship with these leaders of the war of aggression amounts to the realisation of an enduring connectivity between Koizumi, and the Japanese government which he heads on the one hand, and Japan's war of aggression on the other. So, for example, *Renmin ribao*, the official organ of the Chinese Communist Party's central committee, published an article on 16 September, 2005 which exemplifies this position:

> Prime ministerial patronage of the Yasukuni shrine is quite simply an act of glorifying the war of aggression and escaping responsibility for the war. The Japanese state's glorification of past acts of aggression, and the avoidance of responsibility for them mean nothing less than the resurrection of Japanese militarism and the opening of the way to new wars of aggression.

Naturally enough, in their eyes, Koizumi's visits and the concomitant glorification of Class A war criminals, constitute in themselves a major provocation towards the Chinese government.

The political myth that it was the Chinese Communist Party as heroes of the people that, through its counter Japanese struggle, defeated Japanese militarism and redeemed the Chinese people from the cruel atrocities of the aggressor army, serves as one of the ideological pillars supporting the current CCP administration. Inherent in this political myth is the belief that Japanese Class A war criminals are the very symbol of the cruel atrocities perpetrated by the Imperial Japanese Army; they must be portrayed as 'evil demons' in order that the Chinese 'heroes' can shine in all their resplendent glory. That these Japanese leaders were convicted as criminals is proof of the historical victory which the CCP's heroes won. This is why they will never be shifted from their belief in the inherent justice of the verdicts of the Tokyo War Crimes Tribunal in condemning these men as war criminals and sentencing them to death. In order to sustain and reproduce this sort of political myth, the Class A war criminals must be denounced for eternity as criminals. The CCP's line of thinking, though, is that the visits to Yasukuni by Japanese political leaders restore the honour of the Class A war criminals and glorify the cruel atrocities of Japanese militarism, and this, in effect, belittles the CCP's historical achievements. This is the reason why they can never assent to the visits.

This is the political significance which in the eyes of the leaders of the CCP administration always attached to these 'political acts' of Koizumi when he visited Yasukuni as Prime Minister; this is the political motivation which they invariably read into his acts. As a consequence, the CCP leadership was left with very little choice but to denounce Koizumi's visits vociferously as destructive of the political foundation of Sino-Japanese relations. In this context, their opposition to Yasukuni visits which took the purely political means of refusing summit conferences with Japan, makes perfect sense. For the best part of a year between Koizumi's visit to Yasukuni on 17

October 2005 and his retirement from office on 26 September 2006, not a single Sino-Japanese summit took place. At both the aforementioned APEC summit in Pusan, and the subsequent ASEAN summit convened in Malaysia in December 2005, the Chinese made a point of snubbing Japanese requests for a leadership summit. It seems that politics lies at the very heart of the issue of the Yasukuni visits when it comes to their place within Sino-Japanese relations.

The Chinese and the Spirits of the Dead

This Chinese view of the Prime Minister's Yasukuni patronage is not to be understood solely as a take on visits to Japan's Yasukuni shrine. It is actually rooted firmly in the political culture of the Chinese Communist Party, and the way it too manipulates the deceased. One symbolic manifestation of this political culture of manipulation is the Chairman Mao Memorial Hall that stands proudly at the centre of Tiananmen Square in Beijing. Of course, this is a national facility to commemorate the life and achievements of the late Chairman Mao, but even today, right at the centre of the Hall lies the corpse of Mao Zedong who passed away more than thirty years ago. The Chairman's corpse is not buried underneath the Memorial Hall. On the contrary, it was embalmed and is now on permanent display to the public in a clear glass coffin right at the centre of the spacious hall. To a nation that is any sense at all religiously disposed, the idea of placing a body on display for decades inside a glass coffin would be absurdly distasteful to say the very least, but CCP members are able to do so without the slightest compunction. It is worth noting in this context that the Chinese Communist party erected a monument to the heroes of the people in the middle of Tiananmen Square, and designated this as a site of mourning for the war dead. This site has attached to it not a shred of religious significance and is nothing more than a materialistic monument, fashioned out of stone. This single fact demonstrates that the CCP's extraordinary concept of the deceased is as different as it could possibly be from the conventional wisdom of civilised society.

This Memorial Hall emanates from a world far removed from that of religious worship and consolation to the spirits of the deceased. It is not merely a facility designed to lay in state the remains of Mao Zedong. If that were the sole purpose, the body would not be displayed in such a way. The Chairman Mao Memorial Hall is clearly not *for* Mao Zedong. The Chairman Mao Memorial Hall was quite simply erected, and used, by the CCP administration for its own political agenda. It is by honouring the memory of Mao Zedong, the founder of the CCP administration, that the incumbent administration emphasises the legitimacy of the state, and projects that legitimacy to those both within and outside of China. This is the reason why such a splendid, eye-catching Memorial Hall was, and continues to be, necessary. Mao's remains must be on display for all to see. Mao Zedong's Memorial Hall and Mao Zedong's body are nothing more than physical marks of that political legitimising strategy. By visiting the Memorial Hall from time to time, and by being received in audience, as it were, by Chairman Mao's corpse, the CCP leaders proclaim far and wide that they are Mao Zedong's successors, and the legitimate heirs of the CCP of which he himself was the founder. To put it another way, their 'audiences' with Mao are a dramatic performance of their continuing relationship of intimacy with the very person who founded the Party. The Chairman Mao Memorial Hall and the visits to the Hall for an audience with Chairman Mao exemplify the unique political culture in which the CCP leaders are utterly immersed. It is no doubt by this same yardstick that they drew such sinister inferences about the significance of Japan's Yasukuni shrine, and Prime Minister Koizumi's visits to it. In any event, speculating about the motivation for the actions of other people based on the principles governing one's own behaviour is one of the all too common pitfalls of human nature.

From the perspective of the CCP leaders, it is simply not within the bounds of possibility that a politician, a Prime Minister of Japan, could visit the Yasukuni shrine to pay reverence to those enshrined for reasons rooted in religion or in personal sentiment. As far as

Chinese critics are concerned, the visits can only be political acts informed by some manner of political agenda or objective.[1] Prime Minister Koizumi's political intentions were all the more unmistakably political in light of the fact that some of those to whom he paid reverence were the Class A war criminals who led Japan to war against China. This then is a final consideration in understanding the Yasukuni problem as it informs Sino-Japanese relations: the Chinese are simply incapable of understating the religious meaning of any act, and impute to the Prime Minister when he visits Yasukuni the motivations behind their own patronage of Mao Zedong's corpse.

Conclusion

In this chapter, it has been my intention to dig beneath the surface of the Yasukuni problem and shed light on several different ways in which it has served as a political issue in China-Japan relations. In conclusion, the present cultural gap and the conflicting world views that obtain Japan and China are the root causes of this intractable twenty-first century problem. The vast majority of Japanese, having inherited what we might call a traditional 'Shinto culture', believe the consoling of the spirits of the war dead through ritual performances at Yasukuni to be a fundamentally religious act. By contrast, the Chinese Communist Party comprises atheists who are committed to a materialistic view of the universe and who refuse to admit the existence of spirits or the possibility of any religious significance to consoling the spirits of the deceased. The fact that the CCP is possessed by such a curious political culture, which allows them unreserved political use of the deceased, is undoubtedly a major reason explaining why the issue of the Yasukuni visits first assumed and continues to assume, the very serious proportions it does at the start of the twenty-first century.

1 Wang's chapter in this volume is a classic articulation of this position (ed.).

In this sense, there will never be a solution to the antagonism and controversy between China and Japan surrounding the issue of the Yasukuni visits; for it is a clash of civilisations.

5

LEGACIES OF EMPIRE: THE YASUKUNI SHRINE CONTROVERSY[1]

Takahashi Tetsuya

Japan appears to have reached a crossroads today, such as it has not experienced since 1945. The Japanese government under Prime Minister Koizumi and his successor Abe Shinzō has set a revisionist politics in motion which, if realised, will usher in a new kind of pre-war situation. The possibilities that were contained within the settlement at the end of the Second World War and within Japan's post-war condition seem to be receding fast over the horizon. Instead, we are faced with the real danger of new wars. This imminent turning point calls for an urgent and fundamental re-examination of the negative legacies of the Japanese empire that continue to affect contemporary Japan. This chapter attempts such a re-examination by focusing on the Yasukuni shrine and the controversy it has generated.

The nineteenth-century Meiji State created three essential institutions: the military, the Yasukuni shrine, and patriotic education. For a modern nation-state to be able to use war as a means of national

1 A version of this chapter was presented in the summer seminar series of The Japanese Department, School of Languages, Linguistics and Culture, Birkbeck College, University of London, 26 June 2007.

policy, it has to do more than just maintain an army. It has to create a national consciousness such that people feel a strong sense of belonging to the nation, and are therefore willing to offer up their lives for the nation. To foster such national spirit among the people, the Meiji state established the Yasukuni shrine as the central locus of a national religion, and along with the Imperial Rescript on Education of 1890, it implemented a system of patriotic education that had at its core the cultivation of precisely this willingness 'to offer up one's life for the emperor and the country.' The 'Japanese Empire' and its militaristic state were built upon this triadic base.

This system, based on the trinity of the military, Yasukuni shrine, and patriotic education, appeared to be dismantled in 1945 with Japan's defeat in the Asia-Pacific War. But I emphasise, that it *appeared* to be, for it continued to exist in an ambiguous form throughout the post-war era and it seems now to be reconstituted. Advocating a politics of 'breakaway from the post-war regime' (*sengo rejime kara no dakkyaku*), the current Prime Minister Abe Shinzō has set a clear agenda for his premiership. Already, he has succeeded in revising the Fundamental Law of Education, which is designed to reinstate patriotic education. On the strength of that wave, he is planning to tackle the revision of Article 9, that is, the 'no-war' principle of the post-war democratic constitution. According to the plans of the ruling Liberal Democratic Party (LDP), this would make the Self-Defence Forces formally into an army to be deployed for purposes of self-defence, the maintenance of international peace as well as the upkeep of an ill-defined 'public order.' But whatever euphemism is used, this is nothing other than the revival of the Japanese military.

As for the Yasukuni shrine, despite intense criticism from within Japan and neighbouring China and Korea, Prime Minister Koizumi Jun'ichirō officially visited Yasukuni every year for his six years in office, thereby establishing a record of 'real achievement'. Moreover, the plans of the LDP for a revision of the Constitution include a proposal to amend the constitutional principle of the separation of state and religious institutions. This amendment would permit official, prime-ministerial visits to Yasukuni to participate in public ceremonies of mourning the war dead. Most ominous of all is the scenario whereby Yasukuni will be nationalised again, making it possible for the Emperor to pay visits to the Shrine. This plan has been voiced publicly by a number of influential politicians.

The triadic system of a Japanese military, the national shrine of Yasukuni, and patriotic education was established, as mentioned earlier, by the nineteenth-century government with war in mind. Sixty years after the end of the Second World War, a twenty-first-century Japanese government is seeking to reconstitute this system, albeit in a new form.

It should be added that these revisions are pursued within the framework of the U.S.-Japan Alliance and the redefinition of the US-Japan Security Treaty which followed the end of the Cold War. Whether it is Japan's remilitarization, the reinstatement of patriotic education, or the re-nationalization of Yasukuni shrine, all of this can only be attempted with the implicit consent of the United States. In that sense the post-war condition has not ended. Under the post-war settlement, the emperor system was allowed to continue in the form of a constitutionally defined symbolic role of the emperor. In return, Japan's military strength was constrained through the 'no war' clause of Article 9, while Okinawa was offered up as a permanent military base serving US geopolitical and military strategy. The Japanese government came to perceive these arrangements in terms of the mutual benefits they would bring. The current reconstitution of the triadic system can thus be understood as a part of the global strategy of the US-Japan alliance and the reorganization of US bases in Japan.

In recent years, Yasukuni has become one of the biggest issues influencing Japan-China and Japan-Korea relations and has come to symbolize the frictions that derive from differences in historical consciousness between these nations. It has also received increasing attention in Europe and America. It seems, however, that reports and debates about the Yasukuni issue, whether within or without Japan, have so far failed to get to the heart of the matter. The Yasukuni issue is a complex problem that can be examined from various angles; and the angle chosen for analysis reveals a good deal about the historical consciousness of the discussant. In this chapter, I shall examine the Yasukuni shrine issue in terms of the continuing negative legacy of the Japanese empire.

On 20 July 2006, the *Nihon Keizai Shinbun* (the Japanese equivalent of the *Financial Times*) scooped its rivals by publishing on its front page the contents of a memorandum written in 1988 by the Grand Steward of the Imperial Household Agency, Tomita Tomohiko. In these notes, Tomita records that the Shōwa tennō (Emperor Hirohito as he is known abroad) had expressed in a conversation with him strong feelings of displeasure that Class-A war criminals were enshrined at Yasukuni shrine and that for this reason he had stopped visiting it.[2] Hirohito had, of course, visited Yasukuni regularly before and during the war. And even after Japan's defeat in 1945 he had come to the Yasukuni shrine, but his eighth visit since the end of the war in 1975 was to be the last. If Tomita's notes are to be believed, the Emperor ceased to worship at the shrine because in 1978, Yasukuni shrine decided to enshrine those fourteen men executed for Class-A war crimes as 'glorious spirits'.

In the International Military Tribunal for the Far East, commonly known as the Tokyo Tribunal, the top twenty-eight leaders of the war effort were tried and convicted on charges of committing 'crimes against peace', that is crimes of planning and executing a war of aggression. From among these twenty-eight, seven, including Prime Minister Tōjō were hanged, and another seven died in prison. After the occupation, the Ministry of Health and Welfare determined that these fourteen executed war criminals were equivalent to 'ordinary' war dead and they were, therefore, designated as having 'died in the line of duty.' Yasukuni shrine took the matter further and declared

2 'A kyū senpan Yasukuni gōshi; Shōwa tennō ga fukaikan; sanpai chūshi; "Sore ga watashi no kokora da": Moto Kunaichō chōkan', *Nihon keizai shinbun*, 20 July 2006.

that these fourteen had 'laid down their lives for national duty' and should thus be worshipped as 'martyrs of the Shōwa era.'

The forerunner of the Yasukuni shrine was the Tokyo Shōkonsha, the Tokyo shrine to the war dead, which was established in 1869, a year after the Meiji Restoration. Its function was, initially, to honour those men of the victorious Restoration forces who had fought against the preceding Tokugawa regime and had given their lives in these battles to establish the new imperial state. The shrine was built, it is said, at the 'divine behest' of the Meiji Emperor who wished those loyal men to be honoured in death. In 1879, it was renamed Yasukuni shrine. All soldiers who died in wars since then were enshrined at Yasukuni, beginning with the first overseas deployment of Japan's modern military forces in the Taiwan Expedition of 1874, the Sino-Japanese War of 1894, the Russo-Japanese War of 1904, the First World War, the Manchurian Incident of 1931, the Japanese War in China starting in 1937 and, finally, the Asia-Pacific War of 1941-5. All soldiers and civilians in military service who lost their lives in those external battles in which the Japanese empire engaged—2,460,000 war dead in total—were enshrined and worshipped as 'glorious spirits' in the Yasukuni shrine.

During the period of the 'Empire of Japan', the emperor was not only the sovereign, he also had a religious role as he was considered to be a 'living god', that is, the incarnation of Japan's ancestral deity. At the same time, he was the supreme commander of Japan's armed forces. The Japanese people, including the peoples of Japan's colonies, were his subjects and as such were expected to adhere to 'national morality', which demanded that 'in times of crisis of the Japanese state, the subjects offer up their lives to protect the emperor and the nation.' Soldiers who perished in the imperial wars, that is, the 'sacred wars' fought by the Empire, were regarded as having practised 'national morality' and were thus considered to epitomize national subject-hood. They would therefore be enshrined as 'nation-protecting deities' at Yasukuni shrine, where they were revered and honoured by Prime ministers, Army and Navy ministers, and even the emperor himself. This system was essential and instrumental in raising the morale of the Japanese military, and in the spiritual mobilisation of the entire populace for war.

Upon Japan's defeat in 1945, Yasukuni shrine was declared to be 'a symbol of Japanese militarism', a 'war shrine' and a 'shrine of military aggression' in order to neutralise its influence. With the Shinto Directive issued by the GHQ of the occupying forces in December 1945, Yasukuni, like all other shrines, was separated from the state. In line with the new post-war Constitution of 1946 that stipulated specifically the principle of the separation of state and religion, it was then turned, like Christian churches or Buddhist temples, into a private religious entity.

When the Tomita memorandum was published in July 2006, the debate over Yasukuni was poised to reach its climax in Japan, China, and Korea. For it was seen as highly likely that Prime Minister Koizumi would again pay his respects at Yasukuni shrine on 15 August, the anniversary of Japan's surrender and the end of the war. In China, the date is celebrated as the anniversary of victorious resistance against Japan, and in Korea as the day of liberation from Japanese colonial rule. After becoming Prime Minister in 2001, Koizumi visited Yasukuni shrine every year, so that in all, he visited six times. In the process, the Yasukuni issue became the biggest diplomatic problem undermining Japan's relations with China and Korea.

In 1985, when then Prime Minister Nakasone Yasuhiro visited Yasukuni shrine 'officially', the Chinese government filed a formal protest with the Japanese government. The criticism of the Chinese, consistently repeated ever since, was that a Japanese prime minister visiting a shrine in which Class A war criminals were worshipped raised doubts about the Japanese government's recognition of war responsibility. The Chinese went on to say that the Prime Minister's patronage of the shrine also grievously wounded the feelings of those Asian people who had been the victims of Japan's aggressive war. In acknowledgement of the Chinese government's criticism, Prime Minister Nakasone subsequently ceased visiting Yasukuni shrine.

However, Prime Minister Koizumi rejected the Chinese and Korean criticism as 'interference in Japan's domestic affairs', and instead presented his actions as a show of strength: he wanted to impress on the Japanese people the image of a leader who was not going to be swayed by foreign opinion. This strongman image proved also useful for maintaining Koizumi's public approval ratings. Prime Minister Koizumi did indeed visit the Yasukuni shrine on 15 August, the day of war's end, inciting, as was to be expected, vigorous protests by the Chinese and Korean governments. Subsequently, Chinese and Korean leaders refused on several occasions to attend summit meetings with Koizumi, and intergovernmental relations between Japan and China, Japan and Korea hit rock-bottom. Since Koizumi handed over power to his successor as prime minister, Abe Shinzō, Japan's relations with its neighbours have enjoyed a period of brief tranquillity.

Insofar as the Yasukuni question is considered a diplomatic issue, one that is harming Japan's relationships with China and Korea, the problem is typically narrowed down to the question of the enshrinement and worship of Class A war criminals. The majority of Japanese media and politicians approach the problem from this perspective. Politicians taking Chinese and Korean protests seriously have hence thought of ways to get around the problem and proposed, for example, the removal of those Class A war criminals from the Yasukuni registers. Japanese commentators supporting friendly relations with Asian neighbours have made similar suggestions.

The Tomita memorandum has been used in similar ways: on the one side, those who support Yasukuni and prime ministerial visits to the shrine, have sought to downplay and contest the value of the memorandum as evidence, but these attempts have largely failed. On the other side, newspapers such as the *Asahi Shinbun* and the *Nihon Keizai Shinbun*, who opposed the official visits of Prime Minister Koizumi to Yasukuni, have used the Tomita memorandum to strengthen their own stance by arguing that 'since the Shōwa Emperor ceased visiting Yasukuni because of the enshrinement of leading war criminals, Koizumi should not, of course, have visited the shrine either.' Of note was also the positive tenor with which the principal South Korean media, eager to see an end to Koizumi's Yasukuni visits, presented the Tomita memo. Thus, the memo raised various questions of historical consciousness as regards Yasukuni shrine, and it is to these that I shall now turn.

First, when a Japanese prime minister goes in his official capacity to Yasukuni shrine where Class A war criminals are honoured as glorious spirits, it inevitably invites the interpretation that the state of Japan is denying its war responsibility. Of course, none of the Japanese prime ministers who visited Yasukuni has ever publicly denied that Japan has a responsibility for the Pacific war. Prime Minister Koizumi himself affirmed the official position laid out in the statement made by Prime Minister Murayama in 1995, in which he spoke of his 'deep sense of remorse' and expressed his 'heartfelt apology' for Japan having adopted a 'mistaken state policy in the not too distant past.'[3] Japan, Murayama stated, had caused through colonial rule and invasion extreme distress and suffering to the people of neighbouring countries, especially those in Asia.

On the one hand, prime ministers have not denied publicly Japan's war responsibility, but, on the other hand, the Yasukuni shrine which they have patronised states officially that the 'recent great war' was not a war of aggression, but a 'war of self-defence,' in which the very survival of Japan was at stake and which aimed, moreover, at liberating Asia from European and American colonial oppression. Accordingly, the charges of 'war crimes' whether of Class A, B or C were false indictments imposed unilaterally by the Allied victors of the Second World War. In other words, for Yasukuni shrine, these judgements of the Tokyo Tribunal were nothing but examples of victor's justice.[4] As a matter of fact, the Yasukuni shrine has never been

3 The full statement of Prime Minister Murayama is available at http://www.mofa.go.jp/announce/press/pm/murayama/9508.html.

4 See *Yasukuni daihyakka* (Yasukuni Encyclopedia), undated pamphlet distributed by Yasukuni shrine.

merely a place of mourning the war dead; it has always functioned as an apparatus of celebration, one that transfigures the war dead into a sacred, divine existence by enshrining them as 'glorious spirits' and eulogizing their meritorious deeds. In order to celebrate dead soldiers as 'glorious spirits', the war cannot, of course, be described as a war of aggression and invasion. Given this specific function of Yasukuni, it is unsurprising that the official visits of successive prime ministers generate mistrust in the Japanese state's recognition of its war responsibility.

If one reduces the problem of the recognition of history and war responsibility to the issue of the enshrinement of Class A war criminals at Yasukuni, this constitutes a serious diminution of the problem. If it was, indeed, only a question of the enshrinement of Class A war criminals, then the problem could be solved by simply removing those war criminals from Yasukuni's register of deities. To be sure, the government of China, looking for ways of improving diplomatic ties, seemed to hint that this could be the solution to the problem.[5] However, if the Japanese government and media regard official visits of prime ministers or even the emperor to Yasukuni as unproblematic once the Class A war criminals are removed, and thereby implicitly accept Yasukuni's ideology of celebrating the war dead as 'glorious spirits', then this constitutes, either consciously or unconsciously, an act of denial of history.

A second aspect of the denial of history derives from the concept of 'Class A war crimes'. Class A war criminals are those judged by the Tokyo Tribunal to have been responsible for leading Japan into the war of aggression against China, starting with the Manchurian Incident in 1931, and the Pacific War of 1941. The Tribunal judgements took into account the preparations for the invasion of Manchuria, which began in 1928, and so the period covered by the Tribunal

5 In July 2001, immediately before Prime Minister Koizumi made his first 'official' visit to Yasukuni, the Chinese Ambassador to Japan stated that 'if the Prime Minister paid his respects to the war dead in general, there would be no problem. What renders his visit to Yasukuni problematic is the enshrinement there of the Class A war criminals.'

extends from 1928 to the surrender of Japan in August 1945. This means that the Tokyo Tribunal's framework for 'Class-A war crimes' does not cover, and in fact ignores, Japan's history of invading Asia prior to the Manchurian Incident. By 1928, Japan had already established a large colonial empire that included Taiwan and Korea. But, of course, there were several colonial powers—the United States, the United Kingdom, France, and Holland—among the Allies that formed the Tokyo Tribunal, and they apparently had neither the desire nor the legitimacy to indict Japan for its colonial rule.

However, among the war dead enshrined at Yasukuni are the military personnel who died in *all* of Japan's invasions of Asia since the Taiwan Expedition of 1874. Japan established its colonial rule over Taiwan by suppressing with military force both the resistance movement of Sino-Taiwanese and indigenous Taiwanese people. Likewise in Korea, Japan since the Kanghwa Island incident of 1875 continued to deploy military force against Korean resistance for the purpose of solidifying, in 1910, its colonial occupation. Japanese soldiers and civilian military personnel who died in those military campaigns designed to establish and maintain Japan's colonial rule, and the military suppression of resistance movements in those colonies, are venerated at Yasukuni. These 'glorious spirits' are worshipped for giving their lives to the 'sacred' mission of expanding the Japanese empire and the Emperor's divine rule. Thus, Yasukuni shrine forms an inseparable unity with the imperialism and colonialism of the modern Japanese nation-state. Given that Yasukuni is inseparable from Japan's modern colonialism, and given that these war dead continue to be honoured publicly in the same way as the executed Class A war criminals, the extent of the denial of Japan's responsibility for its colonial rule becomes fairly obvious.

It is not just right-wing revisionists who ignore or deny Japan's responsibilities prior to the invasion of China in 1931, that is, the responsibility for Japan's colonialism. Notably, there are also progressive intellectuals and journalists who are in a similar state of denial even though they otherwise recognise fully Japan's responsibility for

Class A war crimes. In their historical narrative, the grandeur of the Meiji state in achieving Japan's equal standing *vis-à-vis* the powerful Western nation-states is highlighted, while the Showa Empire is seen as Japan gone wrong. Likewise, the Japanese military is depicted as upstanding as far as the Sino-Japanese and the Russo-Japanese wars were concerned, but regarded as degrading into an ill-behaved army ever since the invasion of China. This type of historical consciousness is fairly widespread among Japanese liberals.[6]

Narrowing the problem to the enshrinement of Class A war criminals means also that the scope of Japan's war responsibility since the Manchurian Incident goes unrecognized, and leads to a third kind of denial of the past. Insofar as the alleged decision of the Shōwa Emperor to stop visiting Yasukuni is highlighted positively, the impression is strengthened that the blame for Japan's past aggression lies exclusively with the Class A war criminals. This perception is consonant with the political stratagem of the United States that granted the emperor immunity in the Tokyo Tribunal proceedings. Even though the Shōwa emperor was the supreme power throughout the war period and, more importantly, the supreme commander of the Japanese imperial forces and as such undeniably responsible for Japan's acts of aggression, he was nevertheless allowed to evade prosecution. Moreover, by redefining, in Article 1 of the post-war Constitution, the emperor as the symbol of the democratic Japanese nation and the unity of its people, the emperor system retained its exalted position. Meanwhile the Occupation forces used the figure of the emperor in accordance with American Cold War thinking, to thwart Japan from possibly turning Communist. Thus, by emphasizing the issue of the enshrinement of Class A war criminals, the emperor's war responsibility, which had been covered up by the United States and the Tokyo Tribunal, came to be denied altogether.

But the crucial issue of Japan's war responsibility post-1928 is not just minimized in terms of the emperor's role. Rather, the war respon-

6 Shiba Ryōtarō exemplified this trend. See, for example, Shiba, *Meiji to iu kokka*.

sibility of other elite figures at the time as well as the mass media, intellectuals, religious leaders, and educators—that is, the war responsibility of all levels of society—is thereby denied. If the Yasukuni shrine problem were to be regarded as resolved by simply removing Class A war criminals from the shrine's register, the questions of responsibility for pre-1928 military campaigns and, indeed, for Yasukuni shrine itself would be stifled and allowed to be forgotten.

As I have endeavoured to explain how the Tokyo Tribunal gave rise to the perception that the Class A war criminals were scapegoats, whereas the emperor and the Japanese people not only escaped prosecution but were freed, as it were, from their responsibility for the war. Moreover, the war crimes committed by the Allied forces during the Second World War were not examined, which constitutes an important problem at the heart of the institution of the Tokyo Tribunal itself. The question of an unaddressed colonial past is not one to be asked of Japan alone. Take, for example, France's stance on the complicity of the Vichy regime in the persecution of Jews. Only in 1995, half a century after the end of the war, did President Chirac acknowledge France's responsibility and arrange for restitution. However, to this day, the French government has failed to recognise officially France's responsibility for the atrocities committed during its colonial rule of Algeria and to arrange for restitution. I raise this example not to point the finger at particular nations or governments, but to suggest that the working through of the legacies of imperialism and colonialism is a tricky task shared by several nations.

It is not only that Yasukuni denies the aggressiveness of Japan's war and the nation's war responsibility, but it has also served to alter the very nature of 'death in battle' by casting it as a story of 'glorious death'; in the process, it counterfeits history. That is to say, the bloody and merciless reality of soldiers dying on the battlefield is rewritten at Yasukuni into a sanctified narrative of noble, heroic, and thus 'glorious death.' Three cases will serve to exemplify how this history has been counterfeited.

The first and most obvious case is that of Korean and Taiwanese recruits to the Imperial Japanese army. Currently, close to 50,000 former colonial subjects who died in battle are enshrined at Yasukuni, of whom some 20,000 were Koreans mobilized for the Japanese war effort and around 20,000 were Taiwanese. Needless to say, Japan implemented its imperial education also in the colonies, in order that Korean and Taiwanese subjects might internalize absolute loyalty to the emperor and a willingness to offer up their lives for the sake of the imperial state. When the Enlistment Act was enforced in 1944, many Koreans and Taiwanese were forcibly drafted, but there were also those who enlisted voluntarily for military service because they hoped in this way to escape the ethnic and racial discrimination they had had to endure as colonial subjects. In other words, there is no evidence at all that their decision to enlist had anything to do with belief in the promises made by the Yasukuni ideology.

In 1978, well after the liberation from colonial rule, a Taiwanese bereaved family demanded for the first time that their war dead should be withdrawn from the enshrinement registers of Yasukuni. Korean bereaved families followed their example and put forward similar demands. A number of lawsuits were filed against the Yasukuni shrine and the Japanese government, which had provided it with the list of fallen soldiers in the first place. The representatives of these bereaved organisations have argued that 'not only did we suffer the injuries of invasion and colonialism, but to be enshrined in a shrine that symbolizes more than anything the militarism of the perpetrator nation is an unbearable act of humiliation.' Yasukuni shrine has consistently rejected all of these demands, arguing that:

> since they were Japanese at the time of their death in battle, they don't stop being Japanese after death. They fought and died in battle, believing they would be honoured through their enshrinement as Japanese soldiers when they died. For that reason, Yasukuni cannot withdraw their spirits. It is only natural that these men who helped the war effort in the same manner

and spirit as mainland Japanese, and fought alongside Japanese soldiers, are honoured as glorious spirits at Yasukuni.[7]

What becomes apparent in the Yasukuni shrine's argument is that the coercive force of colonial rule and the Enlistment Act is ignored, in order to counterfeit a historical record of 'voluntary, glorious death in battle.'

The second example is that of Okinawa's civilian war dead. Situated between Japan and China, the islands of Okinawa originally made up the independent kingdom of Ryukyu, but in 1879 the Meiji government eliminated the kingdom by the use of military force and established, in its place, Okinawa prefecture. Okinawa, along with Hokkaido and its indigenous population of Ainu, were the first targets of modern Japan's colonial enterprise. They are usually distinguished from Korea and Taiwan and termed 'domestic colonies', but the assimilation policy which the Japanese colonial government employed was no less forceful in these regions than the one imposed on Taiwan and Korea. In the closing days of the Pacific War, the Japanese army embroiled, in the name of the 'unity of army and civilians', non-combatant Okinawans in the savage battle against the American forces as they landed. All this was in the name of the 'unity of army and civilians.' As many as 100,000 Okinawan civilians lost their lives in the Battle of Okinawa: some were executed for allegedly spying on the Japanese military; others were forced to commit mass suicide because surrendering and being taken as a prisoner of war were forbidden, and not a small number fell victim to the military actions of the Japanese army, who were supposedly friendly troops.[8]

The majority of Okinawan civilians who perished in this way are enshrined at Yasukuni. But how is it that civilians are enshrined at Yasukuni, which is dedicated to military personnel and civilian military employees? The answer is that in 1958, the families of those who had 'participated in the war at the request of the army' became

7 *Asahi shinbun* (morning edition), 18.4. 1978.

8 For contrasting views on Okinawa and Yasukuni, see the chapters of Nitta and Breen in this volume (Ed.).

eligible for survivors' pensions and other benefits under the Law for Relief of War Victims and Survivors. The Japanese administration subsequently encouraged applications from the bereaved families of the Okinawan civilian war dead, since with the change in legislation they were now eligible to receive survivor's pensions. Yasukuni then decided to enshrine these war dead, who had 'participated in the war at the request of the army', under the category of civilian military employees. As a result, the residents of Okinawa who were, as a matter of fact, victims of the war waged by Japan, ended up being enshrined as collaborators of the Japanese forces.[9] Even children who died in the forced mass suicides thus came to be enshrined in Yasukuni's pantheon of 'glorious spirits' for having sacrificed their lives for the sake of the nation. This too we may term a case of 'historical fabrication,' since it conceals the military's responsibility for the atrocious realities of the Battle of Okinawa, and for the huge number of civilian deaths to which it gave rise.

My third example relates to Japan's own war dead and the way in which Yasukuni ideology has sought to cancel out the violent nature of death in war by re-imagining it as 'glorious death.' Of the 2,460,000 war dead enshrined in Yasukuni, over two million—the great majority—died in the Asia-Pacific War. However, sixty per cent of that number did not die from conflict on the battlefield, but in a broad sense suffered death caused by starvation.[10] The Japanese military sent large numbers of soldiers to New Guinea and other areas of the South Pacific knowing full well that there was a serious problem with providing adequate supplies of food and water to these troops. Marching through the jungles, the troops ran out of provisions and many starved to death, their corpses abandoned, and left to rot until nothing but skeletons remained. The indescribable misery and cruelty characterising death in war is converted by Yasukuni shrine into the death of brave soldiers confronting the enemy,

9 See also 'Okinawa to Yasukuni (3)' in *Okinawa Times*, 15.9.2005.

10 On death through starvation in the Pacific War, see Fujiwara Akira, *Gashi shita eiyūtachi*, Aoki Shoten, 2001.

and dying in the heroic mission of protecting the imperial state. Yet it was not just the horrific reality of death by starvation, but also the wretchedness of death in action that is rendered invisible by the transfiguration of the war dead into 'glorious spirits'. The violence of dying in battle, the bloodiness, the putrefaction of corpses, all of that is effaced by the Yasukuni narrative and, in their place, death in war is sublimated within the realm of the sacred, divine.

The significance of the ideology and practice of Yasukuni lies thus also in the management of the feelings of the bereaved families. For if the grief and pain of the bereaved families were to be left unaddressed, those feelings could potentially turn into doubts, criticism or even anger towards Japan's leaders who were responsible for waging war. So the special ceremonies of honouring the war dead, which were regularly conducted at Yasukuni during the war, and in which the emperor himself participated, served the purpose of what I have called 'the alchemy of emotion', whereby the grief of the bereaved families was to be converted into feelings of joy. An article in the January 1944 issue of the magazine *Shufu no tomo* ('The housewife's companion') illustrates how this 'alchemy of emotion' was achieved.[11] The article featured the case of Tsutsui Matsu, a woman from Kōchi Prefecture who lost three of her four sons to the war effort. She described her feelings, on receiving the news that her eldest and her second son had both died in battle, how she was driven to despair thinking how cruel the war was, and how tragic the loss of her sons' lives. But when she, as mother to her sons, was invited to the state ceremony where the spirits of her sons were enshrined, and when she witnessed the visit on that occasion by the Emperor, she 'experienced enlightenment'. 'It was as if she had been struck by a bolt of electricity.' Her thoughts were these: 'The Emperor himself has favoured us with his visit precisely because [my sons] died for their country. It is such a blessing. Well done, my sons!' Her pain vanished, and from then on, she felt nothing but happiness and pride.

11 *Shufu no tomo*, January 1944, pp. 94-7. On the dynamics of emotional alchemy, see Takahashi, *Yasukuni mondai*, pp. 43-5.

In this way, Yasukuni rites and the imperial presence played a crucial role in generating a positive attitude towards the war among the population as a whole. It was through a similar process that the deaths of military personnel and civilian military employees were, regardless of the actual historical circumstances, sublimated and rendered sacred as acts of self-sacrifice, of patriotic devotion.

The Tomita memorandum published in July 2006 was, as mentioned earlier, used by those criticizing Prime Minister Koizumi for his repeated official visits to Yasukuni shrine. In the medium to long-term future it is perfectly possible that this memorandum may be used for entirely different ends, namely to revive official visits to Yasukuni shrine by the emperor. Some leading political and intellectual figures argue that the current 'abnormal' situation, created when the Shōwa Emperor ceased his visits, should be 'corrected' so that in future not only prime ministers but also the emperor himself can worship at Yasukuni. For example, in summer 2006, Foreign Minister Aso Tarō and other influential politicians suggested that Yasukuni shrine should be nationalised again, in order to pave the way for imperial visits.[12] Such a proposal by high-ranking, influential politicians ought not to be taken lightly. Between 1969 and 1974, the plan to re-nationalize Yasukuni shrine was presented to the Diet every year, in an LDP bill for the state protection of Yasukuni. At that time, opposition to these plans was strong, as it was feared that this might be seen as direct indication of a revived militarism. Consequently, the bill was never passed. Today, thirty years later, leading LDP politicians are again pushing for a re-nationalization of Yasukuni shrine to allow for the establishment of official visits by the prime minister and, crucially, the emperor. They suggest this can be achieved by removing Class A war criminals and finding an understanding with China and Korea for the re-nationalization of the shrine.

As I have laid out in this chapter, the triadic system of a full-fledged military, patriotic education, and a nationalized Yasukuni Shrine, now

12 *Asahi shinbun* (morning edn), 8.8.2006.

stands a very good chance of being revived, in the following way. First, revision of Article 9 of the Constitution which will pave the way for the establishment of a military that is officially recognised as an army; second, revision of the Fundamental Law of Education already effected in December 2006, building in patriotic education and, third, the possibility of re-nationalizing Yasukuni shrine. This would mean that in future, if soldiers of the Self-Defence Forces or a new, full-fledged Japanese military died in military missions abroad—for instance in Iraq—they might be enshrined at Yasukuni and, if the shrine is renationalised, they could then be worshipped by both the prime minister and the emperor. Moreover, this scenario could possibly be realised without any objections coming from China and Korea.

Today Japan faces the risk of losing the opportunities it was afforded by the 'post-war' settlement. The danger of those opportunities vanishing before our eyes is symbolized by the slogan of Prime Minister Abe to 'break free from the post-war regime'. He argues that without a revision of the post-war Constitution as put into place by the American Occupation, the Japanese people will never be psychologically free of their 'Occupation mentality'. I believe the opposite to be true, namely that the possibilities seen at the end of the war still await full realisation. This in turn can only happen through a further consolidation of the principles embodied in the post-war Constitution and the Fundamental Law of Education as they were originally formulated. Japan is truly standing at a crossroads and, in view of the hugely influential arguments put forward by conservative politicians, there is little reason for optimism. However, there are numerous citizen movements across Japan which have formed in protest against these political currents and which work tirelessly for strengthening of the principles and ideas of the post-war Constitution.

Popular resistance against a revision of the post-war democratic Constitution, especially its Article 9, is strong, and over six thousand citizen groups are now actively protesting against the LDP plans. As for Yasukuni shrine, there are seven ongoing lawsuits filed by citizen groups that charge that former Prime Minister Koizumi's visits to the shrine violated the separation of state and religion as stipulated by the Constitution. The Japanese judiciary is notoriously reluctant to pass judgements when it comes to violations of the Constitution. However, two decisions supporting these charges have been handed down from the Osaka High Court and the Fukuoka District Court respectively, stating that Koizumi's visits to Yasukuni were indeed a violation of the Constitution. Finally, there are also several citizen groups which challenge the Yasukuni ideology itself, that is, the efforts by the shrine to transfigure death on the battlefield into the death of 'heroic martyrs'.'

As mentioned earlier, the bereaved families of the Koreans and Taiwanese who fought and died for Japan have begun to protest Yasukuni's enshrinement of their war dead. But the first movement for the removal of the war dead from Yasukuni took place as early as 1968. The instigator was a Japanese Protestant priest whose two older brothers had died in the war. He opposed his siblings' enshrinement at Yasukuni on religious grounds, saying that he wished to commemorate them in accordance with his own Christian faith. Yasukuni shrine rejected his request for removal. Subsequently, numerous bereaved families demanded, on religious or other grounds, that the enshrinement of their war dead be revoked; since then some of them have filed lawsuits. Finally, and perhaps most importantly, Japanese, Taiwanese and Korean bereaved families have begun to achieve a degree of cooperation in their protest movements and lawsuits against Yasukuni shrine and the Japanese government. In other words, we see emerging today trans-national collaboration among bereaved families of both the colonized nations and the colonizing nation to protest Yasukuni ideology and what it represents.

A fascinating example of such cooperation is featured in the 2005 film *Annyong Sayonara* ('Hello, Goodbye')[13]—a Korean-Japanese co-

13 The 2005 documentary *Annyong Sayonara* was co-directed by the Korean veteran documentary filmmaker Kim Tae Il and Japanese filmmaker Katō Kumiko. It won the Woonpa Award at the 10th Pusan International Film Festival in 2005, and the Seoul Independent Film Festival 2005 Grand Prize for best documentary.

production—which documents the experiences of Lee Hee Ja, a 62-year-old Korean woman, trying to have her father's name removed from Yasukuni's register of 'glorious spirits'. She is helped in her pursuit by Masaki Furukawa, a former Kobe municipal employee, who dedicates every free minute of his life to supporting Korean victims of Japanese colonial rule and their families in their struggle to gain justice. He is joined by members of various Japanese citizen groups. While the film leaves the question of the Yasukuni problem inevitably unanswered, its moving portrayal of the process towards historical awareness, mutual understanding and reconciliation between individuals like Korean woman Lee Hee Ja and her Japanese supporters, conveys a strong sense of hope.

6

AND WHY SHOULDN'T THE JAPANESE PRIME MINISTER WORSHIP AT YASUKUNI? A PERSONAL VIEW

Nitta Hitoshi

The Yasukuni shrine, which was built in 1869, today enshrines around 2,470,000 war dead as *kami* or gods. Some of these men fell during the Meiji Restoration, effected to ensure national reformation and thus Japan's continued autonomy; others were victims of the Russo-Japanese war (1894-5) and the two Sino-Japanese wars of 1894-5 and 1937-45; still others are the fallen from the subsequent Second World War. The shrine takes its name 'Yasukuni' from historian Zuo's Chinese classic 'Commentary on the Annals of Spring and Autumn' (*Chunqiu Zuozhuan)* to mean 'protect the peace of the nation.' Its rites originate from the memorial services held by the loyalists at the time of the Meiji Restoration to enshrine their comrades who had been killed fighting for the imperial cause.

There has been much controversy both within and outside Japan over Japanese Prime Ministers' visits to Yasukuni, but it is my opinion that the Prime Minister should visit Yasukuni, and that doing so is not in any way a dangerous act. I wish to offer a fourfold explanation of why I believe this. First, it is my personal opinion that the Prime Ministers' visits to Yasukuni are of themselves desirable; second, there is the issue of freedom of religion, and the separation of religion and state, as these are prescribed by the post-war Japanese Constitution; the third reason why I advocate prime ministerial visits is related to the enshrinement at Yasukuni of Class A war criminals; my final reason demands that I explore the view of history as narrated by the Yasukuni shrine.

Before embarking on my four-part discussion, there is one point I would like to confirm from the outset. That is, although former Prime Minister Koizumi Jun'ichirō visited Yasukuni every year of his premiership between 2001-6, the Japanese were never heard to utter cries demanding we breach the San Francisco Peace Treaty or the Japan-US Security Treaty; nobody demanded Japan take revenge on the Allied powers, nor that we launch an invasion on the Korean peninsula, or go to war with mainland China, or the rest of Asia.

The Reasons why I Consider Prime Ministers' Visits to Yasukuni to be Desirable

The reason I support the Prime Minister's visits to Yasukuni is extremely straightforward: it is because I believe that it is a citizen's important duty and right to pay respects, and offer thanks, to those who sacrificed their lives for the nation. It is therefore only right and proper that those responsible in the government venerate at the shrine.

After Japan's defeat in the Second World War, the Occupation forces were intent on razing Yasukuni to the ground, but thanks to the objections articulated by two Catholic priests, Father Patrick Byrne of the Maryknoll Mission and the Jesuit, Father Gustav Bruno Maria Bitter, the shrine was preserved. The substance of their objections was as follows:

> It is evident that there are some who believe that Yasukuni, the hotbed of militarism, must be abolished on account of the fact that Japan conducted an unjust war, but that would be a mistake. Whether or not to abolish Yasukuni is a question related to the nature of the shrine, and is unconnected with the rights or wrongs of the recent war. It is every citizen's important

duty, as well as their right, to pay their respects and offer their thanks to those who sacrificed their lives for the nation. Is it not the case, indeed, that people pay their respects at the graves of those killed in action even when they are citizens of an enemy country? It must be mentioned that Yasukuni shrine is now not simply a Shinto mausoleum, but a monument of national respect. The reason we can assert this is that the souls of departed war heroes are enshrined at Yasukuni without prejudice, irrespective of their religion, be they Shinto or Buddhist, or Christianity. Accordingly, would it not be a negation of an important duty and a right of every citizen, were we to abolish such a place?[1]

This thinking was certainly not limited to Catholics. Indeed, is it not common to many who give thought to the relation between religion and the state, founded as it is on natural law? It was in 1978 that the Class A war criminals, who were tried and executed for the crime of leading Japan to war, were enshrined at Yasukuni, but the Yasukuni records show that this had no detrimental effects on shrine patronage by foreign representatives. Since then military personnel, diplomats, politicians, religious figures and educators from places as varied and numerous as the following have continued to visit the shrine: the United Kingdom, the United States, Germany, Cuba, India, Australia, Tibet, Indonesia, Egypt, Palau, Pakistan, the Soviet Union, Chile, Sri Lanka, Finland, Lithuania, Thailand, Myanmar, Iran, Slovenia, former Korean royalty, Turkey, Romania, Malaysia, Israel, Russia, Switzerland, Brazil, Poland, the Solomon Islands, Canada, Italy, Mexico, Taiwan, Azerbaijan, the Republic of Korea, Peru, South Africa and Morocco.[2]

It is incomprehensible to me why, when even foreign nationals are free to pay their respects at Yasukuni shrine, the Japanese Prime Minister alone is not permitted so to do. Of course, Yasukuni is not the only facility that exists in Japan for consoling the spirits of those who died in war. There are also many such facilities for civilian victims, and naturally the Japanese prime minister has made frequent visits to them, including the Memorial Cenotaph for the A-bomb

1 Shimura, *Kyōkai hiwa,* p. 204.

2 Ōhara, *Yasukuni jinja e no jubaku,* pp. 212-17.

victims in Hiroshima. There are those who criticise Prime Ministerial visits to Yasukuni, which primarily enshrines military personnel, on the grounds that Prime Ministers thereby ignore the ordinary people who were victims of the wars. However, those who demand Prime Ministers visit Yasukuni and venerate the war dead there are merely making the case for him to visit Yasukuni in the same way that he visits all of the other facilities. The argument we make is certainly not that we want him to withdraw from paying his respects to the ordinary victims of the wars and shift the emphasis to the military war dead alone.

The question then arises as to why the site for paying respect and offering thanks to the war dead has to be the Yasukuni shrine. The reason is because most of the war dead exchanged vows with their comrades to the effect that, if they were to die, they would meet again at Yasukuni, and because they went to war with promises from their families that they would come and visit them at Yasukuni. In other words, the Yasukuni shrine is the place of such promises. If one makes a promise to the living, the arrangement can be changed as and when the circumstances require, but there can be no such revising of promises made with and received from the deceased. If the living were to change the arrangement to meet a new set of personal circumstances, it would be tantamount to a betrayal. If the living deceive the dead in this way, consoling the spirits of the dead can have no meaning whatsoever.

Freedom of Religion and the Separation of Religion and State as Provided for by the post-war Japanese Constitution

Article 20 of the Japanese Constitution prescribes that: 1. Freedom of religion is guaranteed to all. No religious organization shall receive any privileges from the State, nor exercise any political authority; 2. No person shall be compelled to take part in any religious act, celebration, rite or practice; and 3. The State and its organs shall refrain from religious education or any other religious activity.[3]

There are those who claim that visits by successive Prime Ministers to Yasukuni are a breach of the regulations as set out above in Article 20, but this is not the case. Prime Minister's visits are purely a matter of the Prime Minister himself visiting and venerating at the shrine, and there is no compulsion for Cabinet Ministers, let alone ordinary citizens, to emulate the Prime Minister. As a result, Prime ministerial visits cannot be said to violate the people's freedom of religion in any way. Furthermore, the Supreme Court determined that those religious activities by the government which are prohibited by Clause 3 should be interpreted in such a way that 'this is not the prohibition of *any* relationship between the state and religion, but of actions whose object and outcome is to provide religion with assistance, support, promotion, suppression or interference'. In accord with this so-called 'object and outcome' standard (*mokuteki kōka kijun*), the Supreme Court ruled it constitutional in 1977 when a certain city presided over a Shinto ceremony. The case in question involved a local Communist councillor in Tsu city, Mie prefecture, taking legal action on the grounds that the city presided over a Shinto ground-breaking ceremony designed to pray for the safe conclusion to construction works for a municipal gymnasium and that, in so doing, it was in breach of the Constitution. The Supreme Court's ruling in the Tsu case established legal precedent.[4] And if it is constitutional for a public body to sponsor such a Shinto ceremony as this, then it goes without saying that Prime Ministers' visits to Yasukuni are beyond attack as a violation of the Constitution.

---

3 The Constitution of Japan, House of Councillors, http://www.sangiin.go.jp/eng/law/index.htm.

4 On this case see Seikyō kankei o tadasu kai (ed.), *Seikyō bunri ni kakaru saikō saiban resishu*, Gyōsei, 1996. It is worth pointing out that Japanese politicians and civil servants take part in Buddhist and Christian ceremonies at home and abroad in their official capacities, but it is rare that any other than Shinto-related participation leads to indictment. This fact needs to be better known. See Ōhara, *Yasukuni jinja e no jubaku*, pp. 137–43.

It is often the case that ritual performances enacted to pay respects and offer gratitude to those who gave their lives for the nation are coloured by the traditional religion of that nation. Surely there can be very few people worldwide who would insist that such performances constitute a breach of the separation of religion and state. Indeed, in America where the separation of religion and state is similarly subject to constitutional prescription, ritual performances for the unnamed soldiers at Arlington National Cemetery take the form of Jewish and Christian ceremonies, as Saeki points out.[5]

In this regard, it is interesting to note that memorial services for the seven astronauts who lost their lives when the space shuttle Challenger crashed in 1986 took the form of Jewish and Christian ceremonies conducted at the Kennedy Space Center. One of those killed in this disaster was Lieutenant Colonel Onizuka, a third-generation Japanese American. Onizuka was an adherent of the Buddhist Jōdo Shinshū sect but, even so, his family attended the memorial service at the Kennedy Center, and afterwards conducted their own private Buddhist services in Los Angeles and at his birthplace in Hawaii.[6]

I would like to declare here my respect for the custom of officially adhering to the state's traditional religion while privately practising one's own faith; it is a wise lesson drawn from history. At Yasukuni, too, worship in the main sanctuary (*honden*) must conform to Shinto style, but before the worship hall (*haiden*), people are at liberty to worship privately according to their own religion.

Prime Ministerial Visits and the Enshrinement of Class A War Criminals

If the Yasukuni shrine were a facility only to enshrine those regular soldiers who were mobilised for war and killed in action, then, in all likelihood the Prime Minister's acts of veneration at the shrine would

5 Saeki, 'Kirisutosha wa 'Yasukuni' o katareru ka'. For further reflections on Arlington, see the chapter by Doak in this volume (Ed.).

6 Ōhara *Yasukuni jinja no jubaku*, pp. 136-7.

not have caused such an uproar. However, the fact is that national leaders executed as war criminals by the Allied powers upon Japan's defeat in that great war, that is, the so-called Class A war criminals, are also enshrined at Yasukuni. It is their enshrinement that is the complicating factor in the Yasukuni issue.

The important point to bear in mind when thinking about the Class A war criminals and their enshrinement is this: although there is a natural enough tendency to class them together because they were allies, the crimes for which the Nazi leaders were tried at Nuremberg and those for which the Japanese leaders were tried at the Tokyo War Crimes Tribunal are completely different. At both sets of trials, the German and Japanese leaders were indicted for crimes that had not previously existed in international law: 'crimes against peace,' that is the crimes of planning and executing war of aggression, and 'crimes against humanity,' that is the crimes of executing acts of persecution, such as the Holocaust, on grounds of politics, religion or race. The Japanese leaders were indicted only for the former while for the German leaders it was predominantly the latter.[7] Both of these crimes have in common that they were newly established, but the former referred to the actions of instigating and prosecuting war which leaders of many other countries had carried out previously and which had, for that very reason, not been regarded as criminal; the latter by contrast was established to designate a specific action, namely the Holocaust, which had never before been carried out by the leaders of any country, and for which there could therefore exist no legal precedent. So, although Japanese and German leaders were all lumped together as 'Class A war criminals', the Japanese were never indicted for crimes of unprecedented acts of persecution such as the Holocaust.

On the 21 May 1980, a Mass was celebrated at St. Peter's Basilica in the Vatican for the 1,068 Japanese war criminals, including those designated in Class A. The celebration of this Mass, which can only be explained in terms of Pope John Paul II's understanding

7 Kisa, *'Sensō sekinin' to wa nanika.*

of the difference between Japanese and German war criminals, was the Pope's response to a request submitted to him by Revd Nakata Junna, Chief Priest of the Shinagawa temple, Special Head temple of the Shingon Daigoji lineage. Revd Nakata had throughout the post-war period continued to perform Buddhist memorial services for the war criminals. [8]

The Netherlands representative at the Tokyo War Crimes Tribunal was Judge Bert Röling. He recognised the significance of establishing 'crimes against peace', but even so opposed pronouncing the death penalty on the basis of such crimes, saying:

> One who commits a crime against peace should be considered more an enemy, than a culprit. Accordingly his punishment should be more in the nature of a political measure, than of judicial retribution. Emerging from a war in which they had been on the side of reason and law, and invested with the task of maintaining the peace, the victorious Powers had a right to act against individuals who might prove dangerous to the new order; they could lawfully arrest, try, and punish them, if they were found guilty. A man found guilty of crimes against peace, should not be sentenced to death, but should only receive a term of imprisonment (unless he had committed war crimes as well).[9]

It is of incidental interest that when this same Röling came to Japan in 1983 to attend a symposium relating to the Tokyo Trials, he made a point of visiting Kōa kannon temple on Mount Izu in Atami where Buddhist monks perform commemorative rites for Class A war criminals.

The objective of the Allied Occupation of Japan, as touted by the Americans, was to ensure that 'Japan will not again become a menace to the United States or to the peace and security of the world'.[10] The

8 See Nagoshi, *Shōwa no senso kinenkan*, pp. 16[illegible] and Nagoshi, "Shōwa junnansha" ni sasageru misa', pp. [illegible].

9 Roling and Cassese, *The Tokyo trial and Beyond*, 1993.

10 US Initial Post-surrender Policy for Japan, or basic directive, of 6 September 1945 issued by MacArthur's GHQ. See Kades, 'The American role', pp. 215-47.

seven years of the American Occupation were, then, a period during which the Allied forces, led by the United States, aimed to achieve this objective through a military strategy, albeit one that did not involve resorting to the use of arms. The Tokyo war crimes tribunal was the most important element of this strategy. Accordingly, those who were put to death by this Allied strategy, that is the 'enemies' who were subject to 'political strategy', to borrow Röling's words, were in fact 'war dead' as far as the Japanese were concerned. Consequently, after Japan won back its independence in 1952, the government took legal action in order that these men might be viewed as such. And thus it was that they came to occupy their place in the pantheon of Yasukuni *kami*, alongside the other war dead.

One must appreciate the fact that these Class A war criminals are treated at Yasukuni as war dead, and venerated there just like the other ordinary soldiers who sacrificed their lives for the nation. They are accordingly not praised especially for their achievements; nor are they accorded special treatment in terms of the manner of veneration. It is not the case that their veneration as Yasukuni *kami* has enhanced their reputation in society at large; nor has it been accompanied by the emergence of young people aspiring to be like them; nor, either, have there been any calls for Japan to take revenge on the Allied nations.

It is in the nature of national leaders that their decision-making is not only liable to cause the deaths of many of the nation's citizens, but it may also lead to them surrender their own lives. When a Prime Minister venerates at Yasukuni and thus confronts the cold realities of international politics, it forces him to get a grip, to deepen his understanding of the gravity of his political responsibilities. It is my personal belief that Prime Ministerial patronage of Yasukuni is important in this sense, too.

The View of History as Narrated by the Yasukuni Shrine

Those who criticise the Prime Minister's visits to Yasukuni and the shrine's enshrinement and veneration of the Class A war criminals typically isolate the Yūshūkan war museum located in the grounds of the shrine as a target for further attack. They insist, for example, that its displays glorify combat and mask the atrocious realities of war; or again that the Prime Minister's visits to Yasukuni serve to give the official seal of approval to the view of history as narrated by the Yūshūkan and its exhibits.

It is clearly impossible here to recount in detail each individual aspect of the view of history as narrated by the Yūshūkan, but I think the essential points are covered by the opening statements made by Yuzawa Tadashi, the former Chief Priest of Yasukuni, in the 'Foreword' to the official illustrated guide to Yūshūkan published by the museum:

> Unfortunately, in the process of creating our modern nation state, there were civil wars, the first of which was the Boshin War [of 1868-9]. Then in later years, there were also international military conflicts. There was the Sino-Japanese war [of 1894-5], the Russo-Japanese war [of 1904-5], the First World war and the most recent Greater East Asian war. The emperor's noble wishes and his fervent prayers, and the noble wishes and prayers of those enshrined as the *kami* of Yasukuni were for a peaceful Japan and a peaceful world. In spite of those wishes and prayers, there was no avoiding the wars subsequently fought in order to achieve the establishment of the modern state, to secure Japan's defences, to maintain the dignity of the nation and, in global terms, to achieve a world of freedom and peace, divorced from issues of skin colour. It is the glorious spirits (*eirei*) propitiated here in Yasukuni who gave up their lives, never to be lived again in this world, to serve the nation in its time of crisis. It is the mission and chief purpose of the Yūshūkan to honour the meritorious service and the illustrious memories of these glorious spirits, and to illuminate the realities of the period of modern history which these fallen heroes treaded.[11]

What is typically overlooked in arguments that criticise this discourse is the fact that Yasukuni is a facility for consoling the spirits of the deceased. I don't know how it works in other religious traditions, but in Shinto funeral ceremonies, it is customary for prayers (*norito*) to introduce the history and achievements of the deceased and to single them out for praise. There is surely no one who would take

11 Yuzawa, 'Goaisatsu', p. 11.

issue with that discourse, and insist that 'unless you make mention of the negative side of the deceased, you will have failed to make a just assessment of them'. When speaking of the hardships encountered by the deceased, it is simply not the done thing for a man to stress the evil deeds of his rivals; no civilised person emphasises the wrongdoings of the enemy. In brief, it goes against traditional Japanese religious sensibilities to introduce, or stir up, negative feelings of bitterness and hatred at a place whose purpose is consoling the spirits of the deceased.

Shinto priests and the majority of the Japanese people unconsciously view the Yūshūkan and its display of the exploits of the war dead with the same feelings as they might hear the prayers dedicated to the deceased at funerals. That being so, the focus of the exhibits at the Yūshūkan is placed on the positive significance of the lives of the deceased, and there is no emphasis on the existence of enemies.

In arguments over the Yūshūkan's telling of history, it is also overlooked that the Yūshūkan only positively set about telling history very recently; in 2002, in fact, after the total reconstruction of the museum. The background to this was that an extremely negative view of Japan's modern history, one which emphasised exploitation within Japan and unremitting aggression abroad, had been implanted in people's minds through the Japanese public education system; this resulted in a situation that could only be described as pathological.

It may be difficult to believe from the point of view of international common sense but, till very recently, Japanese governments repeatedly acknowledged Japan's wrongdoings in modern history and apologised to foreign countries, without confirming the facts, or indeed, by ignoring the facts. For example, in 1982, most Japanese newspapers reported that the Ministry of Education, Science and Culture following an inspection of high school history textbooks, had ordered that the account of Japan's 'invasion' (*shinryaku*) into the northern part of China be rewritten as an 'advance' (*shinshutsu*). However, this was misinformation, and there never was any such enforced rewriting. Nonetheless, to ensure the goodwill of its Asian neighbours, the Japanese government responded to the protests from China and Korea, reassuring them that it would take it upon itself to rectify the issue. It even went as far as to establish new standards of inspection that guaranteed to 'pay careful consideration from the viewpoint of international understanding and international emphasis to the treatment of events that occurred in modern history between Japan and its Asian neighbours.'[12] In essence, this meant that the history textbooks used in compulsory education in Japan would prioritise over historical facts the historical perspectives and feelings of its Asian neighbours.

I will illustrate this extraordinary phenomenon using an example from my home prefecture, Mie. In 1998, first year junior high school pupils, just starting to learn properly about Japanese history, were introduced to Japan-Korea relations under the heading 'Study of human rights'. Rather than being taught the complex historical facts of the mutual relations between the two nations, it was considered more desirable to get across the selfishness and unfairness of Japan in exacting for its own benefit the immense sacrifice on the people of Asia, but particularly of Korea. In other words, teachers were educating pupils with lessons designed to instil a sense of guilt in their pupils towards the Korean people rather than teaching them the complex and accurate facts. The approach proved immensely popular among teaching staff in Mie.[13]

This masochistic drift of public opinion within Japan reached its peak in August 1993 when Chief Cabinet Secretary Kōno Yōhei officially acknowledged and apologised for the enforced prostitution of Korean women by the Japanese army: 'With regard to recruitment of comfort women, businesses who took orders from the Army were the key players but, even so, there are many examples of people being

12 Watanabe, *Banken uso ni hoeru,* and Inagaki, 'Asahi kyōdō no kyōkasho henkō hōdō wa kuni no haji', pp. 4-7.

13 Matsuura, *Ii kagen shiro!* That the state education system implants into the minds of primary and middle school pupils a sense of guilt towards Koreans and Chinese will be apparent to anyone who peruses a copy of any primary or middle school history text book.

assembled against their wishes by means of enticements or force. It is clear, too, that the Military Police were also directly involved.' At this time, the Japanese government devoted all of its energies to searching for materials that proved this prostitution was enforced, but none were found. Even so, Japan was issued with strong demands from the Korean government to 'restore the honour of these women by acknowledging that prostitution was enforced on them,' and it subsequently issued an apology based on statements from sixteen witnesses prepared by the Korean government, without even cross-examining them. It is worth noting that the content of these statements has not been made public to this day. Underlying this apology was the preconceived notion that the Imperial Japanese Army had undoubtedly carried out evil actions, and that these Korean women were hardly likely to have lied. Also, there is evidence here of a uniquely Japanese custom of offering an apology in times of trouble by way of an attempt to avoid exacerbating the situation. What is more, the preamble to the Japanese Constitution declares that 'we have [sic] determined to preserve our security and existence, trusting in the justice and faith of the peace-loving peoples of the world.' This has ever since formed the basis for Japan's apologetic diplomacy. [14]

As a result of chief cabinet secretary Kōno's informal remarks, all junior high school history textbooks have since 1997 provided an account of the 'comfort women issue'. However, in that same year, research by the journalist Sakurai Yoshiko showed that Kōno's statement was the outcome of diplomatic considerations, and that no objective proof existed.[15] Consequently, the realisation spread that Kōno's re-

14 The Constitution of Japan, House of Councillors, http://www.sangiin.go.jp/eng/law/index.htm.

15 Sakurai, *Mitsuyaku gaikō no daishō*, pp. 116-26. Note also that Assistant Cabinet Secretary, Ishihara Nobuo, gave evidence before a gathering of Democratic Party activists to the following effect: 'There are no documents or telegrams which support the [allegation] that the government or army forcibly recruited comfort women.' '[As for our acknowledgement of the use of force], it would be a lie to say that diplomatic considerations were absent.

marks could not possibly form the basis of any historical account. But outside Japan, Kōno's remarks were seen as absolute, evidence-based proof of the Japanese government's acknowledgment of guilt. The situation now is one where people take the extreme view and insist, in all seriousness, that to doubt or deny the enforcement of prostitution by the military is on a par with denying the Nazi Holocaust.

At the risk of departing from the issue at hand, I wish to discuss four points essential to an understanding of the comfort women issue. The first concerns Congressman Mike Honda, who has submitted numerous anti-Japanese bills to Congress. The *Sankei shinbun* recently carried an article under the following heading: 'Honda's funds: 30% from Chinese sources; Anti-Japanese funding to Mr. Honda; China seeks to weaken Japan'. The article goes on to state, among other things, that 'what is striking about individual Chinese donations to Congressman Honda is that they come from Chinese activists attached to anti-Japanese organisations. Each of the activists has donated multiple millions of dollars.' 'Honda has tabled successive motions in 2001, 2003, 2006 and 2007 proposing the US seek an apology from Japan over the comfort women issue.' The *Sankei* concludes there is no mistaking the political intent in the background here: 'Chinese authorities are using [these pressure groups] to weaken Japan's morale and split Japan from the US'. In other words the comfort women issue is one prong of China's global strategy, as much as it concerns historical fact. Second, on 26 March 2007 the London *Times* reported that former prime minister Nakasone Yasuhiro had acknowledged that the Japanese army had enforced sexual slavery and rape. It appears though that he never did 'acknowledge' this. With regard to Nakasone's interview, Korea's *Chōsen nippō* (24 March, online edition) said of Nakasone that he had 'no personal knowledge of the Japanese military's enforced deployment of comfort women at all'; he only knew what he read in the press. 'Nakasone's spokesman insisted in an interview with Associated Press in 1997 that the

This was a case of political judgement not judgement of the facts.' (*Sankei shinbun*, 29 March 2007).

comfort stations were operated by local private businessmen; comfort women were not forcibly deployed; only volunteers were recruited.' Third, research by Koreans themselves and by the Japanese historian, Hata Ikuhiko, has made it clear that the confessions of Yoshida Seiji about his rounding up of comfort women on the island of Jeju do, off the coast of Korea, which is regarded as the classic case of sexual slavery, are a fabrication.[16] Fourth, the so-called 'comfort stations' under military control also existed in Germany where compulsion was very much the order of the day.[17] The British army also approved the employment of local prostitutes and brothels and, indeed, made use of the comfort stations of the defeated Japanese army.[18] The American military too used military comfort stations in Hawaii and in Vietnam, and is said to operate them today in the vicinity of the 38th parallel in Korea.[19]

Note, here, that the ethnic mix of the women in Japanese comfort stations is estimated by Hata Ikuhiko as follows: Japanese 40 per cent; local populations, that is, Chinese, Manchurian, Filipino, Indonesian, Burmese, and mixed race women 30 per cent; Koreans 20 per cent; others (Dutch and Taiwanese) 10 per cent.[20] Be that as it may, it is really only from 1998 onwards, the year after the comfort women began to appear in textbooks, that commentators have become increasingly vociferous in their opposition to this state of affairs. People like myself have only recently started to comment on how distinctly odd it is for Japanese to condemn their own forefathers as irredeemably evil, and to offer apologies without regard for the historical facts; how extraordinary, too, the thoughts and words of those who take no exception to all this; how strange the state of history education which gave rise to this

16 Hata, *Ianfu o senjō no sei*, pp. 229-48. See the Korean writer, O. Sonfa, who also denies the possibility that the Japanese could have enforced sexual slavery (*Seikatsusha no Nihon tōchi jidai*, pp. 42-4; 54-5; 223-4).

17 Kisa,, *'Sensō sekinin' to wa nanika;* pp. 84-97.

18 Hata *Ianfu o senjō no sei*, pp. 156-9.

19 Ibid., pp. 163-75.

20 Ibid., pp. 410.

situation; and how all of this is in need of a re-evaluation. As part of this gathering trend of thought, Yasukuni itself began to feel that displays dedicated to the private honouring of war dead were insufficient; the shrine began to favour exhibits that attached importance to the sort of historical view that till now had remained in the background. However, this change in attitude was regarded by the teaching profession as an insignificant matter. Most Japanese children continued to be taught that the American dropping of atom bombs on Hiroshima and Nagasaki could not be helped, since Japan had started the war in the first place. They were taken on school trips to visit the A bomb Cenotaph, inscribed with its commitment: 'We shall not repeat the evil.'[21] Some junior high schools even took pupils on trips to China expressly to visit the Nanking Massacre memorial hall.

Japan's liberal mass media reported only Yasukuni's switch in attitude, and fails to impart the fact that the Japanese education system is in the grip of a pacifist ideology that is so keen to plant in children's minds an anti-war mentality that it is prepared to exaggerate and fabricate the evil of our ancestors. This has made it difficult even for impartial researchers from overseas to comprehend the entire state of affairs in a balanced way, and to appreciate fully the intricacies of the Yasukuni issue.

So, for example, even the editor of this volume, John Breen, whom I respect for his impartial and level-headed approach to research, refers critically to the exhibits in the Yūshūkan in such terms as 'selective memory' and 'the fabrication of myth'. Even he fails to mention that for more than sixty years since the war's end, the Japanese education system has been under the domineering control of the 'selective memory' and 'myth fabrication' that was the product of pacifist ideology. Breen, moreover, speaks of his own interpretation of history as 'historical fact', while dismissing the Yūshūkan's interpretation of history as 'myth'.[22] For example, he writes that the

21 http://www.pcf.city.hiroshima.jp/declaration/English/1999/1999words/vol08E.html.

22 Breen, 'Yasukuni: rekishi kioku' pp. 156-7. See also the chapter by Breen in

Japanese army forced group suicides on the citizens of Okinawa as though it were an established historical fact. But it is not. In my opinion, these stories were fabricated.[23] Breen makes no reference to the fact that the 'enforcement of group suicide', which never took place, is recorded in school textbooks. Instead, he talks only of 'selective memory' at the Yūshūkan.[24]

There is more to say on the question of selective memory. It is precisely because of selective memory that neither school textbooks nor those who oppose prime ministerial patronage of Yasukuni make mention, for example, of the tragedy of Japanese nurses who, made sex slaves of the Soviet army, committed mass suicide to escape their fate;[25] or again of stirring stories like that of the Japanese destroyer *Ikazuchi* which, with no concern for danger, rescued 422 of the crew of a Royal Navy ship that was sunk by the Japanese north of Java in 1942.[26]

How to dilute a large volume of sulphuric acid? The only way is to add pure water. In terms of dynamics, too, the only way to keep an object where it should be in the face of massive opposing force is probably to pull hard in the opposite direction. It is my hope to direct readers' attention to the reality that the Yūshūkan's claims are but feeble resistance, the object of which is to pull back in the opposite direction. I hope too that readers will understand that the prevailing intellectual mood in Japan is still overwhelmingly in the grip of an overbearing pacifist ideology.

As a father of two, I hope that the age in which my children live will be at peace; I don't war to be waged unthinkingly on account of national interest. Nonetheless, we now live a peaceful, prosperous life in this independent nation of Japan, and it is for that very reason that I wish to express my respect and gratitude to our ancestors. For

---

this volume (ed.).

23 Sono, 'Aru shinwa no haikei'.

24 Breen, 'Yasukuni: rekishi kioku', p. 153.

25 Hata, *Ianfu o senjō no sei*, pp. 153-5.

26 *The Times*, 29April 1998; see also Megumi, *Tekihei o kyūjo seyo!*.

it was they who sacrificed their lives to ensure independence; they who, with military force, broke down the global colonial system in order to lay the foundations for resource-scarce Japan to engage in free trade; they who created an environment where it will never again be necessary to engage in fighting with the Western powers; they who constructed the circumstances that have enabled us to devote ourselves wholeheartedly to economic activity. However I look at it, I just cannot see that respect and gratitude to these war dead are dangerous notions that will somehow plunge the world into chaos.

7

YASUKUNI AND THE LOSS OF HISTORICAL MEMORY[1]

John Breen

Yasukuni is a place of memories, both private and public. The comrades of the fallen of the Pacific war, and bereaved family members, visit Yasukuni to remember and to mourn at the Great Spring and Autumn festivals, or on days of special significance for their regiments. They tell how, in their mourning at Yasukuni, their loved ones appear clearly before them and give them much comfort.[2] But Yasukuni like all memorial sites engages actively in the construction of a more public memory that always seeks to accommodate, but may sometimes conflict with the private. This vital mnemonic function of the shrine merits more attention than it has so far been accorded. The present chapter sets out to address this shortcoming, by identifying and exploring the several strategies Yasukuni shrine deploys to construct its particular historical memory; it seeks to ask why it might be that Yasukuni does what it does mnemonically. My focus here falls uniquely on Yasukuni's construction of Pacific War memory.

1 An earlier version of this article was published in *Sekai* (September, 2006) under the title of 'Yasukuni: rekishi kioku no keisei to sōshitsu'.

2 Breen, 'The dead and the living', pp. 88-90.

Yasukuni shrine, in brief, appeals to three mnemonic strategies. The first is 'textual': shrine priests and shrine apologists publish pamphlets, posters, books and a multiplicity of web pages to articulate their understanding of the Pacific war. A second strategy is that of display: the shrine compound accommodates the Yūshūkan, 'Japan's first and oldest war museum', whose exhibits in their selection and arrangement construct a powerful and vivid historical narrative of war. Finally, there is the ritual strategy. Yasukuni is before all else a ritual site; ritual performance is the shrine's, and the priests', *raison d'être*. As Connerton insists, a fundamental operation of ritual is the conveying and sustaining of 'recollected knowledge', that is, of images of the past.[3] No exploration of the shrine as a mnemonic site can therefore omit its ritual operations.

This chapter does not, then, seek to engage directly with the two arenas that have dominated what has come to be known as the Yasukuni problem; it seeks to articulate a third. The first has concerned the constitutionality of prime ministerial visits to the shrine, while the second involves the presence in the Yasukuni pantheon of Class A war criminals like Prime Minister Tōjō Hideki who led Japan to war, and Generals Matsui and Muto, who commanded the Imperial Army in Nanking and the Philippines respectively. Rather, this chapter identifies the shrine's mnemonic operations as problematic in their own right. That Yasukuni as a private juridical person is entirely free to construct whatever memory and tell whatever historical tales it wishes goes without saying; but these operations become problematic when the state, in the form of the prime minister or, indeed, any of his ministers, patronises the shrine, thus according the shrine the guise of a 'national' shrine and the shrine's memory that of 'official', public memory.

Ritual Propitiation as Mnemonic Strategy

Yasukuni priests perform rites every morning and evening of every day of the year. All performances have as their ritual focus the spirits

3 Connerton, *How societies remember*, pp. 3-4.

of the war dead, whom they celebrate as *kami* (usually translated as gods) or *eirei* (glorious spirits). The rites fall neatly into two categories: *reiji hōan sai*, which are dynamic rites of apotheosis involving the transformation of the war dead into sacred beings.[4] The second, known by the generic term of *ireisai*, are rites of propitiation (*irei*) in which these *kami* or *eirei* are honoured as they are propitiated. The vast majority of Yasukuni rites are of this latter category, but by far the most important and the most solemn among them are the two seasonal rites, the Great Rites of Spring and Autumn. What distinguishes these is the dominating presence of the *chokushi*. This is a special emissary dispatched by the emperor from the imperial palace to Yasukuni shrine, where he serves as imperial proxy. In what follows, I set out first to explain the ritual dynamic that obtains between priests, the *kami* and the emissary in these Great Rites of Spring and Autumn, and then I ask what this has to do with questions of memory and historical narrative.[5]

The Great Autumn Rite comprises three different ritual sequences. In the first, priests make offerings to the *kami* residing in the *nainaijin*, the innermost recesses of the main sanctuary. These offerings include beer and the 'Peace' brand of cigarettes, as well as the more conventional offerings of water, rice and rice wine. The chief priest then intones prayers and places his own offerings of the evergreen *sakaki* branch before the *kami*. In the second sequence, the imperial emissary enters the main sanctuary. He makes his offerings of coloured silk from the centre of the main sanctuary and intones his prayers, and finally offers his own sprig of the evergreen *sakaki*. In the final sequence, representatives of the Defence agency, The Japan Society of the War Bereaved (*Nihon izokukai*), the National Association for Shinto Shrines (*Jinja honchō*), the Glorious War Dead Society (*Eirei ni kotaeru kai*) and other organisations make their way

4 Breen, 'The dead and the living', pp. 80-1.

5 In what follows, I draw on the *Shūki reitaisai shiki shidai* the ritual programme for the Autumn rite I attended in 2001.

along the corridor joining Worship hall to the main sanctuary and present their offerings and pray.

The ritual dynamic operating here in this Great Autumn Rite is of great vintage; it draws on the cults of *goryō*, which are traceable back to the Heian period (8th–12th centuries) and possibly earlier. *Goryō* cults involve the belief that the spirits of (usually) noble men and women who died inauspicious deaths are angry and resentful on account of their lives being cut prematurely short and, in their anger and resentment, return to curse the living and wreak havoc upon them. If, however, the living propitiate the angry spirits with the right offerings, then the angry sprits may be persuaded to desist from destruction and, indeed, to deploy their numinous powers to protect and bring solace to the living. The great autumn rite at Yasukuni is a modern 'take' on this ancient tradition which lies at the very heart of Japanese religious culture. The dynamic here is exactly the same: in return for endless propitiation by the living (priests and emperor foremost among them), the dead will be restful and offer no threat to the living; they will, indeed, guarantee them peace and prosperity.[6]

When, however, we focus our attention on the imperial emissary and his ritual role, a complicating dynamic surfaces. The first thing to notice is the ritual tension that obtains between the propitiating emperor (here, his emissary) and the propitiated war dead. The emissary's actions are clear enough: he makes offerings, he intones a prayer and offers *sakaki*, all by way of propitiating the war dead, and venerating them as *kami*. But there is an inescapable reflexive quality to this rite, too, so that the ritual focus shifts subtly between the venerated war dead and the venerating emperor. After all, the emperor propitiates and venerates the war dead for no other reason than that they embodied loyalty towards him, patriotism in the service of the empire, and self-sacrifice in the service of both. It is never entirely clear whether it is the war dead as *kami* that are celebrated

6 Priests of the shrine interviewed by this author are uncomfortable with the idea that the war dead be understood as angry spirits; they prefer to think of them as 'ancestors' and the rites of propitiation as ancestral rites.

in these rites, or the emperor and the imperial values which these men embodied. One Yasukuni priest told this author he felt deeply uncomfortable when people speak of 'the emperor venerating the war dead [in these rites]'. What he feared was the inversion of the cosmic order: the war dead are supposed to be worshipping the emperor; not the other way around. Indeed, the *norito* prayer which the priest intones in the first sequence confirms the ambiguity of the ritual dynamic. It begins by asserting that 'the offerings of this day are enabled by the limitless generosity of the emperor's heart'. It then asks the dead that, in return for those offerings in the form of abundant fruits of the earth and the sea, they protect the imperial nation and ensure the imperial institution flourishes in splendour for ever more. In other words, the rite entrusts to the dead precisely that function which they fulfilled as soldiers and sailors in their living service: to serve emperor and imperial Japan.

This emperor-centred reading of the Great Autumn Rite seems to finds support in the shrine's total symbolism. The mirror which dominates the main sanctuary, a gift from the Meiji emperor, makes the point that the Sun goddess and her descendants, the incumbents of the imperial line, give meaning to the shrine and its practises; the main sanctuary and the worship hall are bedecked with drapes bearing the 16-petal imperial chrysanthemum, as are the lanterns that light up night time ritual performances. The massive wooden gate (*shinmon*) is embossed with a striking golden chrysanthemum, too, which designates the shrine precinct as imperial space. Moreover, the Yasukuni ritual cycle tracks that of the imperial court so the shrine performs what are known as *tōjitsu sai* or 'contemporaneous rites' for the September *kanname* rite, the November *niiname* rite and the February *toshigoi* rite. These rites involve the emperor venerating Amaterasu, the Sun goddess, and offering thanks for her gift of rice to Japan. Again, on the anniversaries of Kōmei (r. 1847-66), Meiji (r. 1867-1912), Taishō (r. 1912-26) and Shōwa (r. 1926-89), Yasukuni priests face the mausolea of these modern monarchs, and venerate them from afar. There is a human dimension to the shrine's imperial linkage, too. Although the Showa emperor last visited Yasukuni in 1975 and never returned, and the present emperor has not visited since his enthronement in 1989, every year one of the Mikasa Princes attends the Spring and Autumn festivals.

My understanding of this Great Autumn Rite is that it is at one level at least a celebration by the living and the dead gathered in Yasukuni shrine of the emperor. The rite serves to generate, and forever re-generate, a sense of awe before the emperor, his institution and those essentially imperial values the war dead are said to have embodied in his name. The question, then, is what history is remembered and what forgotten in all this?

The rites embed within them a narrative that may be summarized like this. Millions of Japanese went to war in the 1930s and 40s on behalf of the emperor and imperial Japan; 2,300,000 of them, after valiant struggle, sacrificed their lives in the cause of the emperor and imperial Japan. To a man, they died embodying those hallowed imperial virtues of loyalty, patriotism and self-sacrifice. Their deaths were thus noble and honourable before they were ever tragic. The war, which created so many heroes, is by definition a heroic and noble undertaking. This uncomplicated ritual narrative is, of course, myth and not history, and it comprises all those elements of myth defined by Connerton: 'struggle', 'death in war' and 'redemption through death'.[7]

What is banished from the memory, then, in the narrating of this myth? What is banished, first of all, are the sacrifices of the common man and woman. The shrine venerates as glorious spirits only the military.[8] So, for example, the 100,000 citizens of Tokyo who lost their lives in the American firebombing of March 1945, those who died in the defence of Okinawa in April of the same year, the non-combatants who died in the atomic bomb attacks on Hiroshima and

7 Connerton, *How societies remember*, p. 43.

8 The multiple categories of *gun*, *gunzoku* and *jungunzoku* (military, quasi-military and quasi-quasi military) are clearly set out in 'Senbotsu sha no gōshi' in Yasukuni jinja (ed.), *Yasukuni no inori*, p. 186.

Nagasaki in August are all denied a place in Yasukuni's pantheon. The shrine is ambivalent about its status as a 'military' site but to the extent that it is such the omission of civilians is inevitable. The omission undermines the shrine's claim to be a national site of mourning. The autumn rite takes as its premise, after all, the historically false proposition that the Pacific War was a war that engaged combatants alone.

The rites of propitiation fail to accommodate within their narrative these complicating facts of undeniable historicity:

1) that, even though there were many, many Japanese soldiers and sailors who exhibited the most extraordinary bravery, there were countless others who died squalid deaths of starvation and disease;
2) that even those who doubtlessly embodied the vaunted imperial virtues of loyalty, patriotism and self-sacrifice, were victims of the militarism that bound Japan in the 1930s and 40s;
3) that the war which took so many lives was, like all wars, brutal and cruel;

The shrine rites' simplistic recall of the Pacific war brings to mind the case of Iida Susumu. Iida, a corporal in the Imperial Japanese army, featured in an NHK retrospective on Yasukuni in summer 2006. The programme, called *Yasukuni o kangaeru: sengo rokujūnen* ('Reflecting on Yasukuni sixty years after war's end'), began inauspiciously with an overlong, uncritical interview with the then Chief Priest, Yuzawa Tadashi. It turned out, however, to be a deeply moving broadcast, not least because of the appearance of men like Iida whose voices have been smothered in the polemic that has defined Yasukuni studies to date. Iida Susumu was arraigned at the Tokyo war crimes' tribunal as a Class B war criminal for his conduct in New Guinea. The programme did not reveal what he had done, but he anyway spent several years in Sugamo prison reflecting on his actions, and those of the Japanese military in that South Pacific campaign. On camera he spoke of Yasukuni and its 'pacifying' and 'honouring' of the 'glorious spirits' of war dead. 'These are fine words indeed,' he said. 'They strike a chord with the bereaved, with comrades and, indeed, with a lot of the Japanese people. But from the perspective of one who fought in the war, I have to ask "Do these men merit honour as the nation's glorious war dead?" I beg to differ.' Referring to the fact that no less than 100,000 Japanese officers and men died of starvation in New Guinea, Iida continued: 'Who did we soldiers despise? It was the military commanders who planned that New Guinea campaign. To reflect on this is to conclude that words like the "glorious spirits of the war dead" are designed simply to avoid the issue of responsibility. This [refusal to accept responsibility] is insufferable.'[9] Yasukuni's rites of apotheosis and propitiation are indiscriminate; and in their failure to discriminate, they deny the value of the individual war experiences of countless men like Iida Susumu.

To the south of the main sanctuary where Iida's commanders and comrades are venerated as *kami*, stands another site, the Chinreisha, literally 'the Spirit pacifying shrine'. Built in 1965, the Chinreisha comprises two *za*, two sites that is, in which two different categories of *kami* reside. The first *za* is dedicated to those who fought and fell in battles with the imperial army during the revolutionary decades of the 1860s and 70s. So, venerated here are many nameless samurai who died in the Boshin civil war, alongside others of renown like Etō Shinpei and Saigō Takamori, men who worked in the imperial government, left, rebelled and finally took their own lives. The second *za* is still more interesting, since it is dedicated to the dead of Japan's erstwhile enemies. Here are venerated as *kami* the British, Americans, South East Asians, Koreans and Chinese. The Chinreisha is very much peripheral to the Main sanctuary, it is true but, priests make offerings there every morning and every evening; the shrine also has its own feast day—on 13 July. What is important about the Chinreisha in this context is that it has the capacity to recall and narrate a past more complex than that of the rites in the main sanctuary: a violent past that had its perpetrators as well as its victims; its win-

9 See Breen, 'Yasukuni: rekishi kioku no keisei to soshitsu', p. 151 and Breen, 'Pacific trauma'.

ners and losers; its horrors as well as its heroism. So much a matter of controversy was this Chinreisha among the priesthood and shrine activists that, within a decade of its construction, it was banished from sight. The shrine encircled it with a high steel fence, secluding it from all but the shrine priests who served it.[10] On 23 November 2006, the *Mainichi* newspaper carried a front page article announcing that the new Chief priest of Yasukuni, Nanbu Tadashi had ordered the steel fence stripped away. The Chinreisha is once more exposed to the gaze of visitors. At the time of writing, it remains unclear what Nanbu's motives are and what opposition he had to overcome. The *Mainichi* did not explore this. Time will tell, but a distinct possibility remains that it is in preparation for the inaugural visit to Yasukuni of the new Prime Minister, Abe Shinzō.

Strategy of Display: the Yūshūkan War Museum

On the opposite side of the main sanctuary to the Chinreisha is the Yūshūkan war museum. It serves as a sort of illustrated commentary on the shrine's rites of propitiation. Museum exhibits impart physicality to some of the most extraordinary of the military men and women apotheosised and venerated in the main sanctuary. To take but one example among thousands: there is Lieutenant Nishi, who won an equestrian gold medal in the 1932 Los Angeles Olympics. Nishi refused to surrender to the American forces in Iwojima, and died in what was effectively a suicidal tank attack against overwhelming odds. The museum displays Nishi's photograph, his Olympic gold medal and certificate; it records his regiment and his rank, and the date and place of his death. The exhibit addresses Nishi as *mikoto*, where *mikoto* is an honorific form of address for the *kami*.

There is nothing unique about the Yūshūkan as a war museum honouring the war dead; this is precisely what war museums exist to do. Nor is there anything distinctive in Yūshūkan using technology to divert the gaze of the visitor away from war's horrors, sanitising,

10 On the history of the Chinreisha, see Breen, 'A Yasukuni genealogy' in this volume.

even glorifying them. So, for example, the visitor to the refurbished, expanded Yūshūkan which reopened in 2003 encounters first of all a fine example of the C56 steam engine, which travelled the Burma railway. There is a plaque explaining the C56 was built in 1936, and was the first steam engine ever to ply the Burma railway; it was, indeed, such a fine example of engineering that it continued to be used in the post-war era as well. But there is no mention here that 90,000 men, prisoners of war and local labourers, were sacrificed in the building of the railway along which the C56 plied its way. The entrance hall grabs the gaze of the visitor with life size models of the Ōka and the Kaiten, both used in special attack or suicide missions. The Kaiten was an underwater version of the Ōka,[11] its purpose being to rise from the depths and shunt its explosive packed body into the hulls of warships. The plaques reveal much about the technology of these extraordinary weapons of war.[12]

There is one feature of the Yūshūkan museum which is, perhaps, unique; and that is the conspicuous absence of the enemy. The visitor to the museum walks the history of the Sino-Japanese war, the Russo-Japanese war, the so-called Manchurian Incident, the China war and the Pacific war, and there is no enemy in sight. There are no representations of American, British or Chinese soldiers; no uniforms, no weapons, no flags or other trophies of war are anywhere to be seen. This offers a striking contrast to the pre-war Yūshūkan and to Imperial War Museum in London where life-size mannequins of German and Japanese soldiers are displayed and Tiger tanks squat beneath German Messerschmitts suspended from the ceiling. I asked a shrine priest about this absence of the enemy, and he explained that the Yūshūkan is not, in fact, a war museum at all; it is a *hōmotsuden* or repository of the relics of the war dead; its sole purpose is to honour the memory of Japanese war dead. This is persuasive to some extent; the museum certainly is such a repository, but it claims to be much

11 Ibid., p. xii.

12 The Yūshūkan website affords an opportunity to view these and many other items on display: http://www.yasukuni.or.jp/english/Yūshūkan.html.

more. In all of its literature, the Yūshūkan defines itself as Japan's oldest and most esteemed war museum; its remit being 'to clarify the truth about Japan's modern history'.[13] The absence of the enemy makes this a daunting challenge.

What the absence achieves splendidly is an amnesia of perpetration, of defeat, and, above all, of the horror of war. The museum's treatment of the battle for Okinawa might serve as an example. On display in the Okinawan panel are the banner used to dispatch the *tokkōtai* or suicide pilots, as they took off on their doomed missions (*hiri hōken ten*); there is the jacket worn by General Ushijima Mitsuru, commander of the 32nd army, who took his own life on 23 June when convinced the battle was lost; there is a photo, too, of a commemoration stone set up to mark the extraordinary courage of the nurses of the Himeyuri unit, who tended to the Japanese wounded as the battle for Okinawa raged about them; it stands by the cave in which they took refuge. There is also this account of the battle for Okinawa:

> The entire population of Okinawa was one as they fought on for months. No wonder the cost was so high. Lieutenant Colonel Ōta Minoru dispatched a final tearful telegram reporting the activities [of his unit]. In the field of battle, suicide attacks were deployed in the air, at sea and on land. The battleship Yamato played its part, as did aircraft, and the infantry units, too, who took on the American tanks. All of these were suicide attacks.

The museum's memory is clearly impaired here. No battle was more ferocious than that fought over Okinawa, but obliterated from the museum's narrative is the contesting memory of many Okinawans who testified that the imperial army used the civilian population as shields, sometimes murdered them, and even drove many to acts of group suicide.[14] There are many records of individual Okinawans who witnessed friends and family cut down by Japanese

13 Yuzawa, 'Goaisatsu' in *Yūshūkan zuroku*, p. 2.

14 Tanaka Nobumasa writes of Okinawan perspectives in the campaign in Tanaka, 'Okinawa kara Okinawa o tou', pp. 109-11. For a contrasting view on Okinawa, see Nitta's chapter in this volume.

soldiers. Yūshūkan does not, and of course cannot, engage with these complicating memories.

When the visitor reaches the panel that treats the end of the Pacific War, it becomes clear that, while the Imperial Japanese Army's enemies are absent, there is, after all, a striking foreign presence. The panel is dominated by a large photograph of Justice Radhabinod Pal, the one Asian judge at the war crimes tribunal in Tokyo, and the one judge, too, who was an authority in international law. It was Justice Pal's considered view that the Japanese were innocent of all war crimes; the real aggressors, he insisted, were not the Japanese at all, but the Americans and British; *they* should be standing trial. Justice Pal's views are set out in large print alongside his photograph:

> If you read my history, you will know that the Americans and British are the loathsome instigators of aggression against Asia. However, many Japanese intellectuals do not read what I have to say. This is why they tell their students that Japan was guilty of war crimes and that Japan launched a war of aggression against Asia.

The Tokyo war crimes tribunal remains highly controversial; non-Japanese as well as Japanese scholars of different persuasions have argued its shortcomings for over a generation.[15] Many historians now talk of the imperialist identity of combatants on both sides; of an imperialist war fought by imperialist powers competing for land and people that did not rightfully belong to either side. The undeniable truth of Justice Pal's insistence on American and British responsibility in perpetrating imperialist aggression against Asia requires recognition of the fact that Japan was hardly alone in committing war crimes and atrocities in the Asia Pacific War. But it does not render any more persuasive the Yūshūkan's reading of the Pacific War as a purely idealist enterprise, or its visual presentation that elides the horrors of war committed and suffered by Japanese soldiers and citizens.[16]

15 An important early example is Minear's 1971 book, *Victor's Justice*. John Dower offers a similar view in *Embracing Defeat*.

16 The identity between Yasukuni, the Yūshūkan and Pal's understanding of

The gallery of the Pacific War concludes with a panel on national liberation movements 1945-60, which imparts further meaning to the Pal-sanctioned memory of the war:

> The flames stirred under Japanese occupation were not doused even after Japan's defeat, and new nation states emerged in rapid succession following wars of independence.

The wars waged by the Japanese army were noble undertakings, according to the Yasukuni logic, not least because they contributed to the liberation of Asia from loathsome Americans and British imperialists. In short, the Japanese military were, to a man, heroes, paragons of loyalty to emperor and imperial Japan; and not a life was lost in vain because Japan contributed to liberation even if it suffered defeat in the process. Neatly obliterated from the historical memory of the Yūshūkan are the historical facts of Japanese war crimes, of Japanese colonialism and aggression, and of Japanese defeat.

Textual Strategy of Memory

History as narrated by the Great Rite of Autumn and reproduced in the exhibits on display in the Yūshūkan is intended to impart meaning to the horror and the waste of war. This same narrative is reproduced over and over again in the many publications of the shrine, of the museum and of its apologists. Representative are books like *Yasukuni no inori* and the pamphlets, posters and web pages authored by organisations like the aforementioned Glorious War Dead Society and the Japan Society for the War Bereaved, as well as the Shinto Political League (*Shintō seiji renmei*). It goes without saying that the recall of these publications is a perfect fit with the narratives of shrine

---

the Pacific war was reinforced in 2005 when the new Chief Priest, Nanbu Toshiaki, unveiled a stone monument and plaque dedicated to Pal outside the museum entrance. The legend says: 'We hereby honour the courage and passion of Dr Pal who remained true to legal justice and historical truth. In order to record his words as a precious lesson to the Japanese people, we have erected this monument, and hope to pass on to future generations [Dr Pal's] great legacy.'

ritual and the Yūshūkan display. Here I want to focus uniquely on a couple of recurring but distinctive textual themes. The first is what might be called 'cornerstone' theory, since it argues that the sacrifices of the war dead constitute the 'cornerstone' of post-war Japan's brilliant success. Ōhara Yasuo's introduction to *Yasukuni jinja: Yūshūkan no sekai* offers one example:

> The lives we lead today are built upon the cornerstone (*ishizue*) of our forefathers... A year has now elapsed since the new, refurbished Yūshūkan opened to the public. What visitor can fail to be moved by the glorious spirits who constitute the cornerstone of modern Japan, by their relics, their love of country and parents, and by the love for them of the bereaved.[17]

The Glorious War Dead Society hands out complimentary packets of first aid plasters at the shrine that bear the legend: 'Are you not forgetting? It is upon the noble cornerstone (*ishizue*) laid by the 2,500,000 glorious spirits that the Japan of today stands, that you stand, and that your family stands.' The Shinto Political League distributes a pamphlet asserting the centrality of Yasukuni as the nation's site of mourning. The pamphlet, styled *Kudan no sakura wa naite iru* ('The Cherry blossoms on the Kudan hill are in tears') includes the following: 'Thus it is that Yasukuni shrine has been treasured by the people of Japan for so long: Yasukuni, which venerates those who became the cornerstone (*ishizue*) of the modern Japanese state, the cornerstone (*ishizue*) of the peace and prosperity that Japan enjoys today.'

It is important to understand that this equation of the sacrifice of the war dead and post-war prosperity is not the monopoly of shrine apologists. Just before he went to Saipan in May 2006, Emperor Akihito voiced the same sentiments. 'It is vital, he insisted, that we all bear constantly in mind that the Japan of today is, indeed, built upon the cornerstone (*ishizue*) of the sacrifice made by the fallen.' Former PM Koizumi Jun'ichirō espoused the same idea most recently on 15 August 2005 at the annual commemorative event in the Budōkan hall in Tokyo. Koizumi in his address said: 'In the last great war, many, many were scattered [like cherry blossoms] on the

17 Ōhara, *Yasukuni jinja Yūshūkan no sekai.*

battlefield, motivated by their love of country and family; some fell in the tragic midst of war, others perished in distant, foreign lands after the war's end. I reflect that it is on the noble sacrifice of the fallen that post-war Japan built its peace. [This thought] deeply moves me, and thus I offer to them all my gratitude and respect.'[18]

Koizumi legitimised his personal visits to Yasukuni with the same logic. Koizumi reiterated his determination to 'take on board historical facts with humility and to keep reflection and sincere apology always embedded in my heart.'[19] So what then are the historical facts? For Koizumi, the kamikaze pilots are especially important; so much so that, in moments of crisis, he tells himself to imagine what the pilots would do in similar critical situations. But what historical evidence is there, after all, that the kamikaze pilots so admired by Koizumi contributed to the foundation of post-war peace and prosperity? No doubt many died desirous of defending the Japan they loved, but this was not the Japan of the post-war era. It was the Japan of the Meiji constitution, over which the emperor, descended from the Sun goddess, ruled as 'sacred and inviolable'; it was the Japan in which the Imperial Army enjoyed extraordinary constitutional privileges; the Japan in which the Imperial rescript on education and its Confucian ethical imperatives were accorded sacred status. This was not the democratic Japan of individual freedoms and rights. Of course, there were kamikaze pilots like Lieutenant Furukawa Masataka who wrote, as he waited to take off on his last mission, of his unsurpassed love of peace; and of his dreams of a world in which all people worked together and loved

---

18 *Mainichi shinbun* 8.15.05. As I check the proofs for this manuscript in August 2007, the Shinto newspaper, *Jinja shinpō*, reports that Prime Minister Abe Shinzō and Emperor Akihito both reiterated the idea of postwar prosperity standing upon the foundations laid by the war dead. The event in question was the national rite for mourning the war dead (*Zenkoku senbotsu tsuitōshiki*) held at the Budōkan, Tokyo, 15 August, (*Jinja shinpō*, 20.8.07).

19 The Japanese Foreign ministry's website carries these and other related statements by Koizumi (last accessed, August 2006): http://www.mofa.go.jp/mofaj/area/taisen/Yasukuni/tachiba.html

one another. There must have been many like him; but to claim that they died for democracy is preposterous.[20]

The premise of cornerstone theory is emotional, not rational. However bravely and selflessly these men sacrificed their lives, it was Japan's defeat by the Allies, the post-war dismantling of Japanese militarism, the implementation of democratic reforms and the restructuring of government under the Occupation, not to mention the hard work of the Japanese people that laid the foundations for post-war prosperity. The consummation of these several processes was none other than the imposition by the Occupation of the post-war Constitution, with its provisions for popular sovereignty and pacifism. Neither the publications of apologists nor, indeed, the Yūshūkan displays is able to accommodate this narrative of war's end.

There is a second recurring theme in the textual memory generated by the shrine which merits consideration here and that is the linkage forged between the shrine and the regeneration of post-war Japanese ethics. The most eloquent proponent of this repositioning of the shrine in post-war society, and perhaps the most prolific of Yasukuni's many apologists, is an emeritus professor of Tokyo University, Kobori Keichirō. Kobori set out his basic position in a recent publication, co-authored with Ōhara Yasuo. 'If only, he began, the prime minister and the emperor would make their way boldly to Yasukuni, this would surely have an extremely positive effect on the morals of the nation at large.' He develops his theme:

> In the Japan of today the young people especially have no sense of gratitude that they have been born into this nation of Japan. If only the Yasukuni problem can be solved [so that the PM and emperor both venerate there], the attitude of the young toward Japan will be quite transformed. I believe they would then come round to the belief that Japan is a nation to be proud of, that we Japanese have something of which we can truly be proud. [...]

20 Two books that serve admirably to humanise the kamikaze pilots are Naitō, *Thunder Gods* and Ohnuki-Tierney, *Kamikaze Diaries*.

To this extent [he concluded] the solution of the Yasukuni problem will have a profoundly beneficial effect on national ethics.[21]

The first thing to note about this striking statement is that it constitutes post-war shrine orthodoxy. The very first item of the Outline of a Proposal for Legislation on Yasukuni (*Yasukuni hōan yōkō*), which was the product of an attempt by the Liberal Democratic Party back in 1956 to reform the legal status of the shrine, makes precisely the same point. Its reads: 'The shrine exists to venerate the dead, to honour their posthumous virtue and thus to bring about a revival in the ethics of contemporary Japan.' The conjunction 'and thus' is of particular interest as it hints that the shrine, in its post-war manifestation, exists first and foremost to regenerate the moral order of Japanese society; that honouring the war dead is subordinate. This same moral position is to be found in the writings of post-war chief priests since the 1950s, and in the publications of satellite groups like the Japanese Society for the War Bereaved and the Glorious War Dead Society.[22] Indeed, the reason why the shrine today insists on the ritual participation of the prime minster and the emperor lies here: for how might the shrine constitute the moral beacon for all of post-war Japanese society without their physical presence? Kobori does not make explicit what he means by 'morals', but they can only be those which the fallen were all said to embody: loyalty towards the emperor, love of imperial Japan and self-sacrifice. If the prime minister as representative of government and people, and the emperor as symbol of Japan go boldly to Yasukuni, then these moral values will establish themselves across Japan. Such is the conviction of Kobori and others. This conviction is fundamental to an understanding of

21 Kobori, *Yasukuni jinja o kangaeru*, pp. 16-7.

22 For a representative selection see the statements by Chief priests Matsudaira and Yuzawa in Matsudaira, 'Yasukuni hōshi', Yuzawa, 'Goaisatsu' respectively, and the websites of the Japan Society for the Bereaved and the Glorious War Dead Society: 'Nihon izoku kai mokuteki': www.nippon-izokukai.jp/index2.html; and 'Warera no shuchō' www.eireinikotaerukai.net/E01Ayumi/E0102.html.

the meaning which the shrine accords to itself and its practices in the post-war.

The problem with the 'Kobori conviction' is that it seeks to appropriate the dead and subvert the shrine as a site of propitiation and mourning. For in his schema propitiation and mourning are secondary; they are reduced to serving the greater good of ethical dissemination. This strategy is problematic in the mnemonic realm too. How can the shrine recall anything other than a past of imperial loyalty, of love of imperial nation and self-sacrifice if it is charged with disseminating these values throughout post-war Japanese society?

Epilogue

The question remains, then, of how to understand the shrine's mnemonic strategies of ritual, display and text: why does Yasukuni do what it does in the realm of memory? The reflections on historical memory by French critics like Eric Santner are suggestive here. Santner, whose attention has focused on museums and memorials of post-war France, points out that, whether they be museums built by Gaullists or memorials sponsored by Communists, they have all failed equally. They have failed in that they have obstructed the process of mourning, which demands an 'elaborating and integrating of the reality of loss and traumatic shock, by remembering and repeating in mediated doses'. These sites fail, as Santner puts it, to 'take the poison that cures'. Post-war French sites of memory have worked together to suppress the trauma of the war experience, of defeat, of occupation and of collaboration. France experienced massive trauma, painful beyond endurance, and these post-war sites deployed various mnemonic strategies in order to ensure its suppression rather than facilitate the remembering that would make it possible to overcome trauma. Santner refers to these strategies as 'narrative fetishism'.

He writes:

> By 'narrative fetishism' I mean the construction and deployment of a narrative consciously or unconsciously designed to expunge the traces of the trauma or loss that called that narrative into being in the first place. Narrative fetishism is a strategy of undoing in fantasy the need for mourning by simulating a condition of intactness, typically by situating the site and origin of loss elsewhere.[23]

Narrative fetishism, or 'myth production', releases one from the burden of having to reconstitute one's self-identity under post-traumatic conditions; in narrative fetishism, to use Santner's coinage, the 'past is indefinitely postponed'.

If Santner's observations do, indeed, apply to post-war sites of memory and mourning in France, they may well do to other nations visited by massive trauma, too. The ritual dynamic in Yasukuni's rites of pacification, the display of artefacts in the Yūshūkan and the principles sustaining cornerstone theory as history may also, perhaps, be understood as constituting a sort of narrative fetishism. Yasukuni in the twenty-first century suppresses the defeat, the loss of 2 million and more military lives, the humiliation of occupation, and the imposition of the constitution which together are the very source of massive trauma. The shrine obliterates from its memory of war all traces of trauma. In their place, it unfolds a fetishised narrative that recalls all Japanese combatants as heroes, paragons of loyalty and patriotism, who sacrificed their lives selflessly for the emperor; it recalls the war as a noble undertaking, fought with heroism to free Asia from American and European imperialist powers; and it recalls the suicide pilots, especially, as the cornerstone of post-war Japan in its peace and prosperity. Santner's theory might lead us to assume that, in its failure to integrate and elaborate the trauma of war, Yasukuni disqualifies itself as a place of mourning.[24]

Yasukuni's shortcomings as a site of mourning render particularly significant Koizumi's declaration of October 2005 that a cross-party committee would convene to consider the creation of a new, non-

23 Santner, 'History beyond the pleasure principle', p. 144.

24 Brower, 'The preserving machine', pp. 87-8.

religious site for honouring the war dead. The idea was first raised by Nakasone in the 1980s and has periodically resurfaced only to be buried again. Prime Minister Abe Shinzō and Foreign minister Aso Tarō have already hinted that they see no need for a new site. Aso suggests rather that the Abe administration set up a review of Yasukuni's status as an independent religious juridical body, with a mind to bringing it and the state into closer proximity. This is precisely the position of right wing intellectuals like Ōhara Yasuo. Ōhara dismisses the idea of a new site on the spurious grounds that Yasukuni has the overwhelming support of the people.[25] But anti-Yasukuni intellectuals like Takahashi Tetsuya are no less opposed. Takahashi writes: 'In the present with the government consistently refusing to pursue the question of war responsibility and instead reconsidering Article 9, which has committed Japan to non-belligerence, there is a real fear that any new peace memorial will be hijacked by the state and become a second Yasukuni.'[26] Takahashi may or may not be exaggerating the dangers, but the advantages of a new site under government jurisdiction and without grounding either in state Shinto or imperial ideology seem to this author to be overwhelming:

1) Such a site has the potential to be liberated from the 'narrative fetishism', the fetishised narrative, of the sort that Yasukuni exhibits in its desperation to bury the massive trauma of war;
2) to the extent that the new site would be liberated from the fetishised narrative of the Asia Pacific War, it would facilitate for the first time the process of unencumbered mourning—mourning minus the politics and the ethics—and thus help to bring closure to the war;
3) finally, such an unencumbered site of mourning would enable the Japanese premier, indeed the Japanese emperor, to stand alongside the heads of state of Japan's former enemies—something which cannot, and should not, ever happen at Yasukuni—and reflect on the horrors of war.

25 See, for example, Ōhara, 'Koizumi shushō', p. 3.

26 Takahashi, *Yasukuni mondai*, p. 214.

8

PLEDGE FULFILLED: PRIME MINISTER KOIZUMI, YASUKUNI AND THE JAPANESE MEDIA

Phillip Seaton

'If I become prime minister, however much criticism there is, I will definitely worship on 15 August.'

(Koizumi Jun'ichirō's pledge made during the LDP leadership race: 18 April 2001)[1]

Introduction

The international media typically frames the Yasukuni issue as a diplomatic dispute between Japan and its neighbours.[2] However, from the Japanese perspective the roots of the issue lie in deep-rooted divisions regarding how to remember and commemorate Japan's wars in the first half of the twentieth century. Japanese views range from progressive (arguing that Japan needs to do more to acknowledge responsibility) to nationalistic (celebrating the

1 Wakamiya and Watanabe, *'Yasukuni' to Koizumi shushō*, p. 94.

2 Seaton, 'Reporting the 2001 textbook and Yasukuni shrine controversies'.

Japanese military's heroism and denying guilt).[3] At the beginning of the twenty-first century, no issue has been more emblematic of Japan's struggles with the history of the Second World War than Yasukuni.

This chapter examines the Yasukuni controversy through the eyes of Japanese newspapers, publishing and television news. The limitations and professional codes of these media influence the way the Yasukuni issue is presented. Journalists face tight deadlines and avoid polemic when relaying government pronouncements, although editorial comment and op-ed articles occupy the middle pages. Books, academic essays or magazine pieces are much longer than newspaper articles and polemics may be considered integral to marketability in contrast to press ideals of 'objectivity'. Television news tends to assume a 'neutral' posture by airing comments from 'all sides of the debate' in interviews with studio guests and 'people in the street'. Thus, media forms heavily influence the nature and content of the information mediated.

Koizumi Jun'ichirō became prime minister on 26 April 2001 after a landslide victory in the LDP leadership election. He stepped down on 26 September 2006 having become Japan's third longest serving prime minister in the post-war period. His tenure was characterized by a flamboyance atypical of Japanese politics: from his flowing silver hair, to his love of the photo opportunity (he famously crooned Elvis Presley numbers in Graceland), and the audacity to call a snap election in August 2005 following a parliamentary defeat for his postal reform bill. Across the Japanese media the phrases *Koizumi gekijō* ('Koizumi's theatre') or *pafuo-mansu* ('performance') symbolized his populist approach to politics. He was a colourful character for the media to debate, not least because he divided public opinion with his stands on issues from constitutional reform to Yasukuni worship, and his attempts to open relations with North Korea and his dispatch of Japan Self-Defence Forces to Iraq.

3 Seaton, *Japan's Contested War Memories*, pp. 20-8.

Yasukuni had all the ingredients of a good media story: a charismatic political leader who was unafraid to do something divisive at home and deeply unpopular abroad; the complexity of the Yasukuni issue itself, which gave commentators numerous angles to debate; and of course the war, which inevitably evokes passionate feelings.

13 August 2001 in the Japanese Press

The pledge Koizumi made to patronise Yasukuni precipitated a chorus of protest. The most prominent cautionary voice in Japan belonged to his Foreign Minister Tanaka Makiko, Koizumi's *de facto* running partner during the leadership campaign. She urged Koizumi to reconsider.[4]

Koizumi was forced into a concession: instead of worshipping on 15 August, the symbolic end-of-the-war anniversary, he did so on 13 August. He also issued a statement of remorse for Japanese war actions, based on the 1995 Murayama communiqué.[5] Nevertheless, this was a milestone, the first unambiguously 'official' worship, since 1985 when Nakasone Yasuhiro provoked controversy by visiting on 15 August. In the intervening period, Hashimoto Ryūtarō had performed deliberately 'private' worship on his birthday (29 July 1996) and there was, of course, Prime Minister Miyazawa Kiichi 's 'secret' visit in November 1992.

The five national and three regional newspapers discussed below all made Koizumi's worship their top headline and the subject of an editorial on 14 August. These editorials expose many key themes within the Yasukuni debate in Japan.

---

4 *The Japan Times*, 'Koizumi wavering on plan to visit Yasukuni: Tanaka', 1 August 2001. Relations with South Korea and China were already strained following the Ministry of Education's approval in April 2001 of a controversial history textbook written by the nationalistic Japanese Society for History Textbook Reform.

5 Both statements are available online: <http://www.kantei.go.jp/foreign/koizumispeech/2001/0813danwa_e.html> and <http://www.mofa.go.jp/announce/press/pm/murayama/9508.html> (accessed 9 February 2007).

The 'Big Five' National Papers

Japan's national newspapers cover a broad range of political opinion and in terms of war stance (from progressive to nationalist) the 'big five' are the *Asahi, Mainichi, Nihon Keizai (Nikkei), Yomiuri* and *Sankei*.[6] At the rightwing is the nationalistic *Sankei* (circulation 2.02 million).[7] A *Sankei* editorial, 'A difficult decision, but a loss of principles', called Koizumi's concession to Chinese and Korean pressure 'regrettable'.[8] The *Sankei* had earlier welcomed Koizumi's pledge, and now said the concession would lose people's trust. The editorial also criticized China and Korea for using the Yasukuni issue as a diplomatic card and bemoaned that their demands would only grow louder. The *Yomiuri*'s stance on war issues is typically close to the government and its editorial, 'Koizumi's decision a wise one', was supportive.[9] The *Yomiuri* (circulation 10.21 million) praised Koizumi's 'clever political stratagem' and said 'it is basically a domestic matter as to when and how country's leader [sic.] offers prayers to the war dead based on the traditions and customs of that country. Other countries have no right to interfere.' The *Yomiuri* continued that it was 'unfortunate that the Japanese people themselves are divided over the issue' and it is 'natural for national leaders to pay their respects to those who made the supreme sacrifice defending their countries'. However, the *Yomiuri* also said it was 'worth studying' the establishment of a new non-religious memorial where even foreign leaders could pay their respects.

Japan's business broadsheet, the *Nihon keizai shinbun* (*Nikkei*, circulation 3.07 million), tends to carry fewer war-related articles than

6 Seaton, *Japan's Contested war memories*, ch. 4, 'Reporting the "Comfort Women" issue'.

7 Circulations are for July-December 2001: Asahi shinbunsha, *Japan almanac*, p. 244.

8 *Sankei Shinbun*, 'Kujū no ketsudan da ga shin o ushinau', 14 August 2001.

9 *The Daily Yomiuri*, 'Koizumi's decision a wise one', 14 August 2001. All analysis is based on Japanese-language papers and most translations are the author's. However, this is the *Yomiuri*'s translation.

the other broadsheets, and is slightly to the left of the government on war issues. While many *Nikkei* readers in the business world are LDP supporters or conservative, they also have much to lose economically through any 'history issue'-induced deterioration in Japan's relations with Asian neighbours. The *Nikkei* editorial, 'Worship on 13th: the Yasukuni compromise', focused initially on how that compromise would satisfy neither supporters nor opponents of official worship.[10] The worship was 'official', the *Nikkei* concluded, from Koizumi's own statement that being prime minister was a 24-hour-a-day job. But the newspaper's ultimate concern lay with Japan's relations in Asia and warned that Koizumi, as the person most responsible for maintaining friendly ties, will have committed a grave 'sin' (*tsumi*), if diplomatic relations and the national interest were damaged. The paper urged Koizumi to seek the understanding of its neighbours as soon as possible.

In contrast to the *Nikkei*'s avoidance of clear support or condemnation, the *Mainichi* (circulation 3.95 million) criticized Koizumi. The editorial, 'The tough part starts now', argued that the concession over the date would 'not satisfy domestic and international criticism', Koizumi's communiqué was 'insufficient', and his worship could not be in the national interest.[11] Koizumi had not clearly stated his reasons for worshipping, and his actions seemed inconsistent with his statement of remorse for the suffering caused by Japanese militarism. The *Mainichi* concluded that Koizumi had a responsibility to rebuild friendly ties with Asian neighbours. Finally, the *Asahi* (circulation 8.29 million) was the most critical. Its editorial, 'Is this the result of careful consideration?', questioned the legality of Yasukuni worship because of the constitutional separation of religion and state.[12] The *Asahi* also criticized Yasukuni's supporting role in militarism as 'the

10 *Nihon Keizai Shinbun*, 'Dakkyō no sue no Yasukuni jinja "13-nichi no sanpai"', 14 August 2001.

11 *Mainichi Shinbun*, 'Taihen na no wa kore kara da', 14 August 2001.

12 *Asahi/International Herald Tribune*, 'Koizumi's thoughtless visit to shrine shatters trust in Japan', 15 August 2001.

centerpiece of state Shinto' and accused Koizumi of 'fail[ing] to give sufficient consideration' to '[p]eople in neighboring countries devastated by military Japan's aggression and colonization [who] still suffer from the wounds inflicted at that time'. Koizumi's peace pledge and communiqué expressing remorse merely 'left the impression' of a 'double standard'.

The Regional Press

Japan also has a flourishing regional press. Strong regional identities, particular war experiences (such as air raids or the conduct of a local battalion), and the relative comfort of remembering 'local victimhood' rather than 'national aggression' all make regional war memories particularly important in Japan.[13] The stances of regional papers can be categorized in terms of which national broadsheet they mirror most closely.[14]

Close in stance to the *Asahi* was the *Okinawa Times* (circulation 204,000). The high civilian death toll during the Battle for Okinawa and the belief among many Okinawans that they were used as sacrificial pawns to save 'Japan proper' has led to widespread antipathy towards the conservative Tokyo elite.[15] Ishihara Masaie argues that most Okinawans reject the conservatism of the Japan Society for the War Bereaved.[16] Unsurprisingly, therefore, the *Okinawa Times* condemned Koizumi's worship.[17] The editorial, 'Rethink the way you mourn', compared Koizumi's statement of remorse for the suffering caused in Asia with the nationalistic version of war history in Yūshūkan (the museum in the grounds of Yasukuni Shrine) and

13 Seaton, *Japan's Contested War Memories*, ch. 8.

14 Sankei shinbun ronsetsu iinshitsu, *Shasetsu no daikenkyū*, pp.101-2.

15 For example Ōta, *Okinawa*, pp.48-50.

16 Ishihara, 'Memories of war and Okinawa', p.88. Japan Society for War Bereaved has campaigned for official Yasukuni worship and is a prominent vote-gatherer for the LDP.

17 Circulations are for 2002: Nihon shinbun kyōkai, *Zenkoku shinbun gaido*.

called them 'completely incompatible'.[18] The *Okinawa Times* called upon Koizumi to be conscious of Japan's responsibility toward Asia.

By contrast, the stance of the *Hokkoku Shinbun* (circulation 332,000) from the Ishikawa region was to the right of the *Yomiuri*. Conservatives and nationalists there like to portray Yasukuni worship as 'natural' (*atarimae* or *tōzen*) given Japanese traditional values and culture, and conservative approaches to the war fit with the Ishikawa region's wider identity. Also important is the participation of local soldiers in the Nanking massacre.[19] This may incline local commemorations and politically-powerful veterans' associations towards nationalistic denial of Japanese guilt. The *Hokkoku shinbun*'s editorial, 'An understandable tough political decision', supported Koizumi's worship: 'People who gave their lives for the state should be officially commemorated. It is an important role and obligation of the state. Many citizens want to offer their respect and gratitude to the war dead, too.'[20] The editorial avoided discussion of war responsibility, questioned the justness of the Tokyo trials and dismissed foreign interference. The paper insisted it would be unconstitutional for politicians to ask Yasukuni shrine to remove the Class A war criminals from its pantheon or enshrine them separately elsewhere. Nevertheless, the paper concluded that the creation of a new non-religious site would 'probably be most desirable'.

The *Chūnichi shinbun* (circulation 2.74 million) is the paper for the Chūbu region around Nagoya, one of Japan's commercial and industrial heartlands. This may help explain why the *Chūnichi* was close in stance to the *Nikkei* in expressing concerns about the economic fallout from Koizumi's worship. The editorial, 'Yasukuni causes large ripples', began 'We do not want this commotion again'.[21] The rip-

18 *Okinawa Times*, 'Tsuitō no arikata o minaose', 14 August 2001.

19 The NHK documentary *Nicchū sensō, naze sensō wa kakudai shita no ka* (13 August 2006) introduced local battalion documents recording the executions of over 6,000 Chinese in Nanking.

20 *Hokkoku shinbun*, 'Rikai dekiru kuchū no seiji ketsudan', 14 August 2001.

21 *Chūnichi shinbun*, '"Yasukuni" wa hamon ga ōkii', 14 August 2001.

ples referred to included the constitutional issue, Yasukuni's role in militarism, and the desire of many families to mourn quietly. Like many papers, the *Chūnichi* called for national debate concerning the establishment of a new non-religious site or an expanded role for the military cemetery at Chidorigafuji.

These editorials disclose many of the basic arguments that make up the 'Yasukuni problem'. Progressives typically raise Yasukuni's role in militarism, war responsibility and the constitutional separation of religion and state as reasons for opposing official worship; conservatives cite the obligation to commemorate those who sacrificed their lives for the nation and reject international interference; pragmatists less ideologically involved in war debates tend to focus on more neutral 'concerns', such as the effects of Yasukuni worship on relations with Asian neighbours. Despite these divisions, a conspicuous point of unity across the press (with the notable exception of the *Sankei*) was the call for a new non-religious commemorative site to replace Yasukuni. However, as the next section discusses, the proposal has faced stiff opposition from both nationalist and progressive wings of the Yasukuni debate.

Opposition to a New Non-religious Site

The proposal for a new non-religious commemorative site to replace or complement Yasukuni shrine formally entered the cabinet agenda in 2002 when an advisory group headed by Chief Cabinet Secretary Fukuda Yasuo recommended such a new structure should be established. The new site, it was argued, would resolve the constitutional issue of state commemoration at Yasukuni violating the separation of state and religion, diffuse the row over the enshrinement of the Class A war criminals, and reassure the Chinese and Koreans while still allowing official mourning of the war dead. However, the idea then stalled due to opposition from the right wings of the LDP and the Japan Society for War Bereaved.[22] Koizumi commented that 'no

22 Although it is a fact that sections of both the LDP and War Bereaved Society support the non-religious site: see Breen, 'The dead and the living in

facility can serve as a substitute for Yasukuni Shrine' and in June 2005 Chief Cabinet Secretary Hosoda Hiroyuki admitted the proposal had been 'virtually shelved'.[23] A cross-party group of 130 LDP politicians and MPs from Kōmeitō and the opposition Democratic Party of Japan (DPJ) was formed in October 2005 to revitalize the idea, but the proposal never got off the ground during Koizumi's tenure.[24]

Nationalist criticisms of the proposed new site can be found in rightwing publications. One principal objection relates to 'traditional' Japanese practices of remembering the dead. Yasukuni Shrine's website explains:

> From ancient times the people of Japan believed that the *mitama* (spirit) of the deceased remained upon the land to be celebrated by their descendants. It was believed that the *mitama* of the deceased would watch over the good fortune of their descendants together with the ancestral *kami*.[25]

Spirits are celebrated in a particular location, which for fallen soldiers means Yasukuni shrine. Nationalist manga artist Kobayashi Yoshinori dismissed the proposed new site in his characteristically colourful vernacular:

> If the spirits of the dead aren't there, it doesn't matter how impressive the newly built thing is, it'll be just a lump of rock or whatever. The spirits of the war dead are at Yasukuni. Everyone died saying 'Let's meet at Yasukuni'. You can say to the war dead, 'We've made this *sooo* beautiful, big new facility, and it's non-religious so the Chinese and South Korean presidents will also come here', but not a single spirit will move over to the new memorial.[26]

Less sarcastic but equally forthright arguments appear in rightwing 'opinion magazines'. In a special edition of *Seiron* in August 2003 about Yasukuni shrine, Nakanishi Terumasa dismissed the proposed

---

the land of peace', p. 86 and 'A Yasukuni genealogy', in this volume.

23 *Japan Times*, 'Koizumi nixes Yasukuni replacement', 18 June 2005.

24 *Japan Times*, 'Yasukuni impasse cracking', 28 November 2005.

25 Yasukuni Shrine: <http://www.yasukuni.or.jp/english/> (accessed 5 February 2007).

26 Kobayashi, *Yasukuni-ron*, p. 25.

non-religious site as 'lacking humanity'. All countries commemorate their war dead in typically religious fashion, he argued, citing how soldiers are honoured in churches in the United Kingdom. It goes against human nature to commemorate the dead divorced from religion: atheist commemoration is merely Marxist revolutionary thought, Nakanishi argued.[27] Nationalistic support for Yasukuni worship is deeply rooted in spirituality, belief and emotion. The *Seiron* special gives numerous insights into the roots of these emotions. There are 40 pages of letters and poems written by soldiers expressing love to their families before they died.[28] These historical documents played an important part in Koizumi's decision to worship. Before becoming prime minister he was famously seen crying while reading final letters from kamikaze pilots to their families at the Peace Museum for Kamikaze Pilots in Chiran, southern Kyūshū.[29] Other essays focused on military horses, dogs and pigeons or the sufferings of the 'maidens of Yasukuni' (nurses, including schoolgirls, in the Himeyuri Corps in Okinawa); they had an intentional sentimental quality to them as they dwelt on the nobility of self-sacrifice, the suffering of innocents, or idealized feminine virtues.[30] Other contributors, like Nakanishi, whose uncle died in Burma, chose to discuss Yasukuni in the context of the family and love for the fallen family member.[31] In sum, the *Seiron* special revealed the construction of the emotional bonds between nationalism and Yasukuni shrine. The nation as family, the emperor as a father to his children the people, Yasukuni as a spiritual home, self-sacrifice for the nation as the protector of one's family, ancestor worship as integral to Japanese culture: these are the core elements of nationalist and Yasukuni doctrine. Takahashi Tetsuya, the leading progressive intellectual currently writing on the Yasukuni issue, captures this essence in his phrase the 'nation as a

27 Nakanishi, 'Yasukuni jinja to nihonjin no seishin', pp. 35-6.

28 *Seiron*, pp. 44-83.

29 Kobayashi, *Yasukuni-ron*, p. 8.

30 *Seiron*, pp. 314-21; pp. 328-42.

31 Nakanishi, 'Yasukuni jinja to nihonjin no seishin', p. 34.

religion'.[32] For believers, a new non-religious site is a blasphemous anathema.

Both nationalists and progressives consider war responsibility issues important in their reservations concerning the non-religious memorial. Nationalists bemoan the 'injustice' suffered by the 'so-called Class A war criminals' at the Tokyo trials and laud the dissenting judgement of Indian Justice Radhabinod Pal.[33] In other words, nationalists view the convictions of the 'so-called Class A war criminals' as problematic, not their enshrinement or commemoration by the state. Takahashi argues that the reduction of the Yasukuni issue to the war responsibility of the Class A war criminals disregards wider responsibility issues.[34] He argues that removing the Class A war criminals, as has been discussed periodically since 1985, implicitly disregards the responsibility of ordinary soldiers and B and C Class war criminals, who committed atrocities across Asia. The establishment of a non-religious site might be less controversial in constitutional terms, but it would hardly resolve the problem of official commemoration of soldiers who committed atrocities.[35] A new site would inherit the role of Yasukuni shrine in persuading soldiers to offer their lives to the state through the promise of state-sponsored honour and respect. '[A]s long as this mechanism is in effect and is accompanied by the rhetoric of "sacrifice," any "non-religious site of national mourning" would nonetheless produce a "national spirit" that supports war.' Takahashi adds: 'One of the reasons why the movement to establish a "new national site of mourning" has grown noticeably in contemporary Japan is that it is expected a new generation of "fallen soldiers" will be produced'.[36]

---

32 Takahashi, 'Nation and sacrifice', p.41.

33 *Asahi Shinbun,* 'Rekishi to mukiau: dai 1-bu, Tōkyō saiban 60-nen', 1 May 2006.

34 See Takahashi's chapter in this volume.

35 Takahashi, 'Nation and sacrifice', pp. 34-6.

36 Ibid.', p. 41.

The draft proposals submitted by a specially convened Committee to Consider the State of Sites such as Cenotaphs to Mourn the Dead and Pray for Peace indicated the new site's founding philosophy would have to include the rhetoric of sacrifice. Unlike Yasukuni, this new site would mourn not just Japanese soldiers but all war dead, civilian and military, across Asia. But, Tanaka Nobumasa, a well-known freelance journalist argues:

> To lump together both the Japanese dead and their victims from the Sino-Japanese war and the Asia-Pacific War, wars of aggression—and to name them 'sacred dead' who built Japan's 'peace/prosperity' - leaves unaddressed the clarification of war guilt and the payment of war compensation.[37]

Many Korean, Taiwanese, Okinawan, not to mention some Japanese, families have demanded the removal from the Yasukuni pantheon of the spirits of relatives who died fighting for Japan, but their demands have been rejected by Yasukuni shrine authorities.[38] The new memorial would commemorate non-Japanese victims without any consultation with or consideration for the feelings of those victims or their descendants. For Tanaka the very non-religious nature of the proposed new site is questionable: 'The frequent use of the word "praying" (*kinen*) [in the draft 'Statement of Ideals'] is evidence that the national site for mourning, supposedly a non-religious site, may become a "new national Yasukuni".'[39] In sum, for progressives like Takahashi and Tanaka, the proposed new memorial hardly represents a solution to the key issues concerning the commemoration of the war dead.[40] The debate about a possible new site exposes the more general emotional—rational dichotomy in Japanese war commemoration. Nationalists' emotional appeals to Japanese identity, traditions and pride, and rejection of external interference insist on

37 Tanaka, 'Yasukuni shrine, Japanese nationalism, and the Constitution'.

38 Takahashi, 'The national politics of the Yasukuni shrine', pp. 177-8.

39 Tanaka, 'Yasukuni Shrine, Japanese Nationalism, and the Constitution'. The report's final text is available at: <http://www.kantei.go.jp/jp/singi/tuitou/kettei/021224houkoku.pdf> (accessed 9 April 2007).

40 For an alternative view, see the chapter by Breen in this volume.

the right of an exclusive, quasi-religious commemorative community to do as it wishes. By contrast, progressives' arguments about the problematic nature of any official commemoration of the war dead may resonate rationally and internationally, but the dispassionate nature of logical reasoning risks alienating significant sections of the Japanese public.

The opinions of 'middle Japan' inevitably incorporate a balance of the rational and emotional. But consistency is elusive: the emotional (identification as Japanese, family bonds, national pride) sits uncomfortably with the rational (20 million people killed across Asia is not something to celebrate). Nevertheless, the mainstream view is that whatever the rights and wrongs of the cause, the state has a duty to remember those who gave their lives for the state. Yasukuni is a contested commemorative site because it asserts a particular view of history and therefore cannot generate unity in a nation divided over the legacy of Japanese war responsibility. Any new site that imposed an alternative historical view would face the same problems. But if the site let individuals decide for themselves whether the war dead should be honoured, respected, mourned, apologized to or even condemned, its very function as a 'national' site would be undermined.

The Osaka High Court Ruling, September 2005

Koizumi's pledge was to worship on 15 August. Even as his worship got further removed from the symbolic war-end anniversary: 21 April 2002, 14 January 2003 and 1 January 2004, he was still fulfilling the second part of his pledge, to worship every year. The hiatus between his fourth visit and his fifth on 17 October 2005 was the longest at twenty-two months. There were domestic reasons for this. In April 2005, violent anti-Japanese demonstrations erupted in China which would have made worshipping on 15 August 2005 explosive. But ultimately other aspects of Koizumi's political agenda overtook Yasukuni. Koizumi called a snap poll on 8 August and the possibility of Yasukuni worship on 15 August was eliminated by election fever.

Koizumi's reduction of the 11 September 2005 election into a 'back me or sack me' referendum on postal privatization was a masterstroke. The rebels were expelled from the LDP and some lost their seats to 'assassin' candidates loyal to Koizumi's reform programme. The LDP won the election with an increased majority. Koizumi had never been politically stronger, but still had to decide when he could worship at Yasukuni in such a sensitive anniversary year. Then came another blow: the Osaka High Court ruled on 30 September that his Yasukuni worship was unconstitutional.

One of the primary aims of the proposed non-religious memorial discussed earlier was to avoid violating the Constitution, Article 20 of which guarantees the separation of religion and the state. Furthermore, Article 89 prohibits the use of public money in offerings made at religious institutions. However, the Constitution also guarantees individual religious freedom. The issue, therefore, centres on whether a prime minister is acting in a private or official capacity when worshipping at Yasukuni shrine.[41] Issues at stake include use of government or private vehicles to reach the shrine; payment for flowers as offerings out of personal income or public funds; 'worship' using the Shintō ritual of two bows, two claps and one bow or an abbreviated, and therefore 'non-religious' form; and statements prime ministers have made about the status of their worship. Filing lawsuits against officials who worship at Yasukuni shrine has been a feature of the anti-Yasukuni movement since the 1960s. Most cases have resulted in either no decision or rejection of the plaintiffs' case,[42] but the Osaka High Court's 2005 ruling overturned on appeal a previous defeat for the plaintiffs and came a day after the Tokyo High Court rejected a similar suit.[43] Unconstitutional rulings are the exception rather than the rule, so they are 'controversial' and generate most media attention.

41 Hardacre, *Shinto and the state*, p. 144.

42 See Tanaka, *Yasukuni no sengoshi*, p. 249.

43 *Japan Times*, 'Koizumi's Yasukuni trips are ruled unconstitutional', 1 October 2005.

The national broadsheets were split over the Osaka High Court ruling, and an earlier ruling in the Fukuoka District Court on 7 April 2004. The *Sankei* called both rulings 'distorted' and urged Koizumi to continue his worship.[44] The *Yomiuri* took a similar line: it asked whether the cabinet's traditional *hatsumōde* (New Year Shrine visit) to the Ise shrines was now going to be considered unconstitutional and urged the courts to take into account 'cultural norms' when making judgements. While accepting that a variety of opinions existed regarding Yasukuni worship, it rejected politically motivated lawsuits through the courts.[45] The other three papers treated the judgements as justification for their reservations or opposition expressed since 2001. The *Asahi* was most direct: its editorial was titled 'Time to stop worshipping'.[46] The *Mainichi* focused more on the 'warning from the judiciary' to Koizumi, while the *Nikkei* wanted to 'take the ruling seriously'.[47]

In sum, courts could not agree whether Koizumi's worship was constitutional, the papers were split over whether 'unconstitutional' rulings were valid, and international observers showed little interest in constitutional minutiae. The man in the middle of the storm, Koizumi Junichirō, was characteristically phlegmatic: 'I do not think paying homage at Yasukuni violates the Constitution,' Koizumi told the House of Representatives Budget Committee. 'I am not paying visits as an official duty. I have difficulty in understanding why they violate the Constitution'.[48] He vowed to continue his worship. Speculation grew concerning his next move, but when

---

44 *Sankei Shinbun*, 'Hanrei o kyokkai shita iken hanketsu', 8 April 2004; 'Nejire hanketsu ni kōsokuryoku nashi', 1 October 2005.

45 *Yomiuri Shinbun*, 'Ise jingū sanpai mo iken ni naru no ka', 8 April 2004; 'Kiwamete gimon no ōi "iken" hanketsu', 1 October 2005.

46 *Asahi Shinbun*, 'Sanpai o yameru shiodoki da', 1 October 2005.

47 *Mainichi Shinbun*, 'Iken hanketsu wa shihōfu no keikoku da', 1 October 2005; *Nihon Keizai Shinbun*, 'Omoku uketometai Yasukuni sanpai iken no hanketsu', 1 October 2005.

48 *Japan Times*, 'Koizumi's Yasukuni trips are ruled unconstitutional', 1 October 2005.

that move came on 17 October it was clear the Osaka High Court ruling *had* affected his thinking.

17 October 2005 on Japanese Television News

Yasukuni's Great Rites of Spring and Autumn are key dates in the shrine's calendar, and were the occasions for the majority of prime ministerial visits in the post-war period; 17 October 2005 was the first day of the Great Autumn Rite. Following the public announcement of his visit at about 8 am, there was a buzz of activity at the shrine. Police were there in force; helicopters circled overhead; the press was everywhere. Koizumi's black saloon arrived at 10:10 am and stopped near the second torii gate. The prime minister got out dressed in a grey suit with a pale blue tie. Despite the light rain, he did not use an umbrella. Surrounded by secret service agents, he strode through the main gate to the worship hall. There he stopped, reached into his pocket and took out a coin, which he threw into the offering box. He clasped his hands in prayer, bowed his head and closed his eyes. Thirty-five seconds passed before he opened his eyes, and about-turned and headed back to his car. His worship had taken under five minutes. That evening, all of the major television news

Channel (Tokyo)	Channel (affiliated newspaper)	Programme	Schedule	Duration
10	TV Asahi (*Asahi Shinbun*)	*Hōdō Station (Broadcast station)*	21:54 – 23:10	26 mins.
1	NHK-General (-)	*News 10*	22:00 – 23:00	24 mins.
6	TBS (*Mainichi shinbun)*	*Chikushi Tetsuya's news 23*	22:54 – 23:55	44 mins.
4	Nippon Television (*Yomiuri shinbun*)	*Kyōno dekigoto (Today's events)*	23:09 – 23:40	10 mins.
8	Fuji Television (*Sankei shinbun*)	*News Japan*	23:45 – 24:10	14 mins.

Table 1. Five news programmes coverage of Koizumi's 17 October 2005 worship.

programmes on terrestrial television made Koizumi's worship their top story. As shown in Table 1, five of the flagship evening news bulletins had a total of 118 minutes of coverage.

The five programmes tabulated above followed some basic practices of Japanese television journalism. Presenters and reporters gave primarily agreed facts, while politicians, 'people in the street' or pundits added opinion via sound-bites or interviews. If pundits or 'people in the street' took sides, the channels tended to use a 'two for, two against' format to maintain reporting balance. Single experts asked for commentary presented an image of learned neutrality. Commentary added by presenters was carefully scripted and expressed a relatively mainstream opinion. All five programmes dwelt on the following:

1) Images of Koizumi's worship: his walk to the worship hall; his offering of a coin and prayer; and his post-worship news conference when he explained his motives.
2) Reaction from various politicians: Kanzaki Takenori of Kōmeitō called the worship 'regrettable'; Koga Makoto of the Japan Society of the War Bereaved expressed his gratitude; Takebe Tsutomu, Secretary General of the LDP, stressed the worship's private nature and said he respected the Prime Minister's decision; Maehara Seiji, President of the Democratic Party of Japan, dismissed the private—public distinction and criticized worship at a site where war criminals are enshrined.
3) The 'deliberately private' nature of Koizumi's worship: the worship route (walking up to the public worship hall rather than being taken by car to the worshipper's entrance and then proceeding to the main sanctuary); his clothing (a suit and tie rather than ceremonial clothes); his offering of one coin rather than his customary 30,000 yen for flowers; not signing his name in the visitor's book; and not being accompanied by any Yasukuni representative.
4) The Constitutional aspect: the influence of the Osaka High Court ruling on the 'deliberately private' nature of worship.

5) Chinese and Korean reaction: diplomatic protests, live reports from correspondents in Beijing and Seoul, and images of small but angry demonstrations outside the Japanese embassies in both capitals.

Despite these common components, the television channels had distinctive approaches.[49] NHK's public broadcasting charter obliges it to be politically neutral. Consequently, its round-up of political reaction included the smaller parties: Fukushima Mizuho of the Socialist Party angrily asking, 'What is he doing, what about views in Asia?', and Shii Kazuo of the Communist Party saying that after his election victory Koizumi feels he can do anything. The commercial channels ignored these parties with only a handful of seats. Furthermore, NHK reporters all followed carefully-worded scripts (even in 'interviews' with studio presenters) and the guest pundit on *News 10*, diplomatic analyst Okamoto Yukio, focused on neutral 'concerns' about what would happen next. The constitutional issue and the proposed non-religious site also featured. NHK epitomizes self-consciously neutral, carefully-scripted, mainstream television journalism.

TV Asahi's *Hōdō station* adopts an infotainment approach to news. Presenter Furutachi Ichirō began by enthusing about an exciting Pacific League playoff game before almost apologetically saying: 'But more on the baseball later, let's start with Koizumi's Yasukuni shrine worship.' Koizumi's worship route was shown using a colourful cartoon map of Yasukuni shrine and caricature of Koizumi; there was a segment about souvenir vendors in Yasukuni shrine's precinct selling 'Koizumi manjū' (sweet bean cakes), and benefiting from his worship. But in line with the stance of its related newspaper, *Hōdō station* also focused on the constitutional issue, and provided commentary from a Shintō scholar. Regular studio commentator Katō Chihiro from the *Asahi* spoke in uncomplimentary tones about Koizumi's 'performance' and his failure to keep his pledge, while Furutachi concluded *Hōdō station*'s twenty-six minutes of coverage with a dismissive 'he's just given another trump card to neighbouring countries'.

---

49 See also Seaton, *Japan's contested war memories*, ch. 5.

News 23 on TBS is the most self-consciously highbrow evening news programme: presenter Chikushi Tetsuya specializes in long interviews set against artistic studio backgrounds. On 17 October, *News 23* was extended and devoted forty-four minutes to Koizumi's Yasukuni worship. The key feature was a panel discussion with three guests: Tasei Yasuhiro of the *Nikkei shinbun*, diplomatic analyst Okamoto Yukio, and Chinese scholar Ye Qianrong of Tōkai University. Chikushi raised an issue and all three guests gave their thoughts in turn.[50] The combination of two 'analysts rather than advocates' (Tasei and Okamoto), a Chinese critic, and Chikushi's well-documented progressivism on war issues inclined the discussion towards calm but critical evaluation of Koizumi's visit. The programme also introduced specialist angles, such as archive footage of Nakasone's 1985 worship, criticism by Yasukuni shrine's head priest of his 'rude' worship that curtailed the full Shintō ritual, and a report about *Junkoku shichishi no haka*, the cemetery, that is, where the cremated remains of the seven executed Class A war criminals are kept. *Today's events* on Nippon television gave the least coverage at only ten minutes. It is close to NHK news in style: reserved, carefully scripted, and with a focus on official news. Its reporting was limited to images of Koizumi crying while reading the last letters of kamikaze in Chiran and comments from Tōjō Yūko, granddaughter of wartime prime minister Tōjō Hideki. Tōjō welcomed the prime minister's worship, but pressed Koizumi to fulfil his pledge by worshipping officially on 15 August. Presenter Oguri Izumi ended the programme by citing a diplomat who said Japan must keep explaining to China and Korea, and she commented that Koizumi understood his private worship would have an effect and that mending relations would take time.

Finally, *News Japan* on Fuji Television had the clearest example of the 'two for, two against' format that television channels use to

50 Chikushi took one opportunity to express his own views: China and Korea are important friends of Japan, and given that the events/people being commemorated at Yasukuni occurred in other countries, Koizumi's comments that Yasukuni worship was an internal matter for Japanese people were extremely debatable.

maintain 'objectivity'. Four experts, Sasegawa Norikatsu of Meiji University (constitutional law, against), Hasegawa Michiko of Saitama University (philosophy, for), Arai Ken of Komazawa University (religion, against) and Ushio Masato, a Christian freelance pundit (for), discussed three points:

1) The constitutional issue: Hasegawa said the problem could be solved by changing the Constitution and removing the provision for the separation of religion and state, and questioned how commemoration could be divorced from religion, citing religious war commemorations in the UK. Sasegawa said changing the constitution, whether revoking the 'renunciation of war' clause or removing constitutional impediments to Yasukuni worship, will inevitably produce more war dead.
2) The diplomatic issue: Ushio said a pledge had been made and Koizumi should not give in to international pressure. Sasegawa used a common saying among progressives: 'People remember more when their foot has been trodden on than when they tread on the feet of others.' Japan should not forget this, he added.
3) How to mourn the dead: Hasegawa said it was normal to mourn those who died defending their country. Arai noted how only soldiers were enshrined, not civilians. Ushio, who was introduced as a Christian, added it was very difficult to mourn the dead divorced from religion; he supported commemoration at a Shintō shrine).

A studio analyst added that Yasukuni worship could be thought of as integral to Koizumi's foreign policy given that this was his fifth worship. Presenter Matsumoto Masaya concluded by saying he hoped China and Korea would take the news calmly, and there could be forward-looking diplomatic relations.

The *News Japan* exchange illustrates why television is the best medium for observing the competing opinions regarding Yasukuni worship going 'head-to-head'. The audio-visual format permits dialogue as well as the 'monologues' predominant in newspapers and publishing. Television as a verbal genre is somewhat limited: time constraints force commentators and politicians to speak in soundbites and distill their arguments. But this is offset by the richness of visual images. The most-watched television news programmes on 17 October were *Hōdō station* (15.5 per cent) and Fuji Television's early evening bulletin *Super news* (13.3 per cent).[51] These ratings constitute a much greater outreach than the highest-selling newspaper, the *Yomiuri*, or publications with readerships in the thousands. The nature of television coverage, particularly the 'arguments for and against' format of most programmes, is central to understanding Japanese public opinion concerning the Yasukuni issue.

A Nation Divided

When Koizumi first pledged to worship at Yasukuni in 2001, opinion poll data indicated that more people supported than opposed his proposed visit: according to an NTV poll nearly 50 per cent supported and under 40 per cent opposed, while a *Yomiuri* poll had 40 per cent supporting and 34 per cent opposed.[52] However, by October 2005, just before Koizumi's fifth worship, an NHK poll pointed to an even split: 43 per cent wanted Koizumi to continue his worship; 45 per cent wanted him to stop.[53] By 2006, three polls indicated 53-7 per cent opposed further worship by Koizumi.[54] The longer term erosion in Japanese public support for official Yasukuni worship is also evident in a poll taken in September 1985, just after Nakasone's worship: then 52 per cent supported 'official worship' while only 25 per cent opposed.[55]

51 Viewing ratings are available from Video Research Ltd. Available online: <http://www.videor.co.jp/index.htm>.

52 *The Independent* 'Koizumi pays tribute to Japan's war dead, provoking fury across Asia', 14 August 2001; Yomiuri shinbunsha yoron chōsa bu, *Nihon no yoron,* 461.

53 NHK, *News 10*, 17 October 2005.

54 BBC online, 'Japanese "oppose PM shrine trips"', 24 July 2006; *Asahi/ International Herald Tribune*, 'Editorial: Koizumi's Yasukuni visit', 17 August 2006.

55 Yomiuri shinbunsha yoron chōsa bu, *Nihon no yoron,* 461.

In the international media and academy, Koizumi's annual Yasukuni worship was often linked to discussion of 'rising nationalism' in Japan. Any discussion of 'rising nationalism' must consider these trends in public opinion concerning Yasukuni. It is true that since the 1990s Japanese nationalists have mounted prominent campaigns, mobilized their supporters and won over many in the younger generations. Koizumi's worship also influenced greater numbers of ordinary people to visit Yasukuni. Nevertheless, nationalist voices remain a minority, albeit a vocal and politically powerful one. In a 2007 *Asahi* newspaper poll about patriotism that asked how Japan should respond to 'Japanese colonial rule and aggression in Asia', 32 per cent answered 'much remorse (*hansei*) is necessary', 53 per cent said 'some remorse is necessary', while the answers 'not much remorse' and 'no remorse' accounted for nine and two per cent respectively.[56] The historical views expressed in Yasukuni's war museum, the Yushukan, are closest to the 'no remorse necessary' answer and are clearly a fringe position.

The key to explaining eroding support for Yasukuni worship is a split among conservatives into pragmatists and hardliners caused by deteriorating relations with neighbouring countries. Pragmatists have called for restraint, arguing that, however desirable the official mourning of the war dead, the wider national interest must take precedence. Meanwhile, hardliners insist on Yasukuni worship regardless of the consequences. In 2005-6 a number of media stories indicated the shift to pragmatism among conservatives. In June 2005 the *Yomiuri* newspaper surprised many by withdrawing its support for Koizumi's continued Yasukuni worship. An editorial on 4 June 2005 stated:

> Koizumi said Thursday at the House of Representatives that he understood the Class A war criminals, those found guilty at the International Military Tribunal for the Far East [...] were war criminals. [...] If this is the case, then Koizumi should not visit Yasukuni shrine, which enshrines Class A war criminals along with other war dead.[57]

56 *Asahi Shinbun*, 'Nihon ni umarete "yokatta" 9-wari', 25 January 2007.

57 *Daily Yomiuri*, 'Govt must expedite new war memorial', 6 June 2005.

Wakamiya Yoshibumi of the *Asahi* was one surprised observer. In a transcribed conversation with *Yomiuri* editor Watanabe Tsuneo, Wakamiya stated:

I had come to believe the *Yomiuri* was in favour of the Yasukuni visits and, based on the editorials of the past several years, I felt the *Yomiuri* had moved excessively to the right, and that now there is very little difference between the Yomiuri and the *Sankei shinbun*. So I was very surprised by that editorial.[58]

Watanabe responded by saying he disagreed with the historical views expressed in the Yūshūkan museum and had warned Koizumi in 2001 about worshipping on 15 August. Given Watanabe's highly influential position as editor of Japan's largest-selling newspaper, his open withdrawal of support for Koizumi's worship was a body blow. A week later came another setback. The Japan Society for the War Bereaved called for 'more consideration' towards Asian neighbours. To have prime ministers paying homage at the shrine 'has been an ardent wish of the association and we appreciate it very much. … At the same time, however, it is most important that the spirits of the war dead rest in peace,' the group said. 'It is necessary to give consideration to neighboring countries and obtain their understanding'.[59]

The Society was not withdrawing its support for prime ministerial worship and President Koga Makoto subsequently welcomed Koizumi's 'deliberately private' worship later in the year, on 17 October. But, calls for 'consideration' were nevertheless a climb down from the Society's previous advocacy of official worship and state patronage for Yasukuni shrine.

Other powerful voices expressed concern at deteriorating relations with neighbouring countries in 2006. The economic fallout from the Yasukuni issue had featured prominently in the Japanese media, whether concerning Chinese boycotts of Japanese goods or attacks on Japanese restaurants in the riots in April 2005. The concerns of the business community were formalized in May 2006, when incom-

58 Wakamiya and Watanabe, 'Yomiuri and Asahi editors'.

59 *Japan Times,* 'War-dead families ask Koizumi to consider Asia', 12 June 2005.

ing chairman of the Japan Business Federation (*Nippon Keidanren*) Mitarai Fujio 'urged the government swiftly to resolve the nation's conflict with its Asian neighbours' and criticized 'Koizumi's lack of consideration of the consequences of his Yasukuni visits'.[60]

But perhaps the most damaging blow to public support for continued Yasukuni worship was a front-page scoop in the *Nikkei* on 20 July 2006: 'Enshrinement of Class A war criminals at Yasukuni: Emperor Hirohito's displeasure'.[61] Among the documents of former Imperial Household Agency grand steward Tomita Tomohiko, a reporter found a document (the 'Tomita memo') which suggested the enshrinement of Class A war criminals in 1978 was the reason why Emperor Hirohito stopped worshipping at Yasukuni (between 1945 and 1975 he had worshipped eight times). The *Nikkei*'s evening edition led with a follow-up story: Chief Cabinet Secretary Abe Shinzō had been grilled by journalists on how the memo would affect Koizumi's worship plans for 2006.[62] The implications were serious: if the emperor considered Yasukuni worship inappropriate, surely the prime minister should reconsider.[63]

The 'Tomita memo' episode is a microcosm of many themes within the Japanese media's treatment of the Yasukuni issue. The story started with a newspaper scoop. The *Nikkei*, like its rivals, is a business and uses scoops or exclusives to attract consumers. The timing was 'ideal': barely a month before Koizumi's last opportunity to fulfil his pledge before stepping down in September 2006. When a 'timely' story breaks with a 'new twist' on an already controversial topic, the rest of the media jumps on the bandwagon. This is indicative of the war's status as a 'current affairs issue' in Japan.

60 *Japan Times*, 'New Keidanren chief urges Asia diplomatic thaw', 25 May 2006.

61 *Nikkei Shinbun*, 'A-kyū senpan gōshi, Shōwa tennō ga fukaikan', 20 July 2006.

62 *Nikkei Shinbun* (evening edition), 'Shōwa tennō hatsugen memo ni hamon', 20 July 2006.

63 On this Tomita memo, see the chapter by Takahashi: and Breen 'A Yasukuni genealogy' in this volume.

The memo gave plenty for the media to debate. For example, TV Asahi's *Television till morning* (*Asa made terebi*, 28 July 2006) staged a marathon four-hour discussion about the Tomita memo. The programme, hosted by prominent political journalist Tahara Sōichirō, adopts a 'confrontational round-table debate' format and invited twelve panelists with diverse views.[64] Rightwing commentator Okazaki Hisahiko doubted the authenticity of the memo and criticized the *Nikkei* for its politically motivated scoop. He called for the media fuss about Yasukuni to stop so that the emperor could worship at Yasukuni shrine without hesitation.[65] Psychologist Kayama Rika thought it strange that the *Nikkei* had discussed the emperor's 'displeasure' (*fukaikan*) when that word did not appear in the original memo.[66] Progressive scholar Komori Yōichi, a leading figure in the 'save Article Nine' movement opposing constitutional reform, said that official commemoration of the war dead, either at Yasukuni or a new site, is unnecessary if Japan has truly renounced war. Mourning should be carried out privately, even at Yasukuni, if individuals prefer.[67] LDP parliamentarian Takemi Keizō welcomed the debate stimulated by the Tomita memo, DPJ parliamentarian Hosono Kōji said he wished the clock could be turned back to before the enshrinement of the Class A war criminals in 1978, while LDP parliamentarian Yamamoto Ichita said that Koizumi changing his pledge as a result of the Tomita memo constituted an unacceptably political role for the emperor.[68] This brief selection of arguments cannot do justice to the four hours of debate. But once again, the Japanese media had demonstrated why prime ministerial worship at Yasukuni shrine, like

64 Tahara also edits his own magazine, *Ofureko* ('Off the Record'). This section is based on an *Ofureko* special edition that contains a transcript of the programme and supplementary materials.

65 *Ofureko*, pp. 170-2.

66 Ibid., p. 173.

67 Ibid., pp. 183-4.

68 *Ofureko* pp. 191-6; pp. 200-2.

Japanese war memories in general, is too divisive an issue for a broad-based consensus to be easily found.

In the end, neither the Tomita memo nor the other media debates could dissuade Koizumi from fulfilling his pledge. Indeed, the lack of domestic consensus probably persuaded Koizumi to ignore all criticisms and follow his convictions. After his worship on 15 August 2006 the international fallout was somewhat muted. There was an air of resignation and the focus shifted to the question of who would succeed Koizumi. As widely expected, Abe Shinzō took over as prime minister after an LDP leadership election in which the candidates' Yasukuni worship plans were a key issue. It was somewhat ironic that Abe, who has a track record of Yasukuni worship and whose views are generally thought to be even more hawkish than Koizumi's, would be entrusted with mending ties with Asian neighbours. The end of Koizumi's tenure concluded a turbulent chapter in the history of the Yasukuni issue, but it did not take Japan any closer to a resolution. Practically speaking, given declining public support in Japan and the anger Yasukuni worship provokes in neighbouring countries, it is difficult to see how ongoing prime ministerial and particularly imperial Yasukuni worship could ever be part of any reconciliation process within East Asia. Any alternative national site faces concerted opposition from both nationalists loyal to Yasukuni and progressives skeptical about the motives of all official commemorations of the Japanese military. State reform of Yasukuni is impossible at present as government intervention in the shrine's affairs breaches the constitutional separation of religion and the state. Even then, Yasukuni shrine and its supporters would fiercely resist any government-imposed degradation of its status. With no resolution in sight, the Yasukuni issue is emblematic of how the struggles to remember and commemorate war history continue to divide both Japan and East Asia more than six decades after the end of the conflict.

BIBLIOGRAPHY

NEWS MEDIA

Asahi shinbun
Asahi/International Herald Tribune (online)
BBC (online)
Chūnichi shinbun
Daily Yomiuri (online)
Hokkaidō shinbun
Hokkoku shinbun
The Independent (UK)
Komei shinbun
The Japan Times (online)
Mainichi shinbun
Nihon keizai shinbun
Okinawa Times
Sankei shinbun
Ofureko (January 2007, special edn, *Shōwashi no karakuri*).
Seiron (August 2003, special edn, *Yasukuni to nihonjin no kokoro*).

BOOKS AND ARTICLES

(All Japanese books and articles are published in Tokyo unless otherwise stated.)

Abe Shinzō, 'Press conference by Prime Minister Abe Shinzō following his visit to China', 8 October 2006, available at http://www.kantei.go.jp/foreign/abespeech/2006/10/08chinapress_e.html.

——, and Noda Seiko, 'Seijika to shite "Yasukuni" o kangaeru', *Seiron*, August 2003.

Akazawa Shirō, *Yasukuni jinja*, Iwanami shoten, 2005.

Asahi shinbunsha, *Japan almanac 2003*, Tokyo: Asahi shinbunsha, 2002.

Bachman, David, 'New leaders, new foreign policymaking procedures?' in Lin Gang and Hu Xiaobo (eds), *China after Jiang*, Stanford, CA: Woodrow Wilson Center Press, 2003.

Breen, John, 'Ideologues, bureaucrats and priests: on Buddhism and Shinto in early Meiji Japan' in Breen, John and Mark Teeuwen eds. *Shinto in history: ways of the kami* Hawaii University Press, 2000.

——, 'The dead and the living in the land of peace: a sociology of the Yasukuni shrine', *Mortality* 9.1 (2004), pp. 76-93.

——, 'Pacific trauma: Yasukuni and the fetishised narrative of war', forthcoming in *Cipango*.

——, 'Yasukuni: rekishi kioku no keisei to sōshitsu', *Sekai* 756 (2006).

——, 'Yasukuni shrine: ritual and memory', *Japan Focus* 293 (2005).

Brower, Benjamin, 'The preserving machine', *History and Memory*, 2 (1999).

Bu Ping, 'Riben jingguo shenshe wenti de lishi kaocha', *KangRi zhanzheng yanjiu*, 4 (2001).

Connerton, Paul, *How Societies Remember*, Cambridge University Press, 1989.

Curtin, J. Sean, 'Koizumi could yet rain on China's parade', *Asia Times*, 8 September 2005, available at http://www.atimes.com.

Dower, John, *Embracing Defeat: Japan in the Wake of World War Two*, New York: W.W. Norton, 2000.

Eto Jun and Kobori Keiichirō (eds), *Shinban Yasukuni ronshu*, Kindai Shuppansha, 2004.

Fackler, Martin, 'Japanese court rules Premier's visits to war shrine illegal', *New York Times*, 1 October 2005 available at http://

www.nytimes.com/2005/10/01/international/asia/01japan.html

Foreign Press Center, Japan, 'Leaders of Japan and China meet for first time in 13 months', *Japan Brief*, 23 November 2004 available at http://www.fpcj.jp/mres/japanbrief/jb_523.html (last accessed 9 November 2005).

Gries, Peter Hays, 'China's "new thinking on Japan"' *China Quarterly*, 184 (2005).

Hardacre, Helen, *Shintō and the State, 1868-1988*, Princeton University Press, 1989.

Harootunian, Harry, 'Memory, mourning and national morality: Yasukuni shrine and the reunion of state and religion in postwar Japan' in Van den Veer, P. and Lehmann, H. (eds), *Religion and Nationalism in East Asia*, Princeton University Press, 1999.

Hata Ikuhiko, *Ianfu to senjō no sei*, Shinchōsha, 1999.

——, *Shōwashi no nazo o ou* (jō), Bunshun bunko, 2000.

Hattori Bushō, *Tokyo shin hanjōki*, Tokyo, 1874.

Hu Jintao, 'Hu Jintao zai jinian Zhongguo renmin kang Ri zhanzheng ji shijie fan faxisi zhanzheng shengli 60 zhounian dahuishang de jianghua', 3 September 2005, available at http://www.fmprc.gov.cn/chn/zxxx/t210209.htm.

Hughes, Chris R., 'Rivalry and Realpolitik: China-Japan Relations at the Start of the Twenty-first Century', *Japan Forum*, 2008 (forthcoming).

Inagaki Takeshi, 'Asahi, Kyōdō no kyōkasho henkō hōdō wa kuni no haji', *Shi* vol. 48 (2007).

Ishihara Masaie, 'Memories of war and Okinawa' in T. Fujitani, Geoffrey M. White and Lisa Yoneyama (eds), *Perilous Memories, the Asia-Pacific War(s)*, Durham, NC: Duke University Press 2001.

Itagaki Tadashi, 'Asahi Kyōdō no kyōkasho henkō hōdō wa kuni no haji', *Shi* vol.48 (2005).

——, *Yasukuni kōshiki sanpai no sōkatsu*, Tokyo: Tentensha, 2000.

Iwami Takao, 'Koizumi Yasukuni seisaku no kūkyo to meisō', *Chūō Kōron*, August 2005.

Jin Xide, 'Canbai, jiu nanqiu jingjie', *Shijie Zhishi*, 12 (2005).

Kades, Charles, 'The American role in revising Japan's imperial constitution', *The Political Science Quarterly*, 104, 2 (1989).

Kisa Yoshio, *'Sensō sekinin' to wa nanika; seisan sarenakatta doitsu no kako*, Chūkō Shinsho, 2001.

Kobayashi Yoshinori, *Yasukuni ron*, Tokyo: Gentōsha, 2005.

Kobori Keiichirō, 'Kaidai', *Yūshūkan zuroku*, Kindai shuppansha, 2004.

——, Ōhara Yasuo, *Yasukuni jinja o kangaeru*, Nihon seisaku senta-shuppan, 2004.

——, *Yasukuni jinja to Nihonjin*, PHP shinsho, 1998.

Kou Chunbao and Wei Hua, 'Qingguo shenshe – zhongri guanxi de yige pingjing' *Guoji guanxi xueyuan xuebao*, 3 (2004).

Kuriyama Takakazu, 'Reconciliation – challenges facing Japanese diplomacy', *Gaikō Foramu*, January 2006.

Lam, Peng Er, 'Japan's deteriorating ties with China: the Koizumi factor', *China: an International Journal*, 3, 2 (2005).

Li Delong (ed.), *Qiang'an Dongyou diary*, Wenjin Press, April 2006.

Lind, Jennifer, 'Sorry states: apologies in International Politics', paper prepared for annual meeting of the American Political Science Association, Washington, DC, 1- 4 September 2005, available at http://www.ssc.upenn.edu/~jlind/LindAPSA2005.pdf.

Matsumoto Ken'ichi, 'Yasukuni to iu nanmon no kai o saguru', *Chūō Kōron*, August 2005.

Matsuura Mitsunobu, *Ii kagen shiro! Nikkyōso*, PHP Research, 2003.

Megumi Ryūnosuke, *Tekihei o kyūjo seyo*, Sōshisha, 2006.

McGreevy, Andrew M., 'Arlington national cemetery and Yasukuni jinja: history, memory, and the sacred', *Japan Focus*, 2005.

Minear, Richard, *Victor's Justice*, Ann Arbor, MI: University of Michigan Press, 1971.

Nagoshi Futaranosuke (ed.), *Shōwa no sensō kinenkan*, Tendensha, 1999.

——, '"Shōwa junnansha" ni sasageru misa', *Yasukuni*, 2007.

Naitō Hatsuho, *Thunder Gods: the Kamikaze Pilots Tell Their Story*, Kōdansha International, 1989.

Nakanishi Terumasa, 'Yasukuni jinja to nihonjin no seishin', *Seiron*, August 2003 special edn, 32-43.

Nakasone Yasuhiro, 'Koizumi kun, gaikō kara popyu-rizumu o haijo shi nasai', *Chūō Kōron*, August 2005.

Nathan, Andrew G. and Bruce Gilley, *China's New Rulers: the Secret Files*, New York: New York Review of Books, 2003.

Nelson, John, 'Social Memory as Ritual Practice: Commemorating Spirits of the Military Dead at Yasukuni Shinto Shrine', *Journal of Asian Studies*, 62, 2 (2003).

Ni Yanshuo, 'Who is Doing the Threatening?' *Beijing Review*, 26 January 2006.

Nihon shinbun kyōkai, *Zenkoku shinbun gaido*, Tokyo: Nihon shinbun kyōkai, 2003.

O Sonfa, *Seikatsusha no Nihon tōchi jidai*, Sankōsha, 2000.

O'Brien, David M. and Yasuo Ohkoshi, *To Dream of Dreams: Religious Freedom and Constitutional Politics in Postwar Japan*, Honolulu: University of Hawai'i Press, 1996.

Ōhara Yasuo *Yasukuni Jinja e no jubaku o toku*, Shōgakkan Bunko, 2003.

——, *Yasukuni jinja: Yūshūkan no sekai, Fusōsha*, 2003.

Ohnuki Tierney, Emiko, *Kamikaze Diaries: Reflections of Japanese Student Soldiers*, University of Chicago Press, 2006.

Okamoto Yukio and Tanaka Akihiko, 'Hannichi Chūgoku ga ochiitta kiki', *Chūō Kōron*, June 2006.

Ōta Masahide, *Okinawa, sensō to heiwa*, Asahi bunko, 1996.

Prsyztup, James J., 'Japan-China relations: Ice breaks at the summit,' *Comparative Connections*, 15, January, 2007.

——, 'No end to history', *Comparative Connections*, July 2005 (available at http://www.csis.org.).

Pye, Michael, 'Religion and conflict in Japan with special reference to Shinto and Yasukuni shrine', *Diogenes*, 50, 3 (2003).

Ren Zhanjuan, 'Canbai qingguo shenshe yu zhongri guanxi zhong de lishiwenti' *Tianfu Xinlun*, 12 (2004).

Röling, B.V.A. and Cassese, A., *The Tokyo Trial and Beyond*, Cambridge: Polity Press, 1993.

Rose, Caroline, *Interpreting History in Sino-Japanese Relations: A Case Study in Political Decision-Making*, London: Routledge, 1998.

Saaler, Sven, *Politics, Memory and Public Opinion: The History Textbook Controversy and Japanese Society*, Munchen: Iudicum, 2005.

Saeki Sadamitsu, 'Kirisutosha wa 'Yasukuni' o katareru ka', in Eto Jun and Kobori Keiichirō (eds), *Shinban Yasukuni Ronshu*, Kindai Shuppansha, 2004.

Sakurai Yoshiko, *Mitsuyaku gaikō no daishō: ianfu mondai wa naze kojireta ka*, *Bungei Shunjū*, April, 1997.

Sankei shinbun ronsetsu iinshitsu, *Shasetsu no daikenkyū*, Sankei shinbunsha, 2002.

Satō Kazuo (ed.), *Sekai ga sabaku Tōkyō saiban*, Ju-pita- shuppan, 1996.

Seaton, Philip. A., *Japan's Contested War Memories: The 'Memory Rifts' in the Historical Consciousness of World War II*, Abingdon: Routledge, 2007.

——, 'Reporting the 2001 textbook and Yasukuni shrine controversies: Japanese war memory and commemoration in the British media', *Japan Forum* 17.3 (2005), pp. 287-309.

——, 'Reporting the "Comfort Women" Issue, 1991-1992: Japan's Contested War Memories in the National Press', *Japanese Studies*, 26.1 (2006), pp. 99-112.

Seikyō kankei o tadasu kai ed., *Seikyō bunri ni kakaru saikō saiban resishu*, Gyōsei, 1996.

Shi Youngming, 'Neighbors at odds', *Beijing Review*, 49, 13, 30 March 2006 (available at http://www.bjreview.com.cn/06-13-e/w-2.htm).

Shiba Ryotarō, *Meiji to iu kokka*. NHK books, 1989.

Shibuichi Daiki, 'The Yasukuni Shrine Dispute and the Politics of Identity in Japan', *Asian Survey*, 45, 2 (2005), pp. 197-215.

Shimura Tatsuya, *Kyōkai hiwa: Taiheiyo sensō o megutte*, Seibo Bunko, 1991.

Sono Ayako, 'Aru shinwa no haikei: Okinawa Tōkashiki no shūdan jiketsu', *Shokun*, 1971 (October) – 1972 (August).

Takahashi Tetsuya, *Yasukuni mondai*, Chikuma Shobō.

———, 'Nation and sacrifice', *University of Tokyo Center for Philosophy Bulletin*, vol. 1 (2003), pp. 33-44.

———, 'The National Politics of the Yasukuni Shrine' in Naoko Shimazu (ed.), *Nationalisms in Japan*, London: Routledge, 2006.

Tanaka Nobumasa, 'Okinawa kara Okinawa to tou "Yasukuni"', *Sekai* September 2004.

———, 'What is the "Yasukuni Problem?"', *Japan in the World*, 2001. (available at http://www.iwanami.co.jp/jpworld/text/yasukuni01.html).

———, *Yasukuni no sengoshi*, Tokyo: Iwanami shinsho, 2002.

———, 'Yasukuni shrine, Japanese nationalism, and the Constitution: prime minister challenged'. *ZMag*, 2003. (Available Online: http://www.zmag.org/content/showarticle.cfm?ItemID=2989).

Tsubouchi Yūzō, *Yasukuni*, Shinchōsha, 1999.

Wakamiya Yoshibumi and Watanabe Tsuneo, *'Yasukuni' to Koizumi shushō*, Asahi shinbunsha, 2006.

———, 'Yomiuri and Asahi editors call for a national memorial to replace Yasukuni'. *ZMag* 2006. (Available online: http://www.zmag.org/content/showarticle.cfm?ItemID=9753 (Accessed 15 February 2007).

Watanabe Shōichi, *Banken uso ni hoeru*, PHP bunko, 1994.

Whiting, Allen, *China Eyes Japan*, Berkeley, CA: University of California Press, 1989.

Whitmarsh, Andrew, '"We will remember them": memory and commemoration in war museums', *Journal of Conservation and Museum Studies*, 7 (2001).

Wu Xinbo and Zhang Lina, 'Canbai qingguo shenshe: yitiao tongwang "guojiazhuyi" de "jingshen suidao"', *Guoji Luntun*, 6, 5 (2004).

Xinhua, 'Sino-Japanese Relations Hard to Develop if Shrine Issue not Resolved', 14 March 2006, available at http://news.xinhuanet.com/english/2006-03/14/content_4302138.htm.

Yasukuni jinja (eds), *Yasukuni no inori: me de miru Meiji, Taishō, Shōwa, Heisei*, Sankei shinbun, 2000.

Yomiuri Shinbun, 'Yasukuni Shrine: Nationalism and Japan's International Relations', *Yomiuri Shinbun,* 4 June 2005 (Available at http://www.japanfocus.org (last accessed 24 September 2005).

Yomiuri shinbunsha yoron chōsa bu, *Nihon no yoron*, Tokyo: Kōbundō, 2002.

Yuzawa Tadashi, 'Goaisatsu' in *Yūshūkan zuroku*, Yasukuni jinja, 2000.

Zhai Xin, 'Riben zimindang reyi canbai qingguo shenshe de guonei zhengzhi beijing fenxi' *Shehui Kexue*, 10 (2004).

Zhou Jianguo, 'Ribenren zenmeyang kan qingguo shenshe' *Shijie Zhishi* 12 (2005).

Zhou Yongsheng, 'Xiaoquan neige de waijiao zhengce xianxi', *Riben Xuekan*, 5 (2006).

INDEX